Congress Under Fire

CONGRESS UNDER FIRE

Reform Politics and the Republican Majority

C. Lawrence Evans *1958—*
COLLEGE OF WILLIAM AND MARY

Walter J. Oleszek
CONGRESSIONAL RESEARCH SERVICE

HOUGHTON MIFFLIN COMPANY   Boston   New York

Senior Sponsoring Editor: *Paul Smith*
Project Editor: *Christina Horn*
Associate Production/Design Coordinator: *Deborah Frydman*
Senior Manufacturing Coordinator: *Priscilla Bailey*
Marketing Manager: *Clint Crockett*

Cover Design: Linda Manly Wade, Wade Design

Printed in the U.S.A.

Library of Congress Catalog Card Number: 96-76898

ISBN: 0-395-76918-3

23456789-B-00 99 98 97

To Lee Hamilton and David Dreier

Contents

Preface

I N THE summer of 1993, the authors of this book met with a top aide to the
House leadership. At the time, we were serving on the professional staff of
a temporary reform committee charged with devising recommendations to
streamline and modernize congressional operations. The leadership aide had
just returned from a difficult staff meeting at the White House, and it
showed. A staunch partisan and congressional loyalist, he had little sympathy for the bipartisan reform effort then underway. We asked the staffer what
the reform panel could do for his boss. His one-word response: *"Disappear."*

Well, reform sentiment never really disappears on Capitol Hill. Congress
is always changing; the reform process is always ongoing. Students of Congress are, by necessity, students of congressional reform.

By all accounts, the 1990s have been a fascinating period in the organizational history of our national legislature. Public confidence in Congress's internal operations plummeted in the wake of burgeoning budget deficits and a
succession of embarrassing scandals—allegations of improper campaign finance activity by the Keating Five, bounced checks in the House bank, and
sexual harassment charges against Senator Bob Packwood. Behind the highly
publicized misdeeds of selected members lurked deep-seated misgivings about
the fundamental fairness and efficiency of many congressional processes.
Throughout the decade, reform topics have been a hallmark of political campaigns across the country. And on Capitol Hill, there has been a flurry of
reform-related activity, first under Democratic management, and then under
the Republicans.

The consequences of all this activity for congressional organization have
been significant. In January 1995, for example, the House adopted the most
sweeping overhaul of its internal operations in many decades. The more

informal, tradition-bound Senate also has been influenced by the widespread calls for organizational change.

This book is an analysis of reform politics on Capitol Hill during the 1990s and the implications for congressional policymaking under the Republican majority. Our discussion covers the landscape of organizational issues, from procedural tactics in committee to the leadership style of Speaker Newt Gingrich. We believe that the 1990s reform process is an important political story in its own right. But the recent wave of institutional change in Congress also sheds light on the forces that shape legislative organization more generally. The tactics and events we describe reveal much about the nature of Congress as an institution.

In our staff work for Congress and in preparing this book, we have accumulated many, many intellectual debts. Ken Nelson has been a valued source of friendship and encouragement. We also benefited from our association with the House members and senators on the Joint Committee on the Organization of Congress (1993), but particularly from the four leaders of that panel: Lee Hamilton, David Dreier, David Boren, and Pete Domenici. Similarly, our understanding of congressional politics has been enriched by our staff colleagues on the Joint Committee, especially Kim Wincup, John Deeken, Phil Grone, Nick Wise, Kelly Cordes, Paul Rundquist, Carol Hardy Vincent, Maureen Groppe, James Saturno, Diane Lampert, and Mary Lou Smullen.

Other current and former congressional staff who helped us during this project include Bill Brown, Joe Crapa, Bob Dove, Tom Duncan, Charlie Johnson, Muftiah McCartin, Tom O'Donnell, Matt Pinkus, Vince Randazzo, John Sullivan, Thomas Wickham, and Don Wolfensberger. Scores of other expert professional staff, too numerous to mention here, expanded our knowledge of the legislative process.

The fingerprints of many academic colleagues also are apparent in the pages that follow, particularly those of Scott Adler, Stan Bach, Roger Davidson, Dick Fenno, Louis Fisher, John Gilmour, Joel Kaji, Fred Kaiser, Tom Mann, Norman Ornstein, Leroy Rieselbach, David Rohde, Barbara Sinclair, Steve Smith, Jim Thurber, Clay Wellborn, and Daniel Wierls. The Renewing Congress project, supervised by Tom Mann and Norman Ornstein, provided valuable insights throughout the reform process. Needless to say, all errors of fact and interpretation are ours alone.

In the course of revising our study, we have benefited from the helpful comments and suggestions offered by Albert D. Cover, State University of New York—Stony Brook, and Paul Gronke, Duke University. We are also indebted to many people at Houghton Mifflin for their assistance in the development of this book, but three deserve special acknowledgment. First, Jean Woy encouraged us to undertake the project. Second, Paul Smith took exceptional care to shepherd this volume to completion. Finally, Christina Horn provided her careful editing and writing skills to the manuscript and contributed significantly to its clarity.

Our families are a constant source of encouragement, patience, and motivation. Once again, Larry Evans thanks Susan, Jack, and Becky for their love and support. Walter Oleszek acknowledges with great affection the special support of Janet, Mark, and Eric.

Finally, we recognize an important debt of gratitude to two highly regarded members of the House who played key leadership roles throughout the 1990s reform process—and who along the way taught us a lot about what Congress and its members can accomplish. For good reason, Rep. Lee Hamilton is one of the most respected lawmakers on either side of the aisle. And Rep. David Dreier's energy and tenacity on behalf of reform has been, and remains, remarkable. With great appreciation, we dedicate this book to them.

C.L.E.
W.J.O.

Congress Under Fire

1 Introduction

O N SEPTEMBER 20, 1994, in the Capitol meeting room of the House Rules Committee, Rep. David Dreier of California waited in frustration with other committee Republicans as Democratic members of the panel caucused in the adjoining office of then chairman Joseph Moakley (D-Mass.). On the committee's agenda that afternoon was congressional reform legislation sponsored by Rep. Lee H. Hamilton (D-Ind.). In 1993, Hamilton and Dreier had served as House chair and vice chair, respectively, of the Joint Committee on the Organization of Congress, a panel created to recommend comprehensive reforms of congressional operations. For six months, along with other members of the joint committee, they had listened to hundreds of lawmakers and outside experts offer ideas for improving Congress.

In the end, the House Democrats and Republicans on the joint committee failed to achieve a bipartisan consensus about reform. After five days of highly contentious meetings, the panel endorsed a package of recommendations that Republicans viewed as insufficiently bold. Along with fellow Republican Bill Emerson of Missouri, Dreier voted with the six joint committee Democrats to report the measure, but only to keep the reform process going. In February 1994, Hamilton introduced the reform package in the House as the Legislative Reorganization Act of 1994. It was then referred to the Rules Committee, which had jurisdiction.[1]

As the Rules Committee began work on the legislation in the spring of 1995, Hamilton and Dreier again found common purpose, as they sought to convince House leaders that a comprehensive reform bill should be brought to the floor. The joint committee recommendations were highly controversial among House Democrats, and Democratic leaders did not view reform either as a public priority or as necessary to improve congressional performance. They dragged their heels.

For the Democratic Congress, the end of the reform process came that September afternoon in the Rules Committee. Speaker Thomas Foley (D-Wash.) joined the meeting in Moakley's office and urged his colleagues to reject reorganization proposals opposed by powerful Democrats. After more than an hour of closed-door discussions, Moakley emerged from his office to announce that the Rules Committee would not reconvene that day. As the 103d Congress sputtered to a close, the panel never resumed consideration of the Legislative Reorganization Act, effectively killing the much-publicized initiative to reform Congress. Hamilton and Dreier expressed deep disappointment at the result but vowed to fight for meaningful reform in January 1995, when the 104th Congress began work.

Just weeks later, on November 8, the voters elected Republican majorities to the House and Senate for the first time in forty years. The GOP gained fifty-two House seats: Prominent among the defeated Democrats were Speaker Foley, House Judiciary Committee chairman Jack Brooks (D-Tex.), and House Ways and Means Committee chairman Dan Rostenkowski, (D-Ill.). In the Senate, Republicans picked up eight seats on November 8 and, within days, a ninth, when Democrat Richard Shelby of Alabama switched parties. "An incredible night," remarked a stunned Rep. Bob Wise (D-W.V.). "It felt less like an election than a plane crash, with [my wife and I] left looking for the names of friends on the list of passengers."[2]

Three weeks after the election, an elated Dreier, now an influential member of the House majority, stepped before an audience of reporters and announced the most sweeping reorganization of the House in almost fifty years. In addition to Dreier's recommendations, which derived in large part from the work of the joint committee, GOP leaders announced other changes during the Republican transition, many consolidating power in the hands of incoming Speaker Newt Gingrich (R-Ga.). In the Senate, the pace of institutional reform was slower, but within months Senate Republicans also were considering significant alterations in their procedures.

Following the landmark congressional elections of 1994, change seemed pervasive on Capitol Hill. Former Ways and Means Committee chairman Rostenkowski, one of the most experienced and politically savvy of Democratic lawmakers before losing his 1994 reelection bid, observed that the GOP was making "basic changes that are a virtual guarantee that the House at the turn of the century will be significantly different than it was at the beginning of this decade, irrespective of how long the Republicans retain control." Rostenkowski believed that these developments would continue even if Democrats regained control of one or both chambers: "The Democrats won't be able to put Humpty Dumpty back together again," he remarked, "and they shouldn't want to."[3]

Indeed, by the end of 1995 (the first session of the GOP-controlled 104th Congress), close observers agreed that the House, if not the Senate, was a remarkably different body compared to the years of Democratic dominance. Speaker Gingrich had emerged as the most powerful congressional leader in decades, perhaps since the early years of the twentieth century. Legislative responsibility had shifted, at least temporarily, from the standing committee system to informal task forces, the Republican leadership, and the huge class of freshman GOP lawmakers. And the appropriations and budget processes had been harnessed (Democrats would say subverted) to advance the most ambitious agenda of domestic policy proposals in a generation.

The overall impact of the GOP congressional majority on public policy remains unclear. However, the consequences of Republican rule for the internal operations of Congress (particularly in the House) clearly have been profound. This book is about the recent wave of organizational change on Capitol Hill. Our focus is on the forces that shaped the contemporary congressional reform agenda, the reasons the Democratic majority in Congress was unable to respond to widespread public demands for change, and the causes and consequences of the important institutional reforms implemented by the Republican majority.

MEANING OF REFORM

Congress is constantly changing. Members enter and leave the institution, chairmanships periodically change hands, and new leaders regularly emerge. The procedures and structures of Congress evolve over time, as members alter the institution in response to internal needs and external demands. At the beginning of each new Congress, for instance, the majority party makes incremental (and occasionally significant) alterations in the standing rules of the House. The policy domains of individual House and Senate committees are constantly evolving, as new issues emerge or expansionist committees encroach on the jurisdictions of competing panels. For congressional observers, the institution is always a moving target.

Periodically during congressional history (and regularly in recent decades), members of Congress have devised concrete plans to transform aspects of congressional operations. Such proposals often are characterized as *reform* or *reorganization* (we use these terms interchangeably).[4]

The meaning of *reform* can be ambiguous because the word typically is interpreted as change for the better. Lawmakers seeking to revamp the Medicare or Medicaid programs, for instance, often call their ideas health care reform; proposals that would change antipoverty policy are often labeled welfare reform. Just as people disagree about health and welfare issues, they also disagree about whether and how Congress should be reorganized or changed. The definition of meaningful congressional reform is subject to political debate. Although it is often difficult to reach consensus on a specific reorganization plan as opposed to endorsing reform in the abstract, it is equally difficult to evaluate whether a package of reorganization initiatives, or even whether an individual reform, represents an improvement over the status quo.

In December 1994, for example, House Republican leaders announced that the purely administrative functions of the chamber would be placed under the authority of Speaker Gingrich. This change, the GOP argued, was a reform that would combat patronage, perks, and other administrative ills on Capitol Hill. House Democrats, in contrast, responded that the proposal was nothing more than a power grab by Republican leaders and not real reform.

Rather than a clearly defined issue area, congressional reform is a positive symbol, or label, that may or may not become associated with a proposal to revamp some aspect of congressional operations. In this book, our interest is in institutional reform as an *active issue area* on the legislative agenda. As a result, we treat a suggestion to alter congressional operations as a reform proposal if a significant number of lawmakers, outside observers, or members of the public view it as such. Consequently, the House GOP administrative changes are presented in this book as reforms, even though Democrats have portrayed them as a step backward for the institution.

Also, the emphasis in this book is on recent attempts to reform the *internal operations* of Congress. Not examined are the important efforts to change the various campaign finance and lobbying laws. These topics relate more to the broader electoral and interest-group environments within which Congress functions, rather than to the internal structures and procedures of the House or Senate. Campaign finance and lobbying reform merit (and have received) book-length treatments of their own and are not dealt with here.

IMPORTANCE OF REFORM

The 1990s reorganization process matters because (1) reform has implications for power relationships within Congress and the content of legislation, (2) reform issues have been important to the public throughout the decade, and (3) the reform process provides students of the institution with a useful glimpse of the broader forces that shape congressional organization.

Power and Policy

Most important, congressional reorganization matters because the procedures and structures of Congress determine who has power in the national legislature, and thus influence over the content of public policy. All House members and senators have one vote in their respective chambers. In practice, however, certain lawmakers have greater access to the resources and prerogatives necessary to influence legislative outcomes. Committee chairs control expert staff resources, which can provide them with important informational advantages in the legislative process. Particularly in the House, the majority party leadership sets the terms for floor debate. More generally, legislative leaders in committee and on the floor determine which issues advance and which ones sink from view.

Looking back on Democratic attempts to revamp Congress, Rep. Lee Hamilton emphasized the linkages between organization and power on Capitol Hill. "Reform in this institution is exceedingly difficult," he observed. "While everybody is in support of 'reform,' almost everybody has a separate idea as to what reform constitutes. When you're talking about seniority, committee assignments, structure, organization, of course you're really talking about the distribution of power." Hamilton might have added that when you redistribute power from who has it to who wants it, you are ultimately talking about the content of legislation.

Public Attention

During the 1990s there has been significant public demand for congressional reform, making the topic a potentially important campaign issue. Voters typically are uninformed about the details of congressional procedure, which tend to be complex and technical. But public opinion polls reveal that most citizens strongly favor reform in the abstract and support specific proposals that are relatively blunt and straightforward, such as term limits or the balanced budget amendment to the Constitution.

Public support for congressional reform reflects the deep-seated anger many citizens feel toward the institution. Voters perceive members of Congress as an arrogant, insular ruling class, out of touch with the concerns of ordinary Americans. Frank Luntz, a top pollster for Newt Gingrich, has described the ugly mood of the electorate toward Congress in blunt terms.

> The editorial writers in Washington, they don't understand the mood out there. They write the word "anger" as if it were a five-letter word. It's not. It's a four-letter word and a three-letter word— "F___ you." In all my focus groups, people are saying "F___ Washington." They don't even bother to correct their language.[5]

Rep. Anthony Beilenson (D-Calif.), who announced in the fall of 1995 that he would not seek reelection in 1996, provided a broader explanation for public discontent with the legislative branch and with politics in general.

> At the base of it all is the fact that Americans feel a little less secure economically and in terms of their personal security and the quality of their lives than they did 20 years ago. People are worried that their children are not going to inherit a country in better shape and with greater opportunities than they themselves inherited. I am sure that is at the base [of the public discontent]. There are not enough well-paying jobs the way there used to be.[6]

One result, according to Beilenson, is generalized support among the public for major changes in the way business is conducted in Washington.

Recognizing this demand for change, Republican strategists included a number of major reform proposals in the Contract with America, the House GOP campaign manifesto for 1994. The preamble of the contract, for instance, contained eight specific reforms, such as applying to Congress the same employment and workplace safety laws that the private sector must follow, and streamlining the congressional bureaucracy. Included in the body of the contract were proposals for term limitations for members of Congress, the balanced budget amendment, and the line-item veto.

By most accounts, the congressional reform proposals included in the contract did not sway the electorate in 1994, but reform issues in general were mentioned often in campaigns across the country.[7] The reform agenda reflected and reinforced the intense public anger toward Washington that characterized the 1994 campaign. Ohio Democrat Eric Fingerhut, for instance, was first elected to Congress in 1992 on a reform platform. Selected by his fellow Democratic freshmen to cochair their task force on reform, Fingerhut tried unsuccessfully to convince Democratic leaders to develop a bold reorganization agenda. He was defeated for reelection in 1994, as was the other task force cochair, Rep. Karen Shepherd (D-Utah). After the election, Fingerhut declared:

> Speaker Tom Foley and his team completely misread the message of the 1992 election. They chose to see it as a vindication of their opposition to the Reagan and Bush administrations rather than a call for sweeping change in Washington. They ignored the calls of many freshman Democrats to move quickly on reform legislation, and some of these leaders even ridiculed our efforts and belittled us personally.

Fingerhut recalled, "I sat in Tom Foley's office together with a dozen other freshmen Democrats and pleaded with him to pursue a reform agenda early in the 103d Congress. He responded that by the 1994 elections, no one would ask us about congressional reform."[8]

In contrast to Democratic leaders, GOP candidates in 1994 made changing Congress a centerpiece of their campaigns, emphasizing the reform provisions included in the Contract with America. A good example is Rep. Sam Brownback (R-Kans.), who was elected that year and quickly emerged as an acknowledged leader of the seventy-three-member GOP freshman class. Asked why he was running for Congress, Brownback replied:

> I want to change the direction Congress is currently leading this country. The basic platform of my Congressional campaign is the three R's: Reduce the size, scope and intrusiveness of the federal government by cutting taxes and cutting red-tape and regulation. Reforming an entrenched Congress with term limits; and Returning to those basic values which built this great nation.[9]

In the fall of 1995, Brownback remarked:

During the [August] recess, I went around to town hall meetings [in Topeka, Kansas]. People want to talk about the deficit, Medicare; but what they really get incensed about are the perquisites and privileges of office. They look at us as a ruling class, not a serving class. Perception is critical here. It's its own reality. We've lost the trust of the American people, and we're going to have to earn it back.[10]

Throughout the 1994 campaign, scores of GOP candidates (most of them Gingrich disciples) trumpeted the same theme: Republicans stand for change and reform. Their "end the status quo" message resonated powerfully with an electorate dissatisfied with President Bill Clinton and the Democratic Congress.

Understanding Organizational Change

Congressional reform also reveals much about how and why the institution changes. In the 1990s, a diverse range of reorganization issues, touching on most aspects of the legislative branch, received serious attention. Members debated major changes in the federal budget process, committee jurisdictions and procedures, and minority party prerogatives, as well as numerous other organizational issues. Concerted attempts to reform Congress provide a valuable window into the broader process of congressional change.

What forces shape the organizational features of Congress? This may be the most important and controversial topic in the contemporary academic literature about Congress. Three competing perspectives (referred to here as *organizational rationales*) have dominated recent attempts to generalize about the foundations of congressional operations: clientele rationales, partisan rationales, and institutional rationales. In this book, we evaluate the relevance of these factors for the congressional reform experience of the 1990s. We also explore the impact of two additional rationales for congressional change—personal power agendas and public opinion.

Clientele Rationales

One view of congressional operations is that the procedures and internal structures of the national legislature are designed to help important constituencies and clientele groups achieve their policy aims.[11] Clientele groups provide reelection-minded lawmakers with valuable electoral resources, such as campaign contributions, voter mobilization, and expert political and policy advice. In return, lawmakers attempt to provide the groups most important to their districts or states with the policy outcomes and other legislative services that these groups value. According to this view, members also focus (and receive deference from their colleagues) on the issues of particular concern to the organized constituencies that determine their electoral fates. On other items, they defer to the lawmakers and groups that care the most about those issues. Many scholars argue that the internal operations of Congress have been molded to promote such legislative exchanges and to enhance lawmakers' electoral connections back home.

There is considerable evidence that clientele incentives do influence aspects of congressional organization. For instance, the demands and concerns of outside groups partially shape the committee systems of the House and Senate. Organized constituencies want their issues to be considered by panels that look favorably on their policy goals. Groups representing America's military veterans fought for the creation of the House and Senate Veterans' Affairs Committees. By most accounts, these panels, which focus on veterans' issues, function as advocates for the veterans community. The House and Senate Small Business Committees were created and are maintained in large measure because of the lobbying efforts of small business groups. Jurisdiction over the bulk of farm policy is consolidated in the House and Senate Agriculture Committees, which are dominated by representatives from rural areas.

Other aspects of congressional organization (for example, floor procedure and the distribution of staff) also help lawmakers service the needs of organized constituency groups, who in turn provide members with the financial and political resources necessary to get reelected. As a result, proposals to modify congressional operations, because of the implications for power and policy, are closely scrutinized by the affected interest groups. Attempts in 1974 to abolish the House Committee on Merchant Marine and Fisheries, for instance, triggered intense opposition from maritime firms and unions, leading to the proposal's defeat. As we shall show, the reform agenda of the 1990s also was influenced by the needs and demands of clientele groups. Only this time, the Merchant Marine Committee fell victim to a new constellation of political forces.

Partisan Rationales

Another perspective is that congressional operations are primarily determined by partisan concerns and that Congress's rules and organization should be viewed as a procedural means through which the majority party promotes its legislative agenda.[12] Compared to other western democracies, partisan ties in the American electorate are relatively weak. Still, voters typically consider a congressional candidate's party affiliation when deciding how to cast their ballots, and public perceptions of the incumbent president can influence the electoral prospects of his fellow party members in Congress. Not surprisingly, the two major political parties play key organizational roles on Capitol Hill.

There is substantial evidence that partisan imperatives significantly influence how Congress conducts business and that the success or failure of reform attempts depends largely on the consequences of reform for the majority party. For example, the Speaker, though formally selected by the entire House, is actually chosen by members of the majority party and functions primarily as an agent for the majority caucus. At various points in congressional history, lawmakers have sought to strengthen the Speaker's formal powers to help advance the majority party's legislative program.

Features of the committee system also reflect the policy priorities of one or both political parties. The jurisdiction, or policy responsibilities, of the House Committee on Economic and Educational Opportunities combines issue areas (education and labor) central to the Democratic agenda. In fact, when Democrats controlled the House, they titled this panel the Education and Labor Committee. After winning majority status in November 1994, House Republicans considered breaking up the committee and creating jurisdictions more in keeping with GOP policy interests. Instead, they renamed the committee to highlight Republican priorities.

Similarly, the evolution of floor procedure in the House and Senate reflects partisan concerns. Beginning in the 1970s, House Democratic leaders began clamping down on the ability of Republicans to offer floor amendments that might undermine fragile Democratic coalitions or otherwise embarrass the majority party. GOP complaints about the unfairness of such restrictive floor procedures were a key feature of the House reform agenda in the 1980s and 1990s. Throughout this period, Republicans lambasted Democrats for the way they ran the House.

Institutional Rationales

Still another view is that the internal operations of the legislative branch are designed primarily to promote the collective needs of the institution as a whole and not the concerns of clientele groups or the majority party.[13] According to the Constitution, each chamber may establish its own rules, which must be enacted by more than one-half of the respective membership.[14] As a result, some scholars argue, congressional procedures and structures will reflect the organizational preferences of the entire chamber rather than target benefits to a particular political party or interest group. Institutional needs, they argue, will dominate partisan and clientele concerns.

The committee system, for example, may be structured so that diverse interests and perspectives are represented on the main policymaking panels of the House and Senate. Such heterogeneity of preferences in committee can ensure that committee reports are ideologically balanced and that the institution as a whole has sufficient information about the implications of committee bills.[15] The House Commerce Committee, for one, has a wide-ranging jurisdiction, drawing the interest of many competing constituency groups. The panel's membership has long been heterogeneous, making it a microcosm of the chamber. Such panels can serve the collective needs of the institution for balanced policy recommendations.

Other aspects of congressional organization may derive from chamber imperatives. For instance, the Legislative Reorganization Act of 1946 (the general blueprint for the modern Congress) was stimulated in large measure by broad bipartisan concern among lawmakers that Congress's authority had declined relative to the burgeoning power of the executive branch. As Rep. Mike Monroney (D-Okla.), who helped draft the 1946 act, said, "Lacking adequate organization and staff, Congress cannot carry out its tasks under the Constitution. Without the right sort of equipment and procedures it must abdicate its job to the executive department" and the president.[16]

Personal Power Agendas

In addition to securing reelection and making policy, lawmakers seek to gain power within the House or Senate.[17] Gaining power facilitates members' attempts to get reelected, shape policy, and achieve other objectives. Legislative analysts have argued that the individual "quest for power" by ambitious members can influence key aspects of congressional organization, from the committee system to leadership prerogatives.[18]

Prior to the 1970s, committee chairmanships in the House were determined solely on the basis of seniority (longevity of continuous service on a panel) rather than loyalty to the Democratic policy agenda. During the 1970s, California Democratic representative Philip Burton, a legendary House liberal who once claimed he could round up 110 votes "to [get] dog____ declared the national food," provided the ideas and mobilized the votes to constrain the chairs, many of whom were more conservative than the typical Democrat.[19] Among other reforms, chairs were made subject to secret ballot elections within the confines of the Democratic Caucus. Burton's efforts transformed the distribution of power within the chamber, increasing his own clout as well as that of his liberal allies. Seeking to capitalize on his reform role, Burton came within one vote of being selected House majority leader in 1976 (the winner was Rep. James Wright [D-Tex.]).

The following decade, Rep. Newt Gingrich of Georgia, unlike Burton a conservative Republican, also emphasized reform issues during his emergence as a national political leader. As discussed in Chapter 2, Gingrich attempted to publicize alleged Democratic mismanagement of the House as part of an overall strategy aimed at undermining public support for congressional Democrats. Among other changes, Gingrich called for greater GOP representation on key House committees, fairer floor procedures, and bipartisan administration of the chamber. Then, after the 1994 elections, incoming Speaker Gingrich embraced organizational changes that significantly increased the formal powers of his new office. The importance of reform to Gingrich's remarkable rise to power is a central element of the reorganization story.

Public Opinion

For obvious reasons, reelection-minded lawmakers will carefully consider intensely held citizen views about the organization of the legislative branch. Most voters, however, seldom develop concrete preferences about specific aspects of congressional operations. Still, there are exceptions. In 1917, for instance, public opinion mobilized in favor of filibuster reform after use of the tactic killed legislation to arm U.S. merchant vessels against German attack. And public support for the elimination of congressional perks and privileges exploded after exposure of the House bank scandal in 1991–1992.

Most often, the publicity surrounding congressional scandals and other institutional ills creates diffuse support among the public for congressional reform in the abstract. Lawmakers then devise concrete proposals for change and seek to convince voters that such proposals constitute meaningful reform. If the public comes to view a reorganization idea as necessary for improving Congress, it can be extremely difficult for individual lawmakers to take positions against that proposal. Thus, although public demands for congressional reform often are inchoate, they can be extremely powerful. Indeed, the reorganization of Congress has been a prominent issue on the legislative agenda in the 1990s primarily because of the intense public desire for institutional change.[20]

Throughout this book, we portray lawmakers as rational and goal-oriented. Their decisions about the organizational design of Congress are made strategically, although they are typically subject to some uncertainty about the ultimate impact of a new procedure or other institutional feature. Faced with a range of options for changing congressional operations, a member will support the alternative that best promotes his or her reelection, policy, and power goals. Lawmakers, however, do not make decisions about reform matters in a vacuum. Instead, their choices about internal organization are conditioned by a range of political forces inside and outside Congress. The organizational rationales described here capture different forces that can affect members' procedural choices. Indeed, the main distinction among the five rationales is in *what lawmakers are responding to* when they make choices among reform alternatives.

Consider each organizational rationale in turn. According to clientele rationales, when lawmakers make decisions about organizational matters, they are responding primarily to the outside environment of clientele groups. Under partisan rationales, the key incentives behind organizational choices derive from the institutional and electoral needs of the majority and minority parties. Institutional rationales hold that the internal operations of the House and Senate are responsive to the organizational interests of the membership as a whole. In contrast, if public opinion is a key rationale for organizational change in Congress, the views of citizens about reform options should have a direct bearing on the reform choices of their representatives in Washington. And if personal power agendas shed significant light on congressional design, the reform decisions of key members should respond to their personal ambition for influence as it relates to other lawmakers.

In this book, we evaluate the relative importance of the five organizational rationales by exploring the sources of the incentives lawmakers faced during the wave of congressional reorganization in the 1990s. To what forces were lawmakers responding when they made their decisions about organizational change? How did these incentives influence member behavior, and thus the outcome at each stage of the reform process? These and related questions orient our approach to congressional reform.

PLAN OF THE BOOK

One of our goals is to present the 1990s reorganization effort as an interesting and important political story. In the chapters that follow, we analyze the reform process as it unfolded over time. Chapter 2 examines the roots of reform, particularly the emergence of Newt Gingrich and the GOP reform agenda. Chapter 3 explores why, following the House bank scandal, the majority Democrats were unable to respond to the public's demand for congressional reform. The important institutional changes adopted by the GOP immediately following the 1994 elections are the subject of Chapter 4. Chapter 5 addresses institutional developments in the landmark 104th Congress. A brief summary of how the five organizational rationales relate to each stage of the reform experience is provided at the end of Chapters 2 through 5; their overall importance to congressional reform during the 1990s is a focus of Chapter 6, the conclusion.

Interestingly, the GOP reorganization has not fundamentally changed the *direction* of institutional reform in Congress. Many of the Republican reforms primarily functioned to reinforce changes previously implemented by reform-minded members from both political parties. What was substantially altered after the 1994 elections, however, was the *pace* of institutional change, which accelerated markedly. We examine this theme in the concluding chapter, providing summary observations about change and reform on Capitol Hill.

Before turning to the emergence of the 1990s reform agenda, a few comments are in order about the approach to studying Congress in this book. The evidence we discuss has been gathered from diverse sources, including congressional documents; internal memoranda, letters, and notes; media accounts; personal conversations with members and staff; and our own close observation of the reform process. In social science terms, we use *participant/observation methods* of the sort popularized by Richard Fenno in his many books about Congress.[21]

We have both served as aides to lawmakers involved in the congressional reform process. One of us (Evans) worked on the personal staff of Rep. Lee Hamilton and also served as a professional aide to the Joint Committee on the Organization of Congress, a key reform panel during the 103d Congress. The other (Oleszek) was policy director of the bipartisan joint committee and, for more than twenty-five years, has advised dozens of lawmakers from

2

Setting the Stage

THE REFORMS implemented by the new Republican majority on Capitol Hill were not devised entirely during the short transition period following the November 1994 elections. Instead, these changes resulted from years of sustained interest in reform issues by lawmakers and substantial public sentiment that the internal operations of the national legislature needed improvement.

Of course, public distrust of Congress is as old as the Republic. For instance, looking back in 1925 on his twenty years of House service, Speaker Nicholas Longworth observed that "during the whole of that time we have been attacked, denounced, despised, hunted, harried, blamed, looked down upon, excoriated, and flayed."[1] Decades earlier, Mark Twain had asked his readers, "Suppose you were an idiot. Suppose you were a member of Congress. But I repeat myself."[2] Throughout American history, lawmakers too have been dissatisfied with congressional operations. Under Article I of the U.S. Constitution, members of Congress determine the internal procedures and structures of the institution, and from the early congresses on, lawmakers have proposed countless changes in the organization of the legislative branch.

Still, the long-standing public concerns about Congress and continual efforts by lawmakers to alter congressional operations do not account for the content of the congressional reform agenda as it emerged in the years preceding the landmark 104th Congress, nor do they explain why reform sentiment has been so intense in the 1990s. The purpose of this chapter is to examine the historical context of contemporary reform politics. Although the institutional changes on Capitol Hill reflect many decades of congressional development, three aspects of recent congressional history primarily shaped the

both political parties about congressional operations. We observed at close hand many of the events described in this book and have tried to provide readers with an "over-the-shoulder" perspective à la Fenno.

Students of Congress have much to learn from the comments and observations of lawmakers and other participants in congressional politics. As a result, this book is full of quotations from members and staff. Unlike Fenno, our observations derive in part from meetings and conversations that occurred while we were congressional employees, and thus should be treated as confidential. Consequently, the vast majority of quotations in this book are from published sources. In the few instances where we do cite comments made directly to us (or in our presence), the remarks are not attributed to a particular member or staff person. We are convinced, however, that other participants and observers of the reform process on Capitol Hill will find the pages that follow to be balanced, accurate, and compelling.

Notes

1. Two other panels, House Administration and Government Operations, also received the measure, but the Rules Committee was widely viewed as the main committee of jurisdiction.

2. Bob Wise, "Diary of a Congressman," *The Washington Monthly,* June 1995, 40.

3. David Rosenbaum, "Strong Speaker, Strong House? One Doesn't Necessarily Follow the Other," *New York Times,* December 4, 1994, 32.

4. Charles O. Jones, "Radical Change in Makeup of Congress Will Occur Regardless of Reform Efforts," *Roll Call,* August 8, 1994, 30. Useful books about congressional reform include Leroy N. Rieselbach, *Congressional Reform: The Changing Modern Congress* (Washington, D.C.: Congressional Quarterly, 1994); Roger H. Davidson and Walter J. Oleszek, *Congress Against Itself* (Bloomington, Ind.: Indiana University Press, 1977); Burton D. Sheppard, *Rethinking Congressional Reform: The Reform Roots of the Special Interest Congress* (Cambridge, Mass.: Shenkman Books, 1985). For a recent edited volume, see James A. Thurber and Roger H. Davidson, eds., *Remaking Congress: Change and Stability in the 1990s* (Washington, D.C.: Congressional Quarterly, 1995).

5. Michael Kelly, "Clinton's Escape Clause," *The New Yorker,* October 24, 1994, 46.

6. "Hill Interview, Rep. Beilenson," *The Hill,* November 8, 1995, 22.

7. The Democrats who lost (and the GOP candidates who won) tended to be in conservative to moderate districts, often in the South, that did not lean toward Bill Clinton in 1992. Particularly vulnerable were Democratic incumbents closely associated with the president's overall legislative agenda. See David W. Brady, John F. Cogan, and Douglas Rivers, *How the Republicans Captured the House: An Assessment of the 1994 Midterm Elections* (Hoover Institution, Stanford University, 1995). Exit polls also suggested that voters placing special emphasis on traditional morality ("belief in God, hard work, patriotism, frugality, personal and family responsibility, and self-reliance") were especially likely to vote Republican in 1994. See Charles E. Cook, "Exit

Poll Analysis Puts GOP Landslide in Whole New Light," *Roll Call,* February 27, 1995, 8.

8. Eric D. Fingerhut, "Clinton and Congress: A Democrat Throws Stones," *New York Times,* December 17, 1994, 23.

9. Quoted in the Junction City, Kansas, *Daily Union,* November 6, 1994, 4.

10. Jeff Shear, "The Other Entitlement," *National Journal,* October 14, 1995, 2532.

11. For example, consult David R. Mayhew, *Congress: The Electoral Connection* (New Haven: Yale University Press, 1973). See also Morris P. Fiorina, *Congress: Keystone of the Washington Establishment* (New Haven: Yale University Press, 1977). A related, "distributive" model of congressional policymaking is developed in an important series of articles by Kenneth A. Shepsle and Barry R. Weingast published in the *American Political Science Review* and the *American Journal of Political Science,* among other journals.

12. The partisan foundations of congressional organization are emphasized in a number of works: David Rohde, *Parties and Leaders in the Postreform House* (Chicago: University of Chicago Press, 1991); Gary Cox and Mathew McCubbins, *Legislative Leviathan: Party Government in the House* (Berkeley: University of California Press, 1993); Barbara Sinclair, *Legislators, Leaders, and Lawmaking* (Baltimore: Johns Hopkins University Press, 1995); Sarah A. Binder and Steven S. Smith, "Acquired Procedural Tendencies and Congressional Reform," in *Remaking Congress: Change and Stability in the 1990s,* ed. James A. Thurber and Roger H. Davidson (Washington, D.C.: Congressional Quarterly Press, 1995).

13. The most significant exposition of this view is Keith Krehbiel's pathbreaking study, *Information and Legislative Organization* (Ann Arbor: University of Michigan Press, 1991). See also Joseph Cooper, *The Origins of the Standing Committees and the Development of the Modern House* (Houston, Tex: Rice University Studies, 1970); and Arthur Maas, *Congress and the Common Good* (New York: Basic Books, 1983).

14. The Senate decided to stipulate in Senate Rule 22 that any amendment to that rule, if filibustered, requires a two-thirds vote to end the talkathon.

15. Krehbiel, *Information and Legislative Organization.* See also Richard L. Hall and Bernard Grofman, "The Committee Assignment Process and the Conditional Nature of Committee Bias," *American Political Science Review,* 84 (1990), 1149–66; and John Londregan and James M. Snyder, Jr., "Comparing Committee and Floor Preferences," *Legislative Studies Quarterly,* No. 192 (1994), 233–66.

16. A. S. Mike Monroney et al., *The Strengthening of American Political Institutions,* (Ithaca: Cornell University Press, 1949), p. 7. Concerns about the institutional capacities of Congress vis-à-vis the executive branch are especially pronounced when two vital legislative powers are involved: the power of the purse and the power to declare war. The House and Senate Budget Committees, for example, were created in the 1970s to provide the institution with the procedures necessary to participate in federal budget policy. Similarly, the War Powers Resolution of 1973 was intended to ensure congressional participation in decisions to place U.S. military forces in hostile situations.

17. Richard F. Fenno, *Congressmen in Committees* (Boston: Little, Brown, 1973). See also Richard L. Hall, "Participation and Purpose in Committee Decision Making," *American Political Science Review,* 81 (1987), 105–28.

18. Lawrence C. Dodd, "Congress and the Quest for Power," in *Congress Reconsidered,* 1st ed., ed. Lawrence C. Dodd and Bruce I. Oppenheimer (New York: Praeger, 1977). For an intriguing argument that the personal power agenda of then Speaker Henry Clay facilitated the rise of the House standing committee system in 1815–1817, consult Gerald Gamm and Kenneth Shepsle, "Emergence of Legislative Institutions: Standing Committees in the House and Senate, 1810–1825," *Legislative Studies Quarterly,* 14, No. 1 (1989), 39–66.

19. John Jacobs, "The Newt Gingrich of the Left," *Roll Call,* October 19, 1995, 14. See John Jacobs, *A Rage for Justice: The Passion and Politics of Philip Burton* (Berkeley: University of California Press, 1995).

20. The difference between clientele rationales and public opinion is that the former refers to the relatively parochial interests of particular constituencies, while the latter refers to the reform attitudes of the general public. Traditionally, the media also have played a key role in molding and shaping public opinion on reorganization issues. Public support for passage of the Legislative Reorganization Act of 1946 was generated in part by a major cover story in the June 1945 issue of *Life* magazine ("U.S. Congress: It Faces Great New Tasks with Outworn Tools"). During the mid-1960s, NBC News ran a prime-time television special ("Congress Needs Help"), which mobilized public backing for the eventual enactment of the Legislative Reorganization Act of 1970, another reform measure. Today scores of media outlets report on the alleged institutional shortcomings of Congress, as well as various proposals for changing the institution.

21. The classic overview of participant/observation methods as they relate to the study of Congress is the appendix to Richard F. Fenno, *Homestyle: House Members in Their Districts* (Boston: Little, Brown, 1978).

context for legislative reorganization in the 1990s: prior reform initiatives, the emergence of a confrontational House GOP minority during the 1980s, and the impact of the House bank scandal on public perceptions of Congress.

We begin by reviewing the principal reform efforts since World War II, because they helped define the problems and solutions considered by contemporary reformers. Next we discuss how, beginning in the 1980s, a group of House Republicans began attacking Democratic control of congressional operations, which they portrayed as corrupt, inefficient, and unfair. Though originating in the House, these efforts would shape the tone and content of the reform debate in both chambers. We then summarize the pivotal role of the early 1990s House bank and post office scandals in raising public disapproval of Congress to historic levels, generating substantial momentum for institutional change. In the fourth section, we describe the immediate fallout from the bank scandal, as Democratic congressional leaders tried to contain the explosion of reform sentiment inside and outside Congress. Finally, we evaluate the relevance of the five organizational rationales presented in Chapter 1 to the emergence of the contemporary reform agenda on Capitol Hill.

PRIOR REFORM INITIATIVES

The reforms of the new Republican majority should be considered within the context of previous reorganization efforts. Many of the 1995 reforms were devised and considered by prior reform entities or reform-minded individuals in previous decades. Consider the matter of proxy, or absentee, voting in committee, which the House abolished in 1995. Previously, House members could miss committee meetings but still cast votes by giving their proxies to a member in attendance, typically their party's leading committee member. Although the practice gave lawmakers scheduling flexibility (allowing them, technically, to be in two places at once), Republicans and many Democrats believed that proxy voting undermined the quality of deliberation in committee. If panel members were not present to hear and participate in debate, they argued, how could these lawmakers cast an informed vote?

The abolition of proxy voting had been a reform issue for decades. A proxy ban was recommended by the 1965 Joint Committee on the Organization of the Congress, a bipartisan reform panel. The ban was included in the Legislative Reorganization Act of 1970, which derived from the joint committee's recommendations, and was signed into law in October of that year. Three months later, at the start of the next Congress, the Democratic Caucus voted to repeal the ban. Republicans then pushed for the inclusion of a proxy ban in the recommendations of the 1973–1974 Bolling committee, a House reform panel named after its chair, Rep. Richard Bolling of Missouri, and proxies were abolished once again when the House adopted the Committee Reform Amendments of 1974. The following year, at the start of the 94th

Congress, the Democratic Caucus overturned the proxy ban a second time. House Republicans continued to advocate the abolition of proxy voting, including the proposal in their congressional reform program throughout the 1980s. Proxy voting was a major issue for Republicans during the work of the 1993 Joint Committee on the Organization of Congress, yet another reform panel. Not surprisingly, the new Republican majority adopted a House rule abolishing proxy voting in committees and subcommittees in January 1995.

Most other congressional reforms adopted by the 104th Congress also had their roots in earlier reform efforts. The recent changes, then, should be viewed as a continuation of longer-term attempts to change congressional operations.

Previous reform actions also shaped the procedures and structures that themselves became the subject of reform. In the mid-1970s, House Democratic reformers increased the policymaking role of subcommittees, further diffusing power within the chamber's standing committees. For the first time, subcommittees were guaranteed fixed jurisdictions and staff allotments. Subcommittee chairs were selected by the majority members of the committee rather than by the full committee chairs. Reformers believed that these changes would democratize the House and open up new points of access for policy innovation.

Two decades later, thoughtful lawmakers in both parties were asking whether the 1970s reforms had gone too far. Observed Rep. David Price (D-N.C.), "It is important for a legislative body like ours to retain numerous points of initiative, places where Members can be active and productive, but the pendulum has swung too far . . . in the direction of decentralization and diffusion."[3] The lesson: One generation's reform can become another generation's problem.

In every Congress, alterations are made in House and Senate operations. The process of congressional reform is ongoing, with proposals coming from diverse sources, including party caucuses, House and Senate standing committees, and the initiatives of individual members. Periodically, the chambers form temporary reform committees or commissions to explore major reorganization issues in a comprehensive fashion. These organized reform efforts provide a useful window into the larger history of congressional reform. For example, the experience of the 1993 Joint Committee on the Organization of Congress reveals why the Democratic majority was unable to pass comprehensive congressional reform during the 103d Congress (1993–1994). Significantly, the joint panel's work largely shaped the reorganization plans of House and Senate Republicans during the 104th Congress. For these reasons, we discuss the events leading up to the establishment of the 1993 joint committee in the closing pages of this chapter and analyze the panel's work as part of Chapter 3. Other major reform undertakings during the modern Congress also had implications for the new Republican majority. The following are particularly noteworthy.

Legislative Reorganization Act of 1946. A comprehensive revision of Congress's organization and operations, this act was the product of extensive hearings conducted by the first Joint Committee on the Organization of Congress (1945–1946). The panel was chaired by Sen. Robert La Follette (R-Wis.), with Rep. A. S. "Mike" Monroney (D-Okla.) serving as vice chair. A primary objective was to modernize Congress to meet contemporary challenges, such as workload increases and the expansion of presidential authority. The 1946 act's major features included a reduction in the number of House and Senate standing committees, the provision of permanent professional and clerical aides for committees, a requirement that committees exercise "continuous watchfulness" of the executive branch, the preparation of a legislative budget, and the registration of lobbyists. Certain provisions of the Legislative Reorganization Act of 1946 quickly atrophied or were ignored, but it remains the most significant reform measure adopted by Congress in the modern era. The act was the blueprint for the contemporary Congress, creating many of the procedures and internal structures that present-day reformers target for change.

Joint Committee on the Organization of the Congress (1965). Two decades later, Congress established a second joint reform committee, which was cochaired by now senator Mike Monroney and Rep. Ray J. Madden (D-Ind.), to conduct another major introspective review of legislative organization and operations. Created during a climate of concern about Congress's effectiveness, the work of the second joint committee, as mentioned earlier, eventually culminated in the passage of the Legislative Reorganization Act of 1970. Three broad themes characterized the 1970 act: to open Congress to further public visibility, to strengthen its decision-making capacities, and to augment the rights of the minority party in Congress. For example, the 1970 act authorized television and radio coverage of committee proceedings, established the Senate Committee on Veterans' Affairs, increased the number of committee staff aides, and permitted minority party committee members to call witnesses of their choosing during one day of hearings.

Congressional Budget and Impoundment Control Act of 1974. Following executive branch challenges to congressional spending prerogatives, as well as concerns that Congress lacked the procedures necessary to participate effectively in fiscal policymaking, the House and Senate in 1972 created the Joint Study Committee on Budget Control to overhaul the budget process. A revision of the panel's recommendations was passed as the Congressional Budget and Impoundment Control Act of 1974, by all accounts a landmark reform measure.

In addition to creating the House and Senate Budget Committees, the 1974 act established the Congressional Budget Office to provide lawmakers with analytical support on fiscal issues. The act also included a timetable for considering budget-related measures, but that schedule has been substantially altered over the years because of the practical exigencies of deficit politics. Although the act itself was not responsible for the massive budget deficits that emerged during the 1980s, few members of Congress are satisfied with current budgetary procedures, and proposals for change remain prominent on the reform agenda.

House Select Committee on Committees, 1973–1974. The House created a select (temporary) committee in 1973 to review the chamber's committee structure. Chaired by Rep. Richard Bolling (D-Mo.), the select committee recommended a complete overhaul of the House's committee system, including balancing committee workloads, limiting member assignments, consolidating related policy jurisdictions into a single committee, and allowing the Speaker to refer a bill to more than one committee. In addition, the Bolling plan called for strengthening congressional oversight of the executive branch, reviewing the workload and jurisdictions of committees on a regular basis, and augmenting committee staffs. In the end, however, the House rejected the major consolidation of committee jurisdictions proposed by the Bolling committee. A committee of the Democratic Caucus, chaired by Rep. Julia Butler Hansen (D-Wash.), crafted a less far-reaching set of committee reforms, which the House adopted. Included were modest jurisdictional changes, proposals that increased the Speaker's authority and enlarged congressional staffs, and various other incremental reforms. In the 1990s, many Bolling committee issues and proposals would resurface as reformers again contemplated an overhaul of the congressional committee system. As with the Bolling/Hansen effort, contemporary reformers disagree about whether a bipartisan panel or the majority party caucus is the appropriate venue for drafting a reorganization plan.

House Democratic Caucus, 1971–1975. In addition to the Hansen committee's role in jurisdictional change, the House Democratic Caucus was the source of many important procedural reforms during the early 1970s. Collectively, these changes reduced the power of full committee chairs, increased the policymaking role of subcommittees, and strengthened the prerogatives of the Speaker. In 1971, for instance, Democrats changed their rules for selecting committee chairs to facilitate challenges to the most senior majority party member, who typically was chosen as chair. Two years later, House Democrats adopted the Subcommittee Bill of Rights, which further institutionalized subcommittees as important arenas for legislative work. The Subcommittee Bill of Rights guaranteed to subcommittees fixed jurisdictions and adequate staff resources, and obligated committee chairs to refer bills to the appropriate subcommittee within two weeks. Also increased during this period was the influence of Democratic Party leaders over the committee assignment process. In addition, the Speaker was given the authority to nominate all majority party members of the important Rules Committee, which sets the parameters for floor debate in the House.

By shifting power from committee chairs downward toward the subcommittee level of the legislative process, as well as upward toward the centralized party leadership, the House Democratic reformers hoped to make the committee system more accountable to the Speaker and to the Democratic Caucus as a whole. Many of the procedural reforms implemented in 1995 by Speaker Newt Gingrich (R-Ga.), majority leader Richard Armey (R-Texas), and the new Republican majority should be viewed as a continuation, though at a much accelerated pace, of these earlier Democratic Caucus efforts to make House committees more responsive to the policy priorities and views of the majority party.

House Commission on Administrative Review, 1976–1977. In the midst of ethical and administrative controversies, particularly Rep. Wayne Hays's (D-Ohio) employment of his mistress as a "non-typing" typist, the House created the Commission on Administrative Review, comprising lawmakers and private citizens. Headed by Rep. David Obey (D-Wis.), the commission was charged with studying and recommending ways to improve the House's administrative services, to enhance members' use of time, and to ensure integrity in the conduct of the House's legislative business. The Obey commission's financial ethics package was substantially approved by the House despite angering many senior House members, who opposed the changes. But other Commission recommendations, such as the centralization of diverse administrative matters into a new Office of House Administrator, were turned down by the House. Interestingly, the Obey commission's administrative recommendations would reemerge in the 1990s in the wake of the House bank and post office scandals, and the essential objectives would be included in the House Republican reorganization of 1995.

House Select Committee on Committees, 1979–1980. Even though the Bolling committee had demonstrated the pitfalls of committee jurisdiction reform, continued frustration with the committee system, particularly in the energy area, led to yet another House effort at committee reorganization. In 1979, a second Select Committee on Committees, chaired by Rep. Jerry Patterson (D-Calif.), was established to recommend changes in committee jurisdictions. Citing the fate of the Bolling recommendations, the Patterson committee instead adopted an incremental approach to change and proposed that the House create a new Energy Committee. Rep. John Dingell (D-Mich.), who as chair of an important energy subcommittee stood to lose the most from the Patterson plan, mobilized opposition to it just as he had to the plan proposed by Bolling. In 1980, the House rejected the Patterson plan and overwhelmingly adopted an alternative plan that largely left intact the wide dispersion of energy jurisdiction on Capitol Hill. With jurisdictional fragmentation rife in energy and other policy areas, and as Democrats considered comprehensive reform in 1993–1994, Dingell would again emerge as a leading opponent of committee restructuring.

Temporary Select Committee to Study the Senate Committee System, 1976–1977. In March 1976, the Senate created its own select committee, headed by Senator Adlai Stevenson (D-Ill.), to conduct a thorough review of the Senate's committee structure and make recommendations for improvement. The Stevenson committee's reform plan, after revision by the Rules and Administration Committee, was adopted by the Senate in 1977, producing the most significant restructuring of the Senate committee system since passage of the 1946 Legislative Reorganization Act. For example, the plan led to a reduction in the number of standing committees and consolidation of broad substantive jurisdictions to promote more comprehensive policymaking. Reforms aimed at limiting senators' committee assignments were codified in chamber rules. But the new committee assignment limitations were quickly ignored, and members' concerns about the Senate committee system resurfaced in the 1980s and 1990s. Interestingly, the Stevenson jurisdictional changes influenced some of the thinking behind the committee restructuring implemented by House Republicans in 1995.

Temporary Select Committee to Study the Senate Committee System, 1984. In June 1984, the Senate established another select committee to recommend improvements in the operation of its committees. Senator Dan Quayle (R-Ind.) was named the panel's chair. The Quayle committee conducted a few hearings and in December 1984 submitted its recommendations for change, which were largely ignored except for its proposal for tighter committee assignment limitations. The following year, some reductions in member assignments did occur. However, by the 1990s, reform-minded senators were again urging limitations on members' committee and subcommittee assignments because Quayle's restrictions were too frequently being waived.

These nine efforts were the most significant organized reform initiatives on Capitol Hill between World War II and the beginning of the 1990s. There were many other attempts to change selected aspects of House or Senate organization during this period—various budget reform acts, the War Powers Resolution, campaign finance changes, the televising of House and Senate floor sessions, seniority revisions, ethics reviews, party caucus inquiries, and modifications in Senate filibuster practices.[4] This history of regular, ongoing attempts to alter congressional operations has shaped the contemporary reform agenda. Collectively, these efforts send a message: There are few truly new reform proposals.

REPUBLICANS CONFRONT DEMOCRATIC RULE

Purposeful efforts to reorganize Congress have always been controversial because reform fundamentally is about the distribution of power on Capitol Hill. But the controversy surrounding previous reform initiatives was generally not dominated by partisan conflict. Committee chairs disagreed with party leaders. Senior members disagreed with junior colleagues. Partisan tensions often were present, but they did not dominate reorganization issues. This changed in the 1980s with the emergence in the House of a partisan Republican reform agenda highly critical of the Democratic majority.

GOP interest in congressional reform is long-standing. Particularly in the House, where Democrats organized the chamber for forty years, Republicans sought to alter congressional operations to increase their policymaking role and maximize their partisan advantage. Beginning in the early 1980s, the reform activities of House Republicans intensified, became more public, and grew substantially more partisan and confrontational toward the Democratic leadership. Dismissed as "bomb throwers" by some, an increasing number of GOP representatives sought to undermine public confidence in Democratic management of the House.

Why did Republicans increase their attacks on the Democratic House during the 1980s? One reason was simple frustration with their long minority status. As minority leader Robert H. Michel (R-Ill.) noted, "I haven't chaired a subcommittee or full committee in my 30 years in Congress. It's a pretty doggone discouraging and debilitating thing."[5] Michel's predecessor as minority leader, Rep. John J. Rhodes (R-Ariz.), wrote that "being in a congressional minority for a long period of time is depressing. . . . Members of the minority grow tired of being constantly against proposed bills and of never being able to enact anything of their own."[6] A moderate Republican, Jerry Lewis of California, once observed, "As far as influencing what happens inside the House, we have just enough votes to be irresponsible."[7]

The frustrations of the House GOP were mitigated somewhat in 1980 by the election of Ronald Reagan as president and by the Republican takeover of the Senate. Although the House remained in Democratic hands, that year Republican strength grew to 189 seats—sufficient to forge majority coalitions with conservative Democrats on major issues such as the Reagan economic program. Going into the midterm elections of 1982, House Republicans hoped to capitalize on the Reagan Revolution and again increase their numbers. Instead, Republicans lost twenty-six seats, and with those seats the possibility of forming bipartisan conservative majorities. As an aide to Representative Michel recalled, "We had more successes and greater activity in [1981–1982] than we'd had in 30 years. We just got a horrible stomach punch in 1982, which set everybody and everything back."[8]

The discouraging results of November 1982, combined with longer-term frustrations with their minority role, led many Republicans to attack the House itself. In increasing numbers, GOP representatives felt little stake in the procedures and processes rooted in forty years of Democratic control. If they could convince the public that the internal organization of Congress was bloated, corrupt, and unfair, they might achieve two important results: House Democrats might be forced to extend more protections to the minority party, and change-oriented voters might elect more Republican lawmakers.

Minority Party Rights

In the immediate post–World War II years, the power structure on Capitol Hill was mostly conservative, and the minority Republicans felt a part of the process.[9] Before the 1970s, House Republicans exerted significant influence during the crucial committee stage, where issues are framed, proposals are refined, and key legislative bargains are struck. GOP ranking minority members often developed close working relationships with the relevant chair. The presence of a substantial bloc of conservative Democrats also gave Republican committee members important ideological allies, increasing their power in committee. And patterns of deference toward committee decisions within the chamber as a whole further solidified the clout of Democratic and Republican conservatives.

Beginning with the landmark congressional elections of 1958, the proportion of conservatives among congressional Democrats, and among the committee chairs, began to decline. Southern Democrats became more ideologically representative of the Democratic Party nationally. At the same time, liberal reformers revitalized the House Democratic Caucus as an organization and sought to impose greater accountability on chairs and rank-and-file committee members. As a result, House Republicans were less able to shape legislation during the committee stage of the legislative process.

As Republican opportunities in committees narrowed, changes occurred in floor decision making that further curtailed the potential role of the House GOP. Prior to the 1970s, recorded votes were taken on the final passage of legislation, but not on amendments offered on the House floor. Consequently, it was difficult to force individual members to take a public position on the issues addressed by floor amendments. The Legislative Reorganization Act of 1970 provided for recorded votes on floor amendments. One result was an explosion in the number of amendments offered in the House.[10] Before the new voting procedure, about eight hundred floor amendments were offered in the chamber each Congress. In the wake of the 1970 act, the number surged to approximately fourteen hundred, with Republicans offering disproportionately more amendments than Democrats. By the late 1970s, the average number of amendments offered by Republicans exceeded the average number for Democrats.

What was happening on the House floor? By most accounts, the advent of recorded voting led Republicans to offer more amendments on divisive matters, particularly on issues that might politically embarrass Democrats. Abortion, school prayer, and busing are among the issues that Democrats traditionally have attempted to keep off the floor. With recorded votes on floor amendments, Republicans could force Democrats to go on the record on matters that divided their constituents. Republican lawmakers hoped that these votes would provide Republican challengers with useful campaign ammunition. The number of floor amendments offered by Democratic members also increased during this period, complicating leadership efforts to manage the schedule and adding greater uncertainty to the legislative process.

In 1975, the Democratic Caucus gave the Speaker the power to nominate all majority party members of the Rules Committee, the panel that essentially determines which, or even whether, amendments can be offered on the floor. This party reform effectively made the Rules Committee an arm of the Speaker. Responding to the surge in Republican amending activity, Speaker Thomas P. (Tip) O'Neill (D-Mass.) directed the Rules Committee to clamp down on the number of floor amendments that members could offer.

In 1977–1978, more than 70 percent of major bills were considered on the floor under open rules. A *rule*, in brief, is a special resolution reported by the Rules Committee that establishes the conditions for debating and amending a bill. Under an *open rule,* members are free to offer any and all substantively relevant floor amendments to the legislation.[11] The percentage of open rules declined to 23.5 percent in 1981–1982, and then to 13.6 percent in 1985–1986, the last Congress under Speaker O'Neill. Throughout this period, few rules were *closed rules* (with no amendments permitted). But the usual approach to House floor decision making soon became the *restrictive rule,* which imposes substantial limitations on the number and content of permissible amendments.

Democrats argued that restrictive amendment rules were critical to managing the flow of business efficiently. Rep. Claude Pepper (D-Fla.), chairman of the Rules Committee from 1983 to 1989, commented that "this is not a highhanded committee. We act in what we think is the best interest of the House."[12] His successor as chairman, Rep. Joe Moakley (D-Mass.), emphasized that all rules must receive majority support by the full House to be binding.

> I think that everyone would agree that it is the prerogative of the majority party leadership to both set the legislative agenda, and to provide for the orderly consideration of legislation in the House. [However] the Rules Committee structures its rules based not only on the view of its members, but also on its perception of what a majority, what 218 members of the House, is prepared to support.[13]

Not surprisingly, House Republicans viewed the increased use of restrictive amendment rules very differently—as a strong-armed attempt by the majority leadership to block potentially popular Republican proposals and protect Democrats from having to vote on potentially troublesome issues. In the mid-1980s, Rep. Trent Lott (R-Miss.), the minority whip (second-ranking Republican leader), charged that the "Democratic leadership is trying to turn the Rules Committee into the stranglehold on this institution that it was 30 years ago."[14] Rep. David Dreier (R-Calif.), a leader among House Republicans on reform issues, argued:

> [The House] is reminiscent of the big city political machines that flourished earlier in this century. . . . I don't think it's a mere coincidence that the growing prevalence of restrictive floor procedures has coincided with the decline in public support for Congress. . . . [My concern] is the way these rules are distorted and manipulated to evade accountability.[15]

By the early 1980s, House Republicans perceived the rise of restrictive rules as part of a larger pattern of Democratic insensitivity to their rights as a congressional minority. Hence, they devised a counterattack.

Beginning with the 98th Congress (1983–1984), the Republican leadership began offering a comprehensive reform plan as an alternative to the House rules changes traditionally proposed by the Democrats on the first day of each new Congress, when the House officially adopts its rules. The rules of the House in a given Congress are primarily drawn from the rules used in previous years, but the majority party often makes incremental changes at the beginning of each Congress. By offering comprehensive reform plans as substitutes for these Democratic changes, the House GOP developed and promoted its own reform agenda and also criticized Democratic management of the chamber. Lott, for example, described the Democratic rules changes in 1983 as the "paranoidal palpitations of an imperiled party. . . . I would urge my colleagues to turn back the cowardly [Democratic] package and [support] the Republican alternative that is designed to make this a more responsible, workable, and accountable Congress."[16] Over the years, the Republican reform program would evolve, eventually addressing a wide range of organizational matters, such as proxy voting, restrictive rules, staff cuts, congressional perks, and minority party rights.

Newt Gingrich and the Conservative Opportunity Society

For years, Republicans regularly complained about House rules and structures and advanced selected proposals for change. Their efforts drew little public support in part because many Republicans were content to work within the system, striking bargains with their majority counterparts on legislation. However, beginning with the 1978 midterm elections, a new breed of Republican began entering the chamber in increasing numbers. These newer members tended to be staunch conservatives who were less willing to accept the institutional status quo. Described by the national media as "partisan fire-eaters," "guerrilla warriors," and "bomb throwers," they sought to portray the Democratic leadership as corrupt and to undermine public confidence in congressional operations. Their informal leader was Newt Gingrich.

As early as his freshman term, Gingrich exhibited remarkably ambitious long-range goals for himself and the House GOP. He believed that two key strategies would enable Republicans to win a majority. First, they must work together to advance a unified, strongly conservative policy agenda and use that agenda to nationalize House campaigns. Second, the Republicans should aggressively confront the Democratic leadership about the House legislative both political parties about congressional operations. We observed at close hand many of the events described in this book and have tried to provide readers with an "over-the-shoulder" perspective à la Fenno.

Students of Congress have much to learn from the comments and observations of lawmakers and other participants in congressional politics. As a result, this book is full of quotations from members and staff. Unlike Fenno, our observations derive in part from meetings and conversations that occurred while we were congressional employees, and thus should be treated as confidential. Consequently, the vast majority of quotations in this book are from published sources. In the few instances where we do cite comments made directly to us (or in our presence), the remarks are not attributed to a particular member or staff person. We are convinced, however, that other participants and observers of the reform process on Capitol Hill will find the pages that follow to be balanced, accurate, and compelling.

Notes

1. Two other panels, House Administration and Government Operations, also received the measure, but the Rules Committee was widely viewed as the main committee of jurisdiction.

2. Bob Wise, "Diary of a Congressman," *The Washington Monthly,* June 1995, 40.

3. David Rosenbaum, "Strong Speaker, Strong House? One Doesn't Necessarily Follow the Other," *New York Times,* December 4, 1994, 32.

4. Charles O. Jones, "Radical Change in Makeup of Congress Will Occur Regardless of Reform Efforts," *Roll Call,* August 8, 1994, 30. Useful books about congressional reform include Leroy N. Rieselbach, *Congressional Reform: The Changing Modern Congress* (Washington, D.C.: Congressional Quarterly, 1994); Roger H. Davidson and Walter J. Oleszek, *Congress Against Itself* (Bloomington, Ind.: Indiana University Press, 1977); Burton D. Sheppard, *Rethinking Congressional Reform: The Reform Roots of the Special Interest Congress* (Cambridge, Mass.: Shenkman Books, 1985). For a recent edited volume, see James A. Thurber and Roger H. Davidson, eds., *Remaking Congress: Change and Stability in the 1990s* (Washington, D.C.: Congressional Quarterly, 1995).

5. Michael Kelly, "Clinton's Escape Clause," *The New Yorker,* October 24, 1994, 46.

6. "Hill Interview, Rep. Beilenson," *The Hill,* November 8, 1995, 22.

7. The Democrats who lost (and the GOP candidates who won) tended to be in conservative to moderate districts, often in the South, that did not lean toward Bill Clinton in 1992. Particularly vulnerable were Democratic incumbents closely associated with the president's overall legislative agenda. See David W. Brady, John F. Cogan, and Douglas Rivers, *How the Republicans Captured the House: An Assessment of the 1994 Midterm Elections* (Hoover Institution, Stanford University, 1995). Exit polls also suggested that voters placing special emphasis on traditional morality ("belief in God, hard work, patriotism, frugality, personal and family responsibility, and self-reliance") were especially likely to vote Republican in 1994. See Charles E. Cook, "Exit

Poll Analysis Puts GOP Landslide in Whole New Light," *Roll Call,* February 27, 1995, 8.

8. Eric D. Fingerhut, "Clinton and Congress: A Democrat Throws Stones," *New York Times,* December 17, 1994, 23.

9. Quoted in the Junction City, Kansas, *Daily Union,* November 6, 1994, 4.

10. Jeff Shear, "The Other Entitlement," *National Journal,* October 14, 1995, 2532.

11. For example, consult David R. Mayhew, *Congress: The Electoral Connection* (New Haven: Yale University Press, 1973). See also Morris P. Fiorina, *Congress: Keystone of the Washington Establishment* (New Haven: Yale University Press, 1977). A related, "distributive" model of congressional policymaking is developed in an important series of articles by Kenneth A. Shepsle and Barry R. Weingast published in the *American Political Science Review* and the *American Journal of Political Science,* among other journals.

12. The partisan foundations of congressional organization are emphasized in a number of works: David Rohde, *Parties and Leaders in the Postreform House* (Chicago: University of Chicago Press, 1991); Gary Cox and Mathew McCubbins, *Legislative Leviathan: Party Government in the House* (Berkeley: University of California Press, 1993); Barbara Sinclair, *Legislators, Leaders, and Lawmaking* (Baltimore: Johns Hopkins University Press, 1995); Sarah A. Binder and Steven S. Smith, "Acquired Procedural Tendencies and Congressional Reform," in *Remaking Congress: Change and Stability in the 1990s,* ed. James A. Thurber and Roger H. Davidson (Washington, D.C.: Congressional Quarterly Press, 1995).

13. The most significant exposition of this view is Keith Krehbiel's pathbreaking study, *Information and Legislative Organization* (Ann Arbor: University of Michigan Press, 1991). See also Joseph Cooper, *The Origins of the Standing Committees and the Development of the Modern House* (Houston, Tex: Rice University Studies, 1970); and Arthur Maas, *Congress and the Common Good* (New York: Basic Books, 1983).

14. The Senate decided to stipulate in Senate Rule 22 that any amendment to that rule, if filibustered, requires a two-thirds vote to end the talkathon.

15. Krehbiel, *Information and Legislative Organization.* See also Richard L. Hall and Bernard Grofman, "The Committee Assignment Process and the Conditional Nature of Committee Bias," *American Political Science Review,* 84 (1990), 1149–66; and John Londregan and James M. Snyder, Jr., "Comparing Committee and Floor Preferences," *Legislative Studies Quarterly,* No. 192 (1994), 233–66.

16. A. S. Mike Monroney et al., *The Strengthening of American Political Institutions,* (Ithaca: Cornell University Press, 1949), p. 7. Concerns about the institutional capacities of Congress vis-à-vis the executive branch are especially pronounced when two vital legislative powers are involved: the power of the purse and the power to declare war. The House and Senate Budget Committees, for example, were created in the 1970s to provide the institution with the procedures necessary to participate in federal budget policy. Similarly, the War Powers Resolution of 1973 was intended to ensure congressional participation in decisions to place U.S. military forces in hostile situations.

17. Richard F. Fenno, *Congressmen in Committees* (Boston: Little, Brown, 1973). See also Richard L. Hall, "Participation and Purpose in Committee Decision Making," *American Political Science Review,* 81 (1987), 105–28.

18. Lawrence C. Dodd, "Congress and the Quest for Power," in *Congress Reconsidered,* 1st ed., ed. Lawrence C. Dodd and Bruce I. Oppenheimer (New York: Praeger, 1977). For an intriguing argument that the personal power agenda of then Speaker Henry Clay facilitated the rise of the House standing committee system in 1815–1817, consult Gerald Gamm and Kenneth Shepsle, "Emergence of Legislative Institutions: Standing Committees in the House and Senate, 1810–1825," *Legislative Studies Quarterly,* 14, No. 1 (1989), 39–66.

19. John Jacobs, "The Newt Gingrich of the Left," *Roll Call,* October 19, 1995, 14 See John Jacobs, *A Rage for Justice: The Passion and Politics of Philip Burton* (Berkeley. University of California Press, 1995).

20. The difference between clientele rationales and public opinion is that the former refers to the relatively parochial interests of particular constituencies, while the latter refers to the reform attitudes of the general public. Traditionally, the media also have played a key role in molding and shaping public opinion on reorganization issues. Public support for passage of the Legislative Reorganization Act of 1946 was generated in part by a major cover story in the June 1945 issue of *Life* magazine ("U.S. Congress: It Faces Great New Tasks with Outworn Tools"). During the mid-1960s, NBC News ran a prime-time television special ("Congress Needs Help"), which mobilized public backing for the eventual enactment of the Legislative Reorganization Act of 1970, another reform measure. Today scores of media outlets report on the alleged institutional shortcomings of Congress, as well as various proposals for changing the institution.

21. The classic overview of participant/observation methods as they relate to the study of Congress is the appendix to Richard F. Fenno, *Homestyle: House Members in Their Districts* (Boston: Little, Brown, 1978).

2

Setting the Stage

T HE REFORMS implemented by the new Republican majority on Capitol Hill were not devised entirely during the short transition period following the November 1994 elections. Instead, these changes resulted from years of sustained interest in reform issues by lawmakers and substantial public sentiment that the internal operations of the national legislature needed improvement.

Of course, public distrust of Congress is as old as the Republic. For instance, looking back in 1925 on his twenty years of House service, Speaker Nicholas Longworth observed that "during the whole of that time we have been attacked, denounced, despised, hunted, harried, blamed, looked down upon, excoriated, and flayed."[1] Decades earlier, Mark Twain had asked his readers, "Suppose you were an idiot. Suppose you were a member of Congress. But I repeat myself."[2] Throughout American history, lawmakers too have been dissatisfied with congressional operations. Under Article I of the U.S. Constitution, members of Congress determine the internal procedures and structures of the institution, and from the early congresses on, lawmakers have proposed countless changes in the organization of the legislative branch.

Still, the long-standing public concerns about Congress and continual efforts by lawmakers to alter congressional operations do not account for the content of the congressional reform agenda as it emerged in the years preceding the landmark 104th Congress, nor do they explain why reform sentiment has been so intense in the 1990s. The purpose of this chapter is to examine the historical context of contemporary reform politics. Although the institutional changes on Capitol Hill reflect many decades of congressional development, three aspects of recent congressional history primarily shaped the process, and attempt to make the internal operations of Congress a public issue. More senior Republicans initially were put off by the backbench firebrands. Sen. Dan Coats (R-Ind.), then a House member, recalled that "Newt's belief that to ultimately succeed you almost had to destroy the system so that you could rebuild it . . . was kind of scary stuff for some."[17] Among Democrats, Gingrich was viewed as a destructive nuisance. Tony Coelho (D-Calif.), the majority whip, described him as "a revolutionary who wants to destroy the system to rebuild it."[18] But the Georgian seldom veered from his two strategies during his sixteen-year rise to power in the House.

After the 1982 elections, Gingrich established an informal organization of young Republican activists; he called it the Conservative Opportunity Society (COS). Gingrich recruited many of the early members, including Coats, Robert Walker (R-Pa.), Vin Weber (R-Minn.), Duncan Hunter (R-Calif.), Dan Lungren (R-Calif.), Connie Mack (R-Fla.), and Judd Gregg (R-N.H.). Although the COS eventually grew to a few dozen members, the core group was usually around twelve. In December 1983, Gregg sent Gingrich a memo describing the COS agenda for 1984. Many of the issues mentioned were reform matters that, a decade later, would be in the Contract with America, including House rules changes, the balanced budget amendment, and the line-item veto.[19] Although senior Republicans were wary of the COS activists, GOP whip Lott, who was not a COS member, presented their views to the leadership. After Lott's election to the Senate in 1988, that role was filled by his successor as whip, Rep. Dick Cheney (R-Wyo.).

Throughout 1984, Gingrich and other COS members began publicizing their agenda and sharply criticizing Democrats during special orders, the period after formal legislative business has concluded for the day. During special orders, members can speak (usually to an empty chamber and for up to one hour) on a subject of their choosing. COS members also participated frequently in the one-minute speeches that members can deliver before legislative business begins. Gingrich, Walker, and Weber took the lead in both periods. Their remarks were carried on C-SPAN, the Cable Satellite Public Affairs Network, which provides gavel-to-gavel coverage of the House, including special orders and one-minutes. Gingrich later explained the tactic: "If people ask, 'Why is he on TV all the time,' my answer is 'That's how you can reach 260 million people. . . . That's how you attract attention so people can tell who's you's and who's them.'"[20]

In their floor statements, COS members argued that House rules were unfair to the minority party and that the Democratic leadership was restricting legitimate debate about pressing national issues. Walker's remarks in one special order are illustrative of the tone and content of the COS statements: "When it comes to the minority seeking to gain an upper hand of any kind, the majority immediately leaps in and uses the power of its majority to crush any minority participation in the legislative process." According to Walker, committee memberships were stacked in favor of the majority Democrats.

> The gentleman made mention of the Ways and Means Committee where at the present time we have less than 35 percent of the membership of that committee, even though proportionately we should have about 45 percent. That is particularly important because virtually every piece of legislation that comes to this floor out of the Ways and Means Committee comes out with a closed rule.

The result, in Walker's view, was that the constituents of GOP members were not being fully represented in the chamber.

> That means that in the committee we are down by such a proportion that the minority has no chance to impose any of its thinking on the bills. . . . We are thereby gagged. We are shutoff from having our constituents participate freely and fairly in the process and, in fact, the stench of unfairness affects this body throughout most of its deliberations.[21]

At first, Democrats ignored the late-night floor speeches of COS members, but over time resentment and anger grew within the majority party. Representative (now Senator) Byron L. Dorgan (D-N.D.), remarked that a "blowup was inevitable. We had special orders night after night after night that painted Democrats as irresponsible."[22]

Camera-Gate?

The blowup occurred in May 1984, with the COS reaping a major media windfall. On May 8, Gingrich and Walker orchestrated a special order during which they quoted and criticized foreign policy statements by House Democrats going back fifteen years. Many Democrats were mentioned by name, including Rep. Edward Boland (D-Mass.), a close friend and former roommate of Speaker O'Neill's. As usual for a special order, the chamber was empty of other members. However, C-SPAN viewers were unaware of this because the camera, following normal practice, focused only on the members speaking. At one point, after reading statements derogatory of Democrats into the record, Gingrich looked out at the empty chamber and asked, "How do you reason with people who think like that?"[23]

Speaker O'Neill was furious.

> I happened to be watching in my office one afternoon as Newt Gingrich was taking advantage of special orders to attack Eddie Boland's voting record and to cast aspersions on his patriotism. The camera focused on Gingrich, and anybody watching at home would have thought that Eddie was sitting there, listening to all of this. Periodically, Gingrich would challenge Boland on some point, and would then step back, as if waiting for Eddie to answer. But Boland had left hours ago, along with everybody else in the place.[24]

Under House rules, the Speaker controls television cameras in the chamber, and O'Neill's response came two days later. During a special order by Walker titled "The Integrity of the Congressional Record," the Speaker, without any notice to Walker, ordered camera operators to pan the chamber to show its emptiness to the viewing public. Viewers were surprised by the vacant room. Said one C-SPAN watcher from Salinas, California, "I didn't realize until . . . they made that pan that there was nobody in the whole place, and that was one of the best acting jobs I've ever seen."[25]

Expressing outrage at the camera change, COS members repeatedly took to the floor to criticize O'Neill. Connie Mack described it as "further escalation of dirty tricks" and "an arrogant abuse of power."[26] Vin Weber argued that the new camera angles were "part of a pattern that has grown . . . under the leadership of Speaker O'Neill . . . a pattern of increasing obstructionism of certain legislative business and of the people's right to know."[27] Walker charged that O'Neill was undermining special orders, "virtually the only time of the legislative day when the minority can control a block of [floor] time."[28] Speaking for the Republican leadership, minority whip Lott described the Speaker's action as an "underhanded, sneaky, politically motivated change" and "the most patently unfair political thing . . . I have seen in the 15 years I have been around here."[29]

The following week, during a floor exchange with Gingrich about the matter, the Speaker lost his temper, yelling at the Georgian, "You deliberately stood . . . before an empty House and challenged these [Democrats'] Americanism, and it is the lowest thing that I have ever seen in my 32 years in Congress."[30] Lott then demanded that the Speaker's words "be taken down" (stricken from the record) because they violated House rules against personally insulting other members. Acting on the advice of the parliamentarian, the Democrat presiding at the time, O'Neill's close friend Joe Moakley, agreed with Lott's interpretation, and the Speaker's words were stricken. O'Neill responded, "I was expressing my opinion very mildly, because I think much worse than what I said."[31]

The O'Neill-Gingrich dialogue was featured that evening on national network news, generating significant publicity for the COS. Later that night, Gingrich once again took to the floor, saying:

> I think we are entering a period of considerable change and that the House will never again be quite the same when we are done with this process. It may take 6 months, it may take 1 year, it may take 5 years. But it is as great a change as the progressive era changes from Speaker Cannon in 1910 [or] the rise of Sam Rayburn [a powerful Speaker] in the 1940's and 1950's. And I think during this period of change we are all going to go through a fair amount of turmoil.[32]

Verbal sparring over what some Republicans called "camera-gate" lingered on for weeks, with O'Neill quoted in the press as referring to Gingrich, Walker, and Weber as "the three stooges" and comparing them to members of the ultra-conservative John Birch Society. On the House floor, Walker complained about the Speaker's comments to the media, accusing O'Neill of "name calling." That skirmish ended with a parliamentary inquiry by Rep. Barney Frank (D-Mass.) directed at the Speaker pro tempore, the member presiding over the House in the absence of the Speaker:

Mr. Frank: I have a parliamentary inquiry.

Mr. Walker: I yield for a parliamentary inquiry.

The Speaker pro tempore: The gentleman will state his parliamentary inquiry.

Mr. Frank: The parliamentary inquiry is dealing with the question of propriety. Is the term "crybaby" an appropriate phrase to be used in a debate in the House?

The Speaker pro tempore: The Chair would hope that the phrase would not be used.

Mr. Frank: I thank the Speaker.[33]

Later, moderate Republican Bill Green of New York observed that "the Speaker made a big mistake when he got into the fight with Gingrich, because he put [the COS] on the map. Up until then, most people weren't paying a lot of attention. They thought it was just a frivolous activity."[34] According to Walker, O'Neill told him when they were together on the Capitol subway, "I made you guys."[35]

By the end of the year, other Republican conservatives were suggesting privately and publicly that the COS tactics were too strident and confrontational to be effective. In a move reportedly welcomed by minority leader Robert Michel, Rep. Mickey Edwards (R-Okla.), chairman of the American Conservative Union, sent other House Republicans a letter arguing that conservatives do not "get elected by Washington hoopla and forming ourselves into one great 'team.'" Gingrich, observed Edwards, had "a small cadre of active Members who have influenced matters by their activity but are irrelevant to the process. And now people are saying, 'Enough is enough. . . . I signed up to be a conservative Republican, not a lemming.'"[36]

An Election Controversy

Edwards's sentiments never gained much force because the Democratic majority continued to hand Gingrich and the COS new political ammunition, which further shifted the balance of sentiment within the House Republican Conference toward confrontation. A major flare-up following the November 1984 elections helped radicalize House Republicans. At the time, Republicans were discouraged because they had gained just fourteen seats, despite the landslide reelection victory of President Ronald Reagan. One of those seats was in the Eighth District of Indiana, where Republican Richard McIntyre led incumbent Democrat Frank McCloskey by seventy-two votes. The Indiana secretary of state, a Republican, certified McIntyre as the victor on December 14, but when Congress convened in January 1985, the Democratically controlled House, on a near-party-line vote, declared the seat vacant pending an investigation by the Committee on House Administration, which had jurisdiction over contested elections.

The House Administration Committee created a task force (two Democrats and one Republican) to investigate the matter. Attention focused on the ballots that had been disallowed on technical grounds, particularly a number of absentee ballots that had not been notarized or signed, which is required under Indiana law. For some reason, sixty-two of the questionable absentee ballots were mistakenly sent to precinct workers for counting, while another thirty-two were correctly retained, under Indiana law, by county clerks. On a partisan 2-to-1 division, the task force voted to count the sixty-two ballots that had been forwarded to the precincts but not the thirty-two ballots that had been held at the county level. The task force also decided to count a number of additional ballots that initially had been thrown out. The result: A four-vote lead for Democrat McCloskey. The House approved his election on May 1 by another near-party-line vote.

The contested election significantly heightened partisan tensions in the House, with Republicans charging that the Democratic majority was using its numbers to steal an election. Gingrich stated that "only the tyranny of the majority would prevent [McIntyre's] seating, and let me say to my colleagues on the Democratic side of the aisle: If you seek to run this House by tyranny, then you give those of us in the minority no alternative except to oppose tyrants."[37]

Outrage about Democratic rule was not confined to the COS but extended to Republicans across the ideological spectrum. Minority leader Michel remarked that "a grave injustice is being done here today. . . . To do anything short of seating Mr. McIntyre, in effect disenfranchises 500,000 Indiana citizens."[38] Moderate Republican Bill Frenzel of Minnesota commented, "I think the Democratic leadership behaved badly, and that has caused an awful lot of deep-seated bitterness among Republicans." The House, charged Frenzel, resembles "the partisan playpen of an arrogant majority."[39]

The Republican leadership appointed Gingrich to design a strategy for publicizing the Democrats' handling of the election controversy. For instance, hoping to catch the majority off guard, the Republican leadership moved to seat McIntyre during a pro forma session when many Democrats were absent, only to lose by one vote. After the House Administration Committee accepted McCloskey's four-vote win, Republicans blocked legislative business on the floor for a week, forcing an all-night session on April 22. When the House voted to seat McCloskey, Republicans walked out of the chamber en masse.

Anger about the McIntyre-McCloskey election coincided with renewed Republican complaints that party ratios in committees and subcommittees, as well as other procedural matters, were being tilted toward the Democratic majority. The matter of party ratios had long been a minority concern, but Republican complaints escalated in 1985. Early in the year, the GOP threatened to systematically boycott panel meetings unless party ratios in committees better reflected Republican representation in the chamber as a whole. Some concessions were made, and no boycott occurred. But Republicans on certain panels staged temporary walkouts over allegedly unfair subcommittee ratios. They also filed unsuccessful federal court suits challenging the partisan division of committee seats.

Gingrich and Wright

Republican concerns about their treatment by the Democrats, simmering throughout the mid-1980s, reached a boiling point in 1987–1989 during the speakership of Jim Wright (D-Tex.), who succeeded Tip O'Neill as the top Democrat in the House. Compared to O'Neill, Wright had a broader and more ambitious policy agenda and was willing to push the procedural prerogatives of the majority to the limit to promote that agenda. Majority leader Thomas S. Foley (D-Wash.) remarked, "This Speaker is not diffident or embarrassed about the power of the speakership. I don't think he is inclined to have a small, cautious speakership."[40] A liberal Democrat emphasized that Wright was a risk taker: "It's like Evel Knievel [the motorcycle daredevil]. As long as you keep jumping over all the cars, it's OK. But if you miss one, it could be costly."[41] O'Neill also had used the rules aggressively to promote his party's program, but Wright lacked the repository of personal goodwill enjoyed by his predecessor, and Republicans perceived that the Texan was more willing to engage in procedural subterfuge and to make the GOP feel their minority status.

By most accounts, the pivotal moment for Wright's relations with the minority occurred on October 29, 1987, when the House voted 206 to 205 to pass a major deficit-reduction package crafted by the Democrats.[42] Wright engaged in a number of hardball procedural moves to eke out the victory, including temporarily adjourning the House and counting a vote cast after he had declared that the time for voting had expired. Infuriated Republicans responded with their own procedural maneuvers, which forced an unusual Saturday session and tied up the chamber for much of the following week. Majority leader Foley argued that the Republican anger was "totally without substance."[43] However, as with the fallout from the McIntyre-McCloskey affair, even less confrontational Republicans were deeply alienated by the majority's tactics. Wright's active participation in U.S.-Nicaragua relations, which included negotiating with leaders of the Sandinista government, further antagonized Republicans because it appeared to them to undercut efforts by the Reagan administration to promote peace in Central America.

As the Wright speakership took shape in 1987, Gingrich began making extensive public statements questioning the Speaker's ethics. He mentioned a wide range of possible misdeeds, many of them quickly discredited. His attention eventually focused on the publishing arrangements for Wright's book, *Reflections of a Public Man,* and reports that the Speaker may have inappropriately intervened with U.S. and foreign officials on behalf of certain oil and gas firms.

Gingrich's individual efforts to instigate an investigation by the Committee on Standards of Official Conduct (the House Ethics Committee) were initially dismissed by congressional Democrats as baseless charges by a political adversary. However, as questions about Wright repeatedly surfaced in the media, particularly about the book deal and the Speaker's relationship with Texas developer George Mallick, the public interest watchdog organization Common Cause also called for a formal investigation. The Common Cause request could not be easily dismissed. After Gingrich filed a formal complaint in May 1988, Wright asked the House Ethics Committee to proceed with an inquiry.

During the months leading up to the Ethics Committee investigation and as the case unfolded, Gingrich spoke with journalist John Barry about his campaign against the Speaker. He emphasized that it was part of his broader efforts to undermine the Democratically controlled House. He remarked, "If Wright consolidates his power, he will be a very, very formidable man. We [have] to take him on early to prevent that." Gingrich also told Barry:

> Wright's a useful keystone to a much bigger structure. I'll just keep pounding and pounding on his ethics. There comes a point where it comes together and the media takes off on it or it dies.
>
> He's from Texas. He's been in politics over thirty years. An aggressive investigator with subpoena powers might find something. . . . If he survives this ethics thing, he may become the greatest Speaker since Henry Clay.

Gingrich explained, "I'm engaged in a long-term struggle. The House is sick and Wright's the symbol."[44]

Asked about Gingrich, the Speaker responded, "My views of him are somewhat similar to those of a fire hydrant toward a dog."[45]

In March 1989, President George Bush nominated Rep. Dick Cheney to be secretary of defense, opening up Cheney's second-ranking whip post in the GOP leadership structure. Gingrich was selected by his fellow House Republicans to replace Cheney as minority whip, defeating by one vote Rep. Edward Madigan (R-Ill.), the candidate of the more pragmatic wing of the party. Gingrich's ascension reflected the growing desire among House Republicans for the activist, confrontational approach to the Democrats that had been his hallmark. It also reflected Gingrich's enhanced prominence as a result of the Wright ethics investigation. Observed Mickey Edwards, "If Newt wins this, you've got to give some credit to Jim Wright."[46]

In the end, the charges Gingrich filed against Wright were dropped. However, as part of its investigation, the Ethics Committee, and the independent counsel it hired, turned up sufficient evidence to identify sixty-nine other instances of possible House rules violations by the Speaker. The panel's report was in the form of a Statement of Alleged Violations, analogous to a grand jury indictment, and thus did not constitute a formal finding of guilt. That would be determined during the next stage of the committee's deliberations. But the panel's finding that there was reason to believe violations had occurred, along with two years of negative media coverage, took an enormous political toll on Wright. The Speaker's support among House Democrats also had been undermined by his decision earlier in 1989 not to allow passage without a floor vote of a 51 percent pay raise for lawmakers. The proposed pay hike lost, angering many members. Wright stepped down as Speaker on May 31, resigning from Congress the following month. On June 6, 1989, the House elected Thomas Foley as Speaker, with Republicans wearing buttons that read "Reform not Revenge."[47]

With Gingrich as minority whip, COS veterans now filled key positions throughout the Republican leadership, an indicator that the Republican Conference as a whole had shifted substantially toward confrontation. Gingrich appointed Robert Walker, former chair of the COS, chief deputy whip, along with party moderate Steve Gunderson (R-Wis.). In addition, two other former COS chairs now held leadership positions: Vin Weber was secretary of the Republican Conference, and Duncan Hunter was chair of the Research Committee.

The Gang of Seven

The congressional elections of 1990 brought to the House a new crop of Republican freshmen drawn to the slash-and-burn tactics of the COS. Seven of the GOP freshmen organized an informal group that became known as the Gang of Seven. Included were Reps. Jim Nussle of Iowa, Rick Santorum of Pennsylvania, John Boehner of Ohio, Scott Klug of Wisconsin, Charles Taylor of North Carolina, and Frank Riggs and John Doolittle of California. Many Democrats perceived Gingrich as the behind-the-scenes leader of the group, which they dismissed as "the seven dwarfs" or even "Gingrich's pet trick act." Klug remarked, "Newt serves as kind of an unofficial cheerleader. I don't think he's orchestrated it. . . . He's been a valuable asset in helping at times to tell us how to accomplish what we want to accomplish."[48] During 1991–1992, the group would meet weekly, with Nussle presiding.

The focus of the Gang of Seven was congressional reform, and during the 102d Congress they advocated a range of reform initiatives, particularly the abolition of congressional perks. The group was derided by Democrats and many outside observers of Congress. For example, *Roll Call,* the Capitol Hill newspaper, editorialized that "often, the attitude seems to be that the Seven feel they have to destroy Congress in order to save it."[49] Rep. Steny Hoyer (D-Md.), chair of the Democratic Caucus, described the Gang of Seven as a "kamikaze crowd in the Republican Conference that is much more interested in making outrageous allegations they cannot back up."[50] Gang member Santorum countered that their Democratic critics were "folks who are fighting to keep their turf. They don't want anyone else to play in their sandbox. We're going in and looking at all the sand on their side of the box and saying, 'We just want to make sure you're not polluting the sand.'"[51] Colleague Boehner declared that "seven freshmen have about as much power around here as the lint on the carpet. Our only chance of succeeding was to get America as mad as we were."[52] In 1991–1992, the Gang of Seven helped orchestrate and rivet public attention on a scandal that rocked the chamber—the House bank scandal.

THE HOUSE BANK AND PUBLIC DISAPPROVAL OF CONGRESS

The American people have generally had a low opinion of the U.S. Congress, although the level of public disapproval has varied over time. For decades, the Gallup Poll has periodically asked citizens whether they "approve or disapprove of the way the U.S. Congress is handling its job."[53] Immediately following the 1974 Watergate scandal, 48 percent of the American people said they approved of congressional performance, but the percentage fell steadily during the remainder of the 1970s, reaching 24 percent in November 1976 and just 19 percent in June 1979. During the 1980s, public approval of Congress rebounded somewhat, varying from 32 percent in August 1980 to 56 percent in January 1987. For the rest of the decade, Congress's job performance rating stayed over 40 percent, but then dropped to the 20 to 30 percent range in 1990. Favorable public perceptions of congressional debate on the Gulf War again lifted the congressional approval rating to 49 percent in January 1991. The rating quickly dropped back to the 20 percent range, where it stayed until the House bank scandal was publicized and the approval rating reached an all-time low of 17 percent.

Public outrage over the House bank began in September 1991, after a report by the General Accounting Office (GAO) revealed that during the twelve-month period ending June 30, representatives had written more than eight thousand checks on insufficient funds at the House bank. These checks were never really bounced because no rules had been implemented by the bank to constrain overdrafts. Instead, bank officials simply covered the bad checks, without penalty, using deposits made by other members. No public money was lost, and all the checks were eventually covered by the offending members. Still, a commercial bank would not have tolerated such shoddy financial practices.

After *Roll Call* reported the GAO findings, news media across the country quickly picked up the story, generating a flurry of negative coverage of Congress. A *Houston Post* headline was typical: "A Washington Solution—If

Your Checks Keep Bouncing, Just Vote Yourself a Raise."[54] Constituents may not understand the nuances of congressional procedure or the subtleties of the federal budget process, but writing checks is part of everyday life for most people. To them, the notion that their representatives were bouncing personal checks without penalty reinforced their beliefs that members were an arrogant, privileged class out of touch with the problems of average citizens. The bank scandal also symbolized the kind of fiscal irresponsibility many citizens believe has caused the budget deficit. The flames of public resentment toward Congress were fanned by other reports that lawmakers were not paying their bills in the House restaurants.

In response to this controversy, Speaker Foley issued a statement saying that he had previously instructed the sergeant at arms (who was responsible for the bank) to stop honoring overdrafts. These instructions, he said, had not been followed. Foley informed the House on September 25 that overdrafts would no longer be covered: "Members will henceforth be treated without exception as they would be in a private depository institution. . . . All Members should start now with a clean slate."[55]

The Gang of Seven, however, was not interested in Foley's clean slate. They wanted stronger actions taken against the kiters. Nussle, Santorum, and Klug made statements on the House floor calling for full disclosure of the names of members with overdrafts. On October 1, in a memorable gesture, Nussle stood in the House chamber wearing a paper bag over his head and announced to the television cameras that "it is time to take the mask off this institution. . . . Mr. Speaker, announce the list of names." Doolittle joined him with a one-minute statement, followed the next day by one-minutes from Boehner, Klug, and Nussle again. On October 3, with public outrage over the bank soaring, the House voted to close the financial institution and instructed the House Ethics Committee to investigate the matter. The Gang of Seven declared partial victory but continued to push for full public disclosure. Nussle reported, "I personally even tried to crash a leadership meeting . . . to let them know we weren't going to let this die."[56] Santorum said, "Maybe sometimes banging spoons on a highchair works."[57]

After a five-month investigation, on March 2, 1992, members of the Ethics Committee proposed that only the names of the twenty-four worst offenders over the past three years be revealed to the public. The Democratic leadership initially embraced the plan, but Republicans and many Democrats argued that full disclosure was critical for repairing the credibility of the House. Again the Gang of Seven took the lead. Nussle remarked, "If constituents across the country are as angry as mine, then a little bit of tar is being boiled and feathers are being readied."[58] President George Bush joined the call for full disclosure. To avoid any entanglement in this controversy, the Senate, by a roll-call vote of 95 to 2, reported a resolution declaring that it did not even have a bank.

Throughout the spring, public anger about the House bank scandal was reinforced by a burgeoning scandal associated with the House post office.

Postal workers admitted to financial misdeeds and peddling drugs in House office buildings. As federal and congressional investigators probed internal post office operations, additional allegations surfaced that members of the House had used the facility to convert campaign and office funds into cash for personal use. These allegations eventually led to the indictment, electoral defeat, and eventual conviction of Rep. Dan Rostenkowski (D-Ill.), chair of the Ways and Means Committee. (The Republican 104th Congress has privatized operations of the House postal system.)

In mid-March 1992, the House voted to disclose the names of all current and former members who had overdrawn their accounts at the bank, even though it was clear that shoddy financial records meant that some innocent members would be mistakenly included in the list. Discussion about the matter on the House floor was corrosive. Amid loud hissing from the majority side of the aisle, Gingrich ridiculed Democratic claims that full disclosure derived from a bipartisan agreement.

> The chutzpa, the hubris, the gall of Democratic leader after Democratic leader coming to the floor tonight and wrapping themselves in bipartisanship. . . . Possibly you have no idea how you behave. Possibly you truly are so overwhelmed by the arrogance of power to such a degree that you simply cannot understand the gap between your words and your actions. . . . All this week the Democratic leadership tried to block full disclosure. Only when public outrage had mounted and the Democratic backbenchers had rebelled did the Democratic leadership agree to full disclosure.[59]

An angry Foley responded to Gingrich's comments.

> The suggestion that we have sought to block this resolution is patently untrue. . . . We have the task of [repairing] the reputation of this House. We have the task to show to the American people that we intend to see that deficiencies in its operation are corrected. I am determined to see that that happens, and I am willing to work with anyone on the Republican side, including the whip from Georgia, if he is serious in his offer.[60]

The names of the 24 worst offenders were revealed on April 1, 1992. Two weeks later, the remaining names—252 current and 51 former members—were released. Included on the list were Speaker Foley (2 overdrafts) and majority leader Richard Gephardt (D-Mo.) (28 overdrafts). Also included were Gingrich (22 overdrafts) and COS leaders Duncan Hunter (399 overdrafts) and Vin Weber (125 overdrafts). Public opinion polls at the time indicated that 80 percent of Americans thought that most members of Congress were personally financially corrupt.

In the November 1992 elections, involvement in the House bank scandal proved to be a significant liability for many Democratic and Republican incumbents.[61] For example, as a campaign gimmick, the Republican running against Rep. Chet Atkins (D-Mass.) handed out rubber checks made out to "Chester Malarkey."[62] Of the forty-six Members who kited one hundred or more checks, more than half were defeated or retired from the House.

Gingrich barely won renomination, in part because of his overdrafts. Fellow COS founder Weber chose not to run for reelection, citing constituent anger over his bad checks.

An important consequence of releasing the names was widespread demand for congressional reform in both the House and the Senate. Representatives and senators wanted to demonstrate publicly that they strongly supported institutional reorganization. Members of the Senate understood that the public fury over the House bank did not distinguish between the two chambers and that public approval of Congress as a whole had reached a historic low—thus their interest in reform. Congress took two immediate actions. First, the House and Senate created a bipartisan, bicameral committee to evaluate the internal operations of Congress and to provide recommendations for change. Second, the House established a bipartisan director of nonlegislative and financial services. The task of the new director was to professionalize the House's purely administrative functions. Neither action would have occurred without the House bank scandal, and both merit discussion because they are integral to the story of reform.

DAMAGE CONTROL

Compared to the pressure for change in the House, momentum for reform in the Senate was less intense for a variety of reasons. Republicans had been in the majority from 1981 to 1987, alleviating the frustrations of long-term minority status. The filibuster tactic, unavailable to House members, means that all senators have enormous procedural prerogatives. Any senator can block legislation unless supporters can muster the sixty votes necessary to invoke cloture and cut off debate. The Senate also is more informal than the highly structured House, reducing the potential gains from altering the chamber's internal organization.

Interestingly, although the general impetus for reform was less marked in the Senate, in 1991–1992 the key catalyst for creating a new Joint Committee on the Organization of Congress to consider comprehensive reform was a member of that chamber, Sen. David Boren (D-Okla.). A former Rhodes scholar, Boren had been elected governor of Oklahoma in 1974 after using a broom as his campaign symbol. Elected to the Senate in 1979, Boren was still considered a maverick and a reformer even into his third term. In 1991, Boren began talking with colleagues about creating a bipartisan, bicameral committee to study the internal operations of Congress and to provide comprehensive recommendations for change. He patterned the idea on the two previous bicameral reform entities, the 1945 and 1965 Joint Committees on the Organization of Congress, which produced the Legislative Reorganization Acts of 1946 and 1970, respectively.

During extensive statements on the Senate floor, including a well-publicized reform vigil in the fall of 1991, Boren argued that comprehensive reorganization was needed to restore congressional credibility, to make the institution more efficient, and to counter the growing popular movement for term limitations. He declared:

> All across this country there are new cries for term limitations of Members of Congress. . . . It is a signal from the people of the United States [about] the level of frustration among citizens who feel that Congress no longer conducts the public business in a proper way. [The] frustration level has now reached the point [where] the public is ready to turn to any solution, even an extreme one, to try to change things.[63]

In the House, Rep. Lee Hamilton (D-Ind.), a respected former chairman of the House Intelligence and Iran-Contra Committees, also was searching for ways to improve the organizational effectiveness of Congress. Boren and Hamilton agreed to cointroduce a concurrent resolution creating a third Joint Committee on the Organization of Congress for the purposes of considering comprehensive reform. Boren approached Sen. Pete Domenici (R-N.M.), a pragmatic Republican leader of the Budget Committee, asking him to sign on to the resolution. At Domenici's suggestion, Rep. Bill Gradison (R-Ohio), a key House Republican leader on budgetary matters, was enlisted as the fourth leading sponsor of the proposal. The lawmakers introduced two identical resolutions (one in each chamber) in August 1991—before public exposure of the House bank and post office scandals.[64]

The four reformers emphasized institutional rationales for creating a third Joint Committee on the Organization of Congress. As Congress approached the twenty-first century, they argued, the proposed reform panel was needed to modernize the internal operations of the House and Senate. Missing from their remarks was the fiery partisan rhetoric about congressional failings used by the COS and the Gang of Seven. Domenici said, "I have developed a great deal of respect for Congress as an institution and for many of its Members, some of whom are among the finest people I have ever known. [But Congress] has become an unwieldy institution." Gradison acknowledged problems with "the protection of minority rights" in the House but emphasized that these and other procedural issues were "symptoms of a larger problem. . . . Short-term thinking . . . is distorting the ability of Congress to address urgent long-term national problems in a deliberate fashion." Hamilton observed that "an increasing number of issues—from global warming to drug trafficking—are both international and domestic and no longer cut neatly across organizational lines." Most important, the four lawmakers believed that "Congress needs to stand back, and take stock of itself from time to time [and it is] time for another comprehensive look at the operations of Congress."[65]

As the bank scandal began to unfold, the resolution to create a Joint Committee on the Organization of Congress gathered support, particularly from less senior members. President Bush endorsed the proposal in October, urging Congress to "trim this overgrown thicket of committees and subcommittees. These four are out front for Congressional reform."[66] Leading newspapers supported the effort, with the *New York Times* urging Congress to "listen to the anger." Democratic congressional leaders, however, were skeptical.

After the Senate Rules Committee conducted hearings on the joint reform panel in November 1991, attention focused on mobilizing support in the House. Hamilton and Gradison met with party and committee leaders, trying to enlist their support. One member of the House Democratic leadership told them that there could not be "two better people [pushing the proposal] given the noisy cluck of detractors against this. [But] every day I step into the dining room and somebody comes up and warns me about this crazy Hamilton-Gradison proposal. It would be dismissed if somebody [else] was pushing it, but you guys are respected." Speaker Foley, however, wanted substance addressed before procedural reform. "It becomes the preoccupation of many Members," he warned, "to reorganize the institutional structure rather than to devote their time and effort to the critical problems of national concern that lie before us, and I would like to give those priority."[67]

More generally, many Democrats were concerned about the proposed joint committee's bipartisan and bicameral structure. Under the authorizing resolution, the panel would have an equal number of Democrats and Republicans and an equal number of House members and senators. Democrats worried that bitter partisan divisions about key reform issues might doom to failure any bipartisan attempt at reform. In light of a decade of GOP attacks on House operations, as well as public fury about the House bank, Rep. David Obey, a long-time reform advocate, observed, "I think there is a poisonous atmosphere in the Congress today that makes this a peculiarly bad time to proceed with this effort." The Wisconsin Democrat added, "I don't think you ought to approve this resolution at this time, unless you really do believe that all four caucuses [House and Senate Democrats and Republicans] are willing . . . to use this as a device to improve the Institution, rather than . . . transfer power to different groups of people."[68]

Committee leaders with important stakes in the institutional status quo also expressed their reservations to Hamilton and Gradison in blunt and frank terms. When Hamilton asked one senior chair why he was against the proposed joint committee, the lawmaker furiously responded, "I don't want any f___ Republicans to have a say about House Rules." Still another chair spoke for many committee leaders when he told Hamilton and Gradison that previous reforms "were s___ then, and they're s___ now. . . . I like the concentration of power if I'm part of the organization. The concentration of power warms my heart." After the meeting, Hamilton jokingly told Gradison to "put him down as undecided."

During the spring of 1992, public approval of Congress continued to plummet because of the bank and post office scandals, the unpaid restaurant bills, and the cumulative effects of other complaints about the institution. A growing number of members looked for reorganization measures to support, hoping to convince constituents that they were pro-reform. After the House voted in March to release the names of the kiters, support for the Hamilton-Gradison proposal took off. Within two weeks, the previously reluctant Foley publicly endorsed the resolution, effectively ensuring that the joint committee would be established.

After pro forma consideration of the Hamilton-Gradison resolution by the Rules Committee, the proposal was overwhelmingly passed by the House in June. Senate action followed in July, with the House accepting the Senate's amended version in August. The resolution creating a joint reform committee provided lawmakers with the opportunity to support the concept of far-reaching reform without requiring them to take positions on specific, often controversial, reform issues. The official mandate of the new joint committee directed it to "make a full and complete study of the organization and operation of the Congress" and to recommend changes for "strengthening the effectiveness of Congress, simplifying its operations, improving its relationships with and oversight" of the other branches of government, and "improving the orderly consideration of legislation." The panel would begin its work after the November 1992 elections. Among most members and congressional observers, expectations for the joint committee ran high.

Following disclosure of the kiters, House members faced an immediate problem. Lawmakers needed to convince their constituents that unnecessary perks and administrative shoddiness had been ended in the House. On March 26, the same day he endorsed the joint reform committee, Speaker Foley announced the creation of a bipartisan administrative reform task force. Its assignment was to produce, within a few weeks, a plan to revamp House administrative practices. In contrast to the proposed joint committee, the sixteen-member task force would concentrate on administrative matters rather than a long-term reorganization of Congress.

Over the next two weeks, task force members met repeatedly, trying to forge a bipartisan consensus. The Democrats quickly coalesced around a recommendation originally proposed by the 1977 House Commission on Administrative Review, chaired by David Obey. Rejected by the House at the time, the recommendation called for the establishment of a bipartisan House administrator to manage the purely administrative, nonlegislative activities of the House (such as the payroll system, the House barbershop and gym, parking services, and the restaurants). The Republicans argued that broader reforms should be included in the package. The GOP members wanted to add proposals drawn from the reform plans they had been introducing at the beginning of each new Congress. For example, the Republicans wanted limitations on proxy voting in committees, more procedural prerogatives and committee staff for the minority party, and greater representation of Republicans on the Rules Committee, whose membership advantaged the majority party.

In the task force's closed-door meetings, Foley initially expressed some willingness to include certain proposals from the Republican list, but the negotiations quickly collapsed into partisan infighting. Democrats charged that although GOP task force members might be conciliatory, backbench Republicans did not want compromise and were forcing Republicans on the panel to continuously up the ante. Rep. Charlie Rose (D-N.C.), chair of the Committee on House Administration, remarked that the Republicans "want to use this as an opportunity for a power grab and they so much as admit it. They want a little ransom and the ransom they want is legislative reform."[69] One GOP task force member, Paul Henry (R-Mich.), described the strong cross-pressures under which the panel worked: "We can't sign on to something without substantial reform or our younger members will explode. [Democrats] can't sign on to something with substantial reform or their Old Guard will explode."[70]

On April 7, the bipartisan task force disbanded without approving any administrative reform plan. Two days later, after a floor debate punctuated by partisan shouting matches, the House passed, on a near-party-line vote, the majority Democrats' proposal to overhaul the day-to-day administrative operations of the House. Republican leaders attempted to stage a walkout, but the tactic fizzled. Instead, sixty-four Republicans voted "present." In addition to creating a House director of nonlegislative and financial services, the proposal called for the appointment of an inspector general, who would be responsible for auditing administrative and financial matters inside the House. These new officials, selected jointly by the Speaker, the majority leader, and the minority leader, would be overseen by a new bipartisan subcommittee of the Committee on House Administration. Democrats argued that the broad reforms sought by Republicans would be dealt with the following year by the new Joint Committee on the Organization of Congress. In short, public and member demands for the reorganization of Congress were largely put off during 1992. They would return.

ORGANIZATIONAL RATIONALES

Our description of the rise of congressional reform issues on the national agenda indicates that all five organizational rationales played some role in that process. Congressional operations are complex and multifaceted, and the institution's organizational structure is shaped by a wide range of political forces. Focusing entirely on clientele factors, partisan concerns, or any other single cause can result in key elements of the reform story being lost. Still, certain organizational rationales are more important than others in understanding the tactics and events that set the stage for the 1990s reform effort in Congress.

Public opinion was critical in focusing congressional attention on reorganization in the abstract. The House bank scandal crystallized and intensified public skepticism about the national legislature, fueling widespread demands for institutional change. For the most part, popular sentiment in favor of reform did not translate into widespread public support for specific reorganization proposals. (Exceptions included proposals to abolish congressional perks and otherwise overhaul administrative practices on Capitol Hill.) Although public opinion seldom determines the specifics of organizational choices in Congress, it can create incentives for lawmakers to embrace reform and to embark on sustained efforts to alter the legislative branch.

Institutional factors had a limited impact on the rise of reform. The four main sponsors of the 1990s joint reform committee (Boren, Domenici, Hamilton, and Gradison) began mobilizing support for their proposal before the explosion of public anger over the House bank. Though aware of the potential partisan and clientele implications of procedural change, these four legislators mostly emphasized the need to improve the effectiveness of Congress as an institution. Overall, however, such sentiments were a secondary reason for the emergence of reform on the congressional agenda.

Clientele factors also played a limited role during this stage of the reform process. The procedural and structural interests of clientele groups often center on the committee system, the locus of power for so many outside interests. Clientele concerns vary by committee, depending on the particular groups and constituencies interested in a panel's jurisdiction. As a result, deliberations about committee reform typically do not evoke strong clientele pressures until concrete proposals affecting specific committees are on the table. By design, detailed committee reform proposals were not advanced during the early 1990s by lawmakers attempting to focus attention on the need for reorganization. At this stage, the discussion was simply too vague to activate pressure groups for or against reform.

In contrast, partisan factors did launch congressional reform as a national priority. Following the 1982 congressional elections, backbench GOP House members intensified their emphasis on reform to diminish the majority party and to increase the standing of their party in Washington and at home. By characterizing Democratic management of the House as unfair, inefficient, and corrupt, they hoped to build support for enhanced minority party prerogatives in committee and on the floor, and thus alter the internal balance of power in their favor. House Republicans also viewed reform as a valuable campaign issue that might persuade voters that Republicans should be placed at the helm of the House. In addition, partisan concerns were behind Democratic efforts to restrict floor participation during the 1970s and 1980s. Ironically, by alienating Republican moderates, these tactics fostered partisan unity for the GOP reform agenda of the 1990s. Democratic leaders resisted Republican calls for internal change, fearing that an empowered minority party would impede their legislative agenda.

Another organizational factor that helped propel congressional reform onto the national agenda was the personal power agendas of individual law-makers.[71] Throughout the 1980s and 1990s, Newt Gingrich repeatedly used institutional issues to shift the House GOP toward confrontation, thereby steadily increasing his prominence within the party. Gingrich's successful campaign, via the ethics process, to bring down Speaker Wright was pivotal to his selection as minority whip in 1989. Without Gingrich, reform still would have become a congressional priority because of widespread public demands for change. But the impact of Gingrich and other House Republican firebrands on the tone and content of the reform agenda was significant. Congressional reform was central to Gingrich's climb to influence, a pattern that would continue in the 1990s.

The rise of reform illustrates how strategic, ambitious politicians can use reorganization issues to achieve influence within Congress. Lawmakers respond to clientele, partisan, and other pressures, but they can also have a significant, independent impact on organizational politics. In the next chapter, our attention turns to the Democratic response to widespread calls for institutional change on Capitol Hill.

Notes

1. Paul Boller, *Congressional Anecdotes* (New York: Oxford University Press, 1991), pp. 15–16.

2. Morris K. Udall, *Too Funny to Be President* (New York: Henry Holt and Company, 1988), p. 7.

3. Testimony before the Joint Committee on the Organization of Congress, S. Hrg. 103–11, 103d Cong., 1st sess., 4.

4. For example, in 1975 the Senate created the Commission on the Operation of the Senate, composed of private citizens, to conduct a comprehensive review of the Senate's administrative operations, information resources, and other related topics. The commission submitted its final report on December 31, 1976, but the Senate largely ignored its proposals. Similarly, the Senate took no action on the reform recommendations of the two-person Study Group on Senate Practices and Procedures (1982–1983). Former senators Abraham Ribicoff (D-Conn.) and James Pearson (R-Kans.) composed the Study Group.

5. Janet Hook, "House GOP: Plight of a Permanent Minority," *Congressional Quarterly Weekly Report,* June 21, 1986, 1393.

6. John J. Rhodes, *The Futile System* (McLean, Va.: EPM Publications, 1976), p. 4.

7. John M. Barry, *The Ambition and the Power: A True Story of Washington.* (New York: Penguin Books, 1989), p. 304.

8. Hook, "House GOP," 1395.

9. William F. Connelly, Jr., and John J. Pitney, Jr., *Congress' Permanent Minority?* (Lanham, Md.: Littlefield Adams, 1994), pp. 70–75.

10. See Steven S. Smith, *Call to Order* (Washington, D.C.: The Brookings Institution, 1989).

11. Ibid.

12. See Andy Plattner, "Rules Under Chairman Pepper Look Out for the Democrats," *Congressional Quarterly Weekly Report,* August 24, 1985, 1671.

13. Testimony before the Joint Committee on the Organization of Congress, S. Hrg. 103–19, 103d Cong., 1st sess., 60–61.

14. Janet Hook, "GOP Chafes Under Restrictive Rules," *Congressional Quarterly Weekly Report,* October 10, 1987, 2449.

15. Testimony before the Joint Committee on the Organization of Congress, S. Hrg. 103–19, 103d Cong., 1st sess., 198–202.

16. *Congressional Record,* January 3, 1983, 41.

17. Dan Balz and Charles R. Babcock, "Gingrich, Allies Made Waves and Impression," *Washington Post,* December 20, 1994, A14.

18. Richard Cohen, "Gingrich: From Gadfly to Whip," *National Journal,* March 25, 1989, 743.

19. Ibid.

20. Ibid.

21. *Congressional Record,* January 23, 1984, 96.

22. Diane Granat, "The House's TV War: The Gloves Come Off," *Congressional Quarterly Weekly Report,* May 19, 1984, 1167.

23. *Congressional Record,* May 8, 1984, 11430.

24. Tip O'Neill, *Man of the House* (New York: Random House, 1987), 354. Gingrich and Walker argued that they had previously mailed letters to the Democrats mentioned in the special order, warning them of their plans. But the Democrats claimed that the letters did not arrive until after the special order had occurred. The two Republicans responded that the Democrats managed the House and were thus responsible for any delays in internal House mail.

25. Granat, "The House's TV War," 1167.

26. *Congressional Record,* May 14, 1984, 12041.

27. Ibid., p. 12074.

28. Ibid.

29. *Congressional Record,* May 10, 1984, 11898.

30. *Congressional Record,* May 15, 1984, 12201.

31. Ibid., p. 12202.

32. Ibid., p. 12298.

33. *Congressional Record,* May 31, 1984, 14623.

34. Diane Granat, "Deep Divisions Loom Behind House GOP's Apparent Unity," *Congressional Quarterly Weekly Report,* March 23, 1985, 563.

35. Balz and Babcock, "Gingrich, Allies Made Waves," A14.

36. Richard Cohen, "Family Feud," *National Journal,* December 15, 1984, 2402.

37. *Congressional Record,* February 20, 1985, H528.

38. *Congressional Record,* January 3, 1985, H6.

39. Granat, "Deep Divisions Loom," 535.

40. Janet Hook, "Jim Wright: Taking Big Risks to Amass Power," *Congressional Quarterly Weekly Report,* March 12, 1988, 623.

41. Ibid., p. 625.

42. Janet Hook, "Bitterness Lingers from House Budget Votes," *Congressional Quarterly Weekly Report,* November 7, 1987, 2712–13.

43. Ibid., p. 2713.

44. Barry, *The Ambition and the Power,* pp. 162, 369, 668.

45. *Congressional Quarterly Almanac 1988,* 35.

46. Janet Hook, "Battle for Whip Pits Partisans Against Party Pragmatists," *Congressional Quarterly Weekly Report,* March 18, 1989, 563.

47. *Congressional Quarterly Almanac 1989,* 40.

48. J. Jennings Moss, "GOP Gang Shakes Up Hill," *Washington Times,* May 26, 1992, A8.

49. "The Gang of Seven," *Roll Call,* August 17, 1992, 4.

50. Moss, "GOP Gang Shakes Up Hill," A8.

51. Ibid.

52. Richard S. Dunham, "The Hill's Young Turks," *Business Week,* June 1, 1992, 79.

53. Kelly D. Patterson and David B. Magleby, "Public Support for Congress," *Public Opinion Quarterly* (Winter 1992), 543–44.

54. Phil Kuntz, "Uproar Over Bank Scandal Goads House to Cut Perks," *Congressional Quarterly Weekly Report,* October 5, 1991, 2844.

55. *Congressional Record,* September 25, 1991, H6850.

56. Dunham, "The Hill's Young Turks," 79.

57. Ibid.

58. *Congressional Quarterly Almanac 1992,* 25.

59. *Congressional Record,* March 12, 1992, H1255.

60. Ibid., H1256.

61. Timothy Groseclose and Keith Krehbiel, "Golden Parachutes, Rubber Checks, and Strategic Retirements from the 102nd House," *American Journal of Political Science,* 38, No. 1 (1994), 75–99; Gary C. Jacobson, and Michael A. Dimock, "Checking Out: The Effects of Bank Overdrafts on the 1992 House Elections," paper presented at the annual meeting of the Midwest Political Science Association, Chicago, 1993; Charles Stewart, "Let's Go Fly a Kite: Correlates of Involvement in the House Bank Scandal," *Legislative Studies Quarterly,* 19, No. 4 (1994), 521–35.

62. Craig Winneker, "Heard on the Hill," *Roll Call,* April 16, 1992, 23.

63. *Congressional Record,* October 23, 1991, S15042.

64. The resolutions were S. Con. Res. 57 and H. Con. Res. 192.

65. Statement of Rep. Lee H. Hamilton, *Congressional Record,* June 18, 1992, H4893.

66. Craig Winneker, "Boren Renews His Call for a Hill Reform Panel, *Roll Call,* October 28, 1991, 20.

67. Craig Winneker, "Majority of Freshmen Join Push to Reform Hill Subcommittees, Staffs, and Schedules," *Roll Call,* October 31, 1991, 8.

68. Hearings and Markup Before the Committee on Rules, U.S. House of Representatives, 102d Cong., 2d sess., May 20, 21, 28, 1992, 142–55.

69. J. Jennings Moss, "Democrats, GOP Wrangle Over Reform," *Washington Times,* April 7, 1992, A3.

70. Janet Hook, "Approval of Administrator Creates More Rancor," *Congressional Quarterly Weekly Report,* April 11, 1992, 930.

71. The opposition of key committee chairs to organizational change was already apparent when Hamilton and Gradison lobbied members to back creation of the Joint Committee on the Organization of Congress. To some extent, then, the personal power agendas of individual members also impeded creation of the reform panel.

3

Reform and the Democratic Majority

FOLLOWING THE elections of 1992, politicians, pundits, and the general public expected significant changes in the internal operations of American government, particularly on Capitol Hill. Speaking to an inauguration day crowd of 250,000 people, President Bill Clinton pledged "an end to the era of deadlock and drift." The new president underscored the need for reform:

> This beautiful capital, like every capital since the dawn of civilization, is often a place of intrigue and calculation. Powerful people maneuver for position and worry endlessly about who is in and who is out, who is up and who is down, forgetting the people whose toil and sweat sends us here and pays our way. . . . Let us resolve to reform our politics, so that power and privilege no longer shout down the voice of the people.[1]

In March 1993, Clinton appointed Vice President Al Gore to direct the National Performance Review, a commission charged with "reinventing government." Its job was to propose reforms to cut red tape, streamline the Washington bureaucracy, and make the federal system more responsive to the needs of ordinary Americans.

When the 103d Congress began, lawmakers also called for reform. The 1992 elections brought 110 new members to Congress, the largest number of freshman legislators in forty-four years. These new lawmakers, like many of their more senior colleagues, had campaigned on platforms of reform and renewal. Anticipating the public's change-oriented mood, three months before the election the House and Senate had created the Joint Committee on the Organization of Congress, which would spend 1993 studying the institution and providing recommendations for change.

However, when the 103d Congress staggered to a close, a front-page headline in *Roll Call,* the Capitol Hill newspaper, read, "Hill Reform in Graveyard." From staff reductions to minority party rights to an overhaul of the budget process, all the major congressional reorganization initiatives of 1993–1994 had ended in obstructionism or defeat. The demise of reform in 1994 reinforced popular perceptions that the Democratically-controlled Congress was incapable of producing change—that ill-defined priority of many voters in the 1990s.

A proper understanding of the causes of institutional change on Capitol Hill requires that we explore reform initiatives that fail as well as those that are adopted. Why was the Democratic majority on Capitol Hill unwilling to address the widespread public disenchantment with Congress by passing comprehensive internal reforms? How useful are the five organizational rationales for explaining the forces for and against major institutional change during the 103d Congress? Why did reform opponents tend to dominate during this period? Our purpose in this chapter is to answer these questions.

REFORM AREAS

The internal operations of Congress are a diverse collection of procedures, structures, resources, and informal practices. Still, the complex landscape of reform options and proposals can be simplified into six broad areas of reform, which typically have been the focus of past reorganization efforts.

Leadership Prerogatives. Surfacing periodically on Capitol Hill are proposals to increase or decrease the clout of key party leaders relative to committee and subcommittee leaders and other potential rivals for power within the institution. The formal powers of top party leaders in Congress, such as the House Speaker, have varied over the course of American history. From roughly 1890 to 1910, for instance, the Speaker had enormous power. Among other prerogatives, he appointed the chairs of the standing committees and controlled and chaired the Rules Committee, leading historians to characterize this period as one of "czar rule" in the House. In the second decade of the twentieth century, insurgent lawmakers stripped Speaker Joseph Cannon (R-Ill., 1903–1911) of many formal prerogatives, and power shifted from party leaders to the committee chairs. Sixty years later, in the mid-1970s, yet another wave of reform enhanced somewhat the powers of the Speaker, though not nearly to the levels achieved in 1890–1910. Because of concerns about the unwieldy, often chaotic nature of House decision making, proposals to strengthen further the Speaker's office remained prominent on the reform agenda during the 1980s and 1990s.

Committee System. Since the 1820s, the key structural components within Congress have been the standing, or permanent, committees. In each chamber, the responsibility for preliminary legislative action on most measures is delegated to one or more committees comprising some subset of the entire membership. It is within the committees of jurisdiction that legislation typically is drafted and refined, alternatives are suggested, and key bargains are struck. In 1993, a lawmaker remarked, "Much of the real legislative work that is done day in and day out is done in the committees, and if that were not so, Congress simply would not be able to function."[2] House and Senate committees, because they are such critical arenas for policymaking, have been a perennial target for reform and change.

Floor Deliberations and Scheduling. A third general area of reform concerns the procedures used to structure deliberations on the House and Senate floors and to set the overall legislative schedule, or agenda, for each chamber. The central issues here often relate to the distribution of floor prerogatives between the majority and minority parties, particularly the presence or absence of restrictions on debate and amendment. However, certain proposals to revise floor procedures and scheduling practices relate to bipartisan concerns about the overall efficiency of the legislative process. In the 1990s, for instance, many members from both political parties expressed an interest in scheduling reforms aimed at improving the use of their time, reducing uncertainty, and fostering a more family-friendly environment.

Congressional Integrity. Throughout congressional history, concerns have been raised about the institutional integrity of Congress. In 1942, for instance, as the nation mobilized for war, Congress voted to make members and staff eligible for civil service pension benefits and to allow lawmakers to purchase unlimited gasoline, even though fuel for ordinary citizens was strictly rationed. Citizens were outraged. The Jaycees created a Bundles for Congress program, collecting "old clothes, discarded shoes, and assorted trash for the apparently destitute and avaricious members."[3] Lawmakers, wary of their next campaign, quickly repealed the privileges. They also created the first Joint Committee on the Organization of Congress, which in turn produced the Legislative Reorganization Act of 1946. Almost fifty years later, public outrage over the House bank, yet another perk, was pivotal in establishing the third joint reform panel. In addition to the abolition of perks, topics that address congressional integrity include lawmakers' salaries and pensions, the openness of congressional proceedings to public scrutiny, and the application to Congress of labor laws covering the private sector.

Policy-Driven Reforms. Certain procedural reforms are aimed primarily at altering substantive policy outcomes in a particular issue area. Consider the gag rules used in the House during the 1830s. These rules precluded abolitionist lawmakers from introducing antislavery petitions on the House floor and were part of broader efforts to keep the slavery issue off the congressional agenda. Here, the linkages between procedure (imposition of the gag rule) and substantive policy (slavery) were direct and significant.[4] Such procedural devices can be labeled policy-driven. In the 1980s and 1990s, the substantive policy area drawing the most attention from procedural reformers has been the federal budget deficit. As the imbalance between spending and revenues has grown, interest in so-called procedural fixes also has climbed. Included here are proposals to reorganize the budget process, various versions of the line-item veto, and proposed balanced budget amendments to the Constitution.

Congressional Resources and Interbranch Prerogatives. A final category of reform pertains to the resources and prerogatives of Congress, particularly relative to the executive branch. The War Powers Resolution of 1973, for instance, was intended to ensure congressional participation in decisions to place U.S. military forces in hostile situations. Other reform proposals affecting the institutional resources of Congress have focused on the quantity of staff and analytical assistance available to individual members, committees, and the institution as a whole. In the 1990s, reforms to increase legislative branch resources or protect congressional prerogatives have not been prominent on the reorganization agenda. Indeed, many reform leaders from both political parties have asked whether the intense public disenchantment with Congress might lead to the passage of punitive changes that would weaken, rather than strengthen, the national legislature.

During the 103d Congress, the Democratic majority failed to implement comprehensive changes in all six of the reform areas mentioned here. The incentives for and against change varied by reform area. However, from leadership prerogatives to congressional resources, the benefits from concrete reform proposals seldom exceeded the costs for a majority of the House and Senate— even though the public wanted major changes. In 1993–1994, reorganization issues were considered in diverse arenas within Congress, from informal task forces to the bipartisan, bicameral Joint Committee on the Organization of Congress. Action began within the majority party caucus of the House.

THE HOUSE DEMOCRATIC CAUCUS

The House Democratic Caucus is the formal organization of all Democratic members of the chamber. It is responsible for electing Democratic leaders, appointing Democrats to committees, and a range of other organizational matters. Following decades of relative inactivity, the Caucus was revitalized in the late 1960s through the efforts of the Democratic Study Group (DSG), an organization of reform-oriented party liberals. At the request of DSG members, the caucus in 1970 began to hold regular monthly meetings (more frequently if needed) to discuss policy and strategy. The next year, again because of DSG efforts, the caucus formed a committee to study and recommend possible changes in House operations. The panel was named the Committee on Organization, Study and Review (OSR), but early in its existence it was also known as the Hansen committee, after its first chair, Rep. Julia Butler Hansen (D-Wash.).

The Work of the OSR

The key vehicle through which the OSR and the Democratic Caucus altered congressional operations was the biennial ratification of House rules at the beginning of each Congress. In recent decades, this procedural vote has been along straight party lines. For most Congresses, the rules adopted on the opening day closely resemble the rules used in previous years. But from Congress to Congress, the majority Democrats usually made incremental adjustments in the rules to streamline procedure or otherwise promote their party's agenda.[5] The Senate, in contrast, is considered to be a continuing body, and its rules carry over from Congress to Congress.

In 1992, House Democrats expected—accurately, as it turned out—that they would retain their majority status in 1993–1994. The OSR, chaired by Rep. Louise Slaughter (D-N.Y.), began work on a reform plan for consideration by the full Democratic Caucus in December 1992, when party members would meet to organize for the next two years. For a number of reasons, lawmakers expected that the rules package considered by the Democratic Caucus in 1992 would be much more significant than in prior years. Following the House bank and other congressional scandals, reform sentiment in the electorate was very high. Members also recognized that a large class of reform-minded freshman legislators would be elected in the fall and might arrive in Washington clambering for a reorganization of Congress. Many senior Democrats believed that a credible reform package from the Democratic Caucus would restrain these change-oriented new members from proposing radical reforms. The leadership also hoped that the reforms implemented by the caucus in December 1992 might reduce the momentum for a major overhaul of congressional operations in 1993, when the Joint Committee on the Organization of Congress would consider comprehensive changes.

During 1992, groups inside and outside Congress also were working to provide the House Democratic Caucus with an ambitious reform agenda. Off Capitol Hill, scholars at the American Enterprise Institute (AEI) and the Brookings Institution, two Washington-based think tanks, established the Renewing Congress project, with the goal of providing an independent assessment of how Congress should be reformed. Under the leadership of Thomas Mann of the Brookings Institution and Norman Ornstein of AEI, two well-known congressional scholars, the project drew on the advice of top legislative analysts from around the country. Their first report was directed to the OSR and House Democratic leaders and contained dozens of reform proposals touching on all six reorganization areas.[6] The Renewing Congress suggestions were widely discussed on Capitol Hill, with Mann and Ornstein lobbying Democratic leaders such as Speaker Thomas Foley (D-Wash.) as well as rank-and-file members and staff.

Inside Congress, reform-minded legislators also were developing reorganization agendas. Members of the DSG, chaired by Rep. Bob Wise (D-W.V.), began meeting to develop a reform program for submission to the OSR. A

DSG memo described the group's goals as "to strengthen the ability of the party and its leadership to develop an effective policy agenda; and to enhance the accountability of those who serve in positions of authority as agents of the Caucus." Among other reforms, the DSG proposed that a Working Group on Policy be created that would "assist the leadership in defining a core policy agenda for each session, working with the committees to outline general legislative goals on key issues and plan a schedule for legislative consideration of that agenda." Members of the working group would be appointed by the Democratic leadership.

During the summer of 1992, the chairs of the House standing committees, worried that reformers might seek to curb their power, also began meeting regularly to discuss how they could influence the reorganization process. Of particular concern to the committee chairs was the DSG's proposed Working Group on Policy, which was intended to coordinate the legislative priorities of House committees and thus potentially reduce the chairs' traditional control over their agendas. According to Ways and Means Committee chairman Dan Rostenkowski (D-Ill.), "We're the ones who are going to have to work under the effects of what these proposals are going to be. Those of us who are committee chairmen ought to be able to give those people [the DSG] the benefits of our experience."[7] Responding to this pressure, Slaughter's OSR panel initially endorsed a watered-down version of the DSG recommendation. As Democratic leaders reassured worried committee chairs that they would retain their agenda-setting prerogatives, the chairs backed off, and Slaughter and Wise compromised their differences regarding the proposed Working Group on Policy.

The final OSR recommendations were not trivial (seventeen subcommittees were slated for abolition, among other changes), but the package clearly did not constitute comprehensive or major reform. During the second week of December 1992, House Democrats met in closed session to consider the proposals, as well as other organizational issues. On December 9, the Democratic Caucus adopted the rules package, with only minor amendments. About the changes, *Roll Call* would editorialize, "In an astounding display of the power of Congress to socialize incoming Members of every stripe, scores of Democrats, elected on a theme of 'change' . . . voted overwhelmingly for the status quo."[8]

Democratic Divisions and the Freshman Fizzle

Why did the House Democratic Caucus not adopt a major reorganization plan in December 1992? One reason for the incremental nature of the caucus reforms was that incoming freshman Democrats failed to become a cohesive force for congressional reorganization. They simply lacked the knowledge, time, and staff support necessary to craft a comprehensive alternative to the OSR rules package. As second-term representative Glen Browder (D-Ala.)

observed, the freshmen "feel they've got an important vote coming up next week about congressional reform, and they need more time to study."[9] In addition, almost three-quarters of the new members were current or former elected officeholders, and they arrived in Washington bent not on transforming Congress but on pursuing their policy interests and further climbing the political ladder.

Also, within days of the election, top Democratic leaders took steps to contain reform sentiment among the freshmen. On November 9, Democratic leaders, including Speaker Foley and majority leader Richard Gephardt (D-Mo.), held regional meetings with the freshman Democrats in Los Angeles, Chicago, and Atlanta. Rep. Vic Fazio (D-Calif.), vice chair of the Democratic Caucus and a participant in the regional meetings, said, "We want to know what this class is thinking, particularly as they get together and compare notes for the first time. What is it that they are expecting from their leaders? . . . What is it that they hope to accomplish in terms of . . . rules changes?"[10] At one meeting, Foley, recalling remarks made decades earlier by Speaker Sam Rayburn (D-Tex.), warned the incoming freshmen, "It takes a skilled carpenter to build a barn. Any jackass can kick it down." Concerning one freshman suggestion, he remarked, "That's not reform, that's nonsense."[11]

At the regional meetings, the new members expressed more concern about substantive policy issues and securing good committee assignments than about congressional reorganization.[12] Efforts to organize a bipartisan summit of reform-minded freshmen in Omaha, Nebraska, following the election mostly fizzled. No Democrats and only fourteen Republicans showed up.[13] In December, Democratic leaders did grant the Democratic freshmen a ninety-day extension during which they could propose reforms for consideration by the Democratic Caucus. But during the crucial organizational sessions, the large class of Democratic freshmen was not a significant force for institutional change.

There were more fundamental reasons for the incremental nature of the Democratic Caucus reforms. Political conditions within the caucus simply were not conducive to a major redistribution of power. Party members, for instance, did not want a divisive internal battle at a time when a Democrat had just been elected president.

The caucus's potential role was most important in one reform area—strengthening the prerogatives of the House leadership. Decisions about leadership prerogatives (relative to the committee chairs) primarily relate to the distribution of power within the majority party. As a result, the main forum—if not the only forum—for considering changes in this area is the majority party caucus.

In 1992, many House Democrats, as well as informed observers of the institution, argued that the committee system should be more accountable to party leaders and the Democratic Caucus as a whole. For example, various lawmakers suggested giving the Speaker the power to appoint and remove committee chairs, limiting the terms of committee chairs to eight years, and providing the Speaker with substantial control over the legislative agendas of the standing committees. These reformers believed that centralizing power within the institution would facilitate efforts to formulate and pass a coherent policy agenda. Interestingly, such changes would form the core of the organizational changes implemented by the new Republican majority in 1995.

In the Democratically controlled 103d Congress, however, there was not sufficient support for centralizing reforms among either rank-and-file Democrats or party leaders. Generally, the majority caucus will act to transfer power from the committee chairs to party leaders when (1) majority party members are relatively unified on the major policy issues of the day and (2) they perceive that important committee chairs may oppose these positions and obstruct the party's program.[14] However, when the majority party is divided over policy and the committee chairs reflect this diversity of views, rank-and-file lawmakers generally see few benefits from strengthening party leaders.

House Democrats were divided on key policy issues, from health care reform to budgetary policy. As a result, any efforts to shift power significantly from the chairs to the Democratic leadership were unlikely to succeed. The committee chairs intensely opposed such changes for obvious reasons. And rank-and-file Democrats, lacking a cohesive agenda for their party leadership to promote, did not perceive significant benefits from reining in the independent chairs. Recognizing these political dynamics, Speaker Foley rejected suggestions that the formal prerogatives of his office be significantly expanded. Foley opposed, for instance, proposals that he be allowed to appoint and remove committee chairs.

In the 103d Congress, the lack of support for significant enhancement of leadership prerogatives also was apparent in the centralizing reforms that were adopted by the Democratic Caucus. Consider the Working Group on Policy, originally proposed by the DSG. Reformers hoped that the working group would enable party leaders to better coordinate the agendas of the standing committees rather than allow policy priorities to bubble up at their own pace from the committee system, depending on the personal interests of the chairs and other committee members. As charged by the Democratic Caucus, the working group simply lacked the leverage necessary to alter substantially committee agendas. Democratic leaders also sent strong signals to the committee chairs that they had little to fear from the working group. Indeed, although members were appointed to the agenda-setting panel at the beginning of the 103d Congress, it quickly faded into obscurity, lacking the formal powers and political support to bind the committee chairs to a caucus- or Speaker-driven policy agenda.

The mostly incremental nature of the OSR recommendations ensured that the package received overwhelming support within the Democratic Caucus. However, the package included certain changes that Republicans perceived as further infringements on their procedural rights. One example was a proposal to extend floor voting privileges to the previously nonvoting delegates who represent the District of Columbia and four U.S. territories. At the time, all five of the delegates were Democrats, and Republicans charged that the change was aimed at padding Democratic margins in the House. Faced with a brewing insurrection among party conservatives, Democrats passed a scaled-down version of the original proposal, which provided the delegates with limited floor voting rights.[15]

Another caucus proposal would have limited special orders presentations to three hours per day and capped one-minute speeches at twenty per day. According to caucus chairman Steny Hoyer (D-Md.), the proposed limits on special orders and one-minutes would have saved money and "seemed to [allow] reasonable time for each side to make the points they want to make."[16] Republicans vigorously disagreed. Because of restrictive floor amendment procedures, they argued, special orders and one-minutes provide minority party members with an essential opportunity to present their views to the nation. This is "an effort on the part of the majority to stifle the voice of the minority," said minority leader Robert Michel (R-Ill.). "If it passes, we have mechanisms where we can be disruptive."[17] Faced with Republican threats to obstruct legislative business in the House, the Democratic leadership dropped the debate-restricting proposals.

Partisan controversy aside, the Democratic Caucus failed to pass a comprehensive reform agenda at the beginning of the 103d Congress. Particularly in the area of leadership prerogatives, where the majority caucus has a special role, there was insufficient support to alter substantially the institutional status quo. Indeed, the primary impact of the caucus rules package may have been to fuel partisan tensions in the House. These tensions would not subside in the 103d Congress and would significantly complicate the work of the Joint Committee on the Organization of Congress.

THE JOINT COMMITTEE

Created by Congress in 1992, the Joint Committee on the Organization of Congress was mandated to study the institution and make recommendations for reform by the end of 1993. Membership on the panel was divided equally between the two chambers and the two political parties, with appointments being made by the appropriate party leaders. As expected, the four chief sponsors of the resolution to create the joint committee were asked to lead the panel. Sen. David Boren (D-Okla.) was appointed cochair for the Senate. Rep. Lee Hamilton (D-Ind.) became the House cochair. Senator Pete Domenici (R-N.M.) was named vice chair for the Senate; Rep. Bill Gradison (R-Ohio) initially became his House counterpart. Because of the breadth of the joint committee's formal mandate, as well as the potential for partisan and interchamber cleavages, the four leaders were viewed as critical to the success or failure of the panel. The four committee leaders, as well as the other lawmakers appointed to the joint committee, are listed in Table 3.1.

TABLE 3.1 Joint Committee Members

Democrats	Republicans
Senate	**Senate**
David L. Boren (cochair)	Pete V. Domenici (vice chair)
Jim Sasser	Nancy L. Kassebaum
Wendell H. Ford	Trent Lott
Harry Reid	Ted Stevens
Paul S. Sarbanes	William S. Cohen
David Pryor	Richard G. Lugar
George J. Mitchell (ex officio*)	Robert Dole (ex officio)
House	**House**
Lee H. Hamilton (cochair)	David Dreier (vice chair)
David Obey	Robert S. Walker
Al Swift	Gerald B. H. Solomon
Sam Gejdenson	Bill Emerson
John M. Spratt, Jr.	Wayne Allard
Eleanor Holmes Norton	Jennifer Dunn
Richard A. Gephardt (ex officio)	Robert H. Michel (ex officio)

*Ex officio means "by virtue of office or position." In this case, these are the majority and minority leaders in the Senate and the House.

The members reflected diverse backgrounds, reform interests, and levels of partisanship. However, as the joint committee began its work, most observers viewed the House contingent as substantially more polarized along party lines than the Senate contingent. Senator Boren, for instance, had demonstrated a willingness to break with his leadership on major issues, such as U.S. aid to the Nicaraguan Contras. There would be few partisan barriers to his developing a cooperative relationship with Domenici and the other GOP senators on the joint committee, which included party moderates such as William Cohen (R-Maine) and Nancy Kassebaum (R-Kans.). Also, the Senate is generally less partisan than the House and very protective of minority rights, and most senators are used to working cooperatively with their colleagues from across the aisle.

In contrast, the more structured House, with its emphasis on majority rule, is often a highly partisan chamber, a characteristic reflected in the

House appointments to the joint committee. Cochairman Hamilton was a moderate Democrat with a bipartisan legislative style, as was Rep. John Spratt (D-S.C.). But the other four Foley appointees were strong partisans. The House Republican quadrant of the joint committee, with the initial exception of Gradison, comprised staunch party loyalists. When Gradison resigned from Congress in early 1993, he was replaced as vice chair by Rep. David Dreier (R-Calif.), a member of the extended Republican leadership from his position on the House Rules Committee. Freshman Republican Jennifer Dunn (R-Wash.) was appointed to fill the open seat.

During the first half of 1993, the joint committee conducted extensive hearings on the broad landscape of reform alternatives.[18] The House Speaker and the majority and minority leaders of both chambers appeared before the panel on January 26 to offer their perspectives on reform. Senator Boren described that meeting as "historic . . . the first time in our 200 years that the members of the joint congressional leadership from both the House and the Senate have presented testimony [at a single hearing]."[19] Representative Hamilton told the leaders, "Expectations for this committee are very high, and in a sense we are all on the spot."[20]

As the panel explored reorganization issues and alternatives during the spring of 1993, the response from many Democratic leaders increasingly was a mixture of skepticism and concern. After widely publicized testimony by billionaire Ross Perot, during which he criticized a number of congressional practices, a close observer of Washington politics reported that "the Perot hearing has increased fears that the committee has become a loose cannon and that its members, divided evenly by party, may propose more sweeping changes than Democratic leaders are willing to accept."[21]

Reform Issues

The nature of the controversy created by the joint committee's work varied by reorganization issue. Leadership prerogatives, primarily an intraparty concern, were not prominent on the panel's agenda. But the joint committee's deliberations dealt extensively with the other areas of reform, and the main proposals and issues that emerged merit a brief overview because they were central to the reorganization agenda under the Democratic and Republican majorities.

Committee System

Committee reorganization was a major source of conflict during the 1990s. For example, some lawmakers, as well as outside observers, argued that committee jurisdictions should be realigned. Current committee boundaries mostly derive from the Legislative Reorganization Act of 1946, and national priorities have changed since that time. Major issues such as health care and the environment no longer fit cleanly within existing jurisdictional lines. A 1975 House rules change also allowed the Speaker to refer a bill to more than one committee, further obscuring jurisdictional responsibilities.

According to many reformers, overlapping and obsolete committee jurisdictions impede the formulation of coherent public policy, promote committee-based obstructionism, and complicate efforts to hold individual committee members accountable when things go wrong.[22] Rep. Dan Glickman (D-Kans.), then chairman of the Intelligence Committee and later Secretary of Agriculture, commented:

> Too often, once important bills are introduced, they simply get lost in the process of committee jurisdictions. Good ideas are tossed aside without discussion because overlapping jurisdictions make progress on a bill too difficult. Ironically, in an institution where turf is so important, the lines of demarcation [between committees] are drawn and implemented too loosely.[23]

In a 1993 joint committee survey of House members' reform attitudes, more than 50 percent of the lawmakers favored a "comprehensive realignment of the committee system," with another 30 percent supporting "a more modest consolidation of selected committees." However, when attention within the joint committee turned to abolishing specific committees or to transferring specific issues from one panel to another, the broad support for jurisdictional reform in the abstract quickly crumbled.[24]

Opponents of jurisdictional reform argued that a comprehensive committee realignment would generate intense conflict within the majority caucus, pitting chair against chair and committee against committee.[25] Speaker Foley often said that the bitterness and anger provoked by the 1974 Bolling committee (charged with modernizing House jurisdictions), with lawmakers swearing to get revenge on colleagues no matter how long it took, exceeded even the in-chamber passion triggered by the Vietnam War. In a 1989 interview, he remarked, "I wouldn't suggest touching [committee reform] with a 10-foot pole."[26]

The most formidable coalition against reforming committee jurisdictions comprised the House committee chairs, who continued to meet regularly to plan a common response to the reform effort. As a defensive posture, the chairs agreed among themselves to fight any jurisdictional changes. They preferred the certainty of the turf they controlled to the uncertainty and risk associated with a major overhaul.

As in previous years, the leading opponent of committee realignment was Rep. John Dingell (D-Mich.), chairman of the Energy and Commerce Committee. Dingell's panel had a massive jurisdiction, ranging from energy issues to health care to regulatory policy. He realized that if jurisdictional alterations were to occur, the prime target would be Energy and Commerce. Chairman Dingell, nicknamed "Big John" and "The Truck," also believed that altering committee jurisdictions would not significantly improve decision making in the House. He said, "Fights over jurisdiction . . . almost always reflect real policy differences. . . . Jurisdictional tension and competition between committees, if not carried to excess, can be healthy. . . . Most importantly, all the jurisdictional changes in the world will never substitute for strong leadership."[27] Senate committee chairs also questioned the importance of realigning jurisdictions, although they were less organized and less vocal in their opposition.

During the spring of 1993, partially as an attempt to divert attention from jurisdictional issues, the House chairs coalesced behind a committee reform plan that focused on reductions in the size of committees and stricter limitations on the number of committee assignments per member. During the post–World War II period, congressional committees had grown substantially in size. In the Senate, the average committee rose in size from 14.9 members in 1945 to 18.4 members in 1992. During the same period, the average House committee increased from 20 members to 38.7. Particularly in the House, lawmakers argued that thoughtful deliberation and meaningful debate were difficult in large panels such as Appropriations (60 members in 1993) and Public Works (63 members in 1993). Committee chairs also argued that building coalitions is more difficult in larger committees because of the greater diversity of perspectives and personal ambitions that must be aggregated.

A related issue was the number of assignments allowed per member. Democratic House members, in theory, were restricted by party rules to two full committee and five subcommittee assignments, unless they were members of Appropriations, Rules, or Ways and Means, in which case that was usually their only assignment.[28] During the 103d Congress, however, waivers from the assignment limits were so common that they had been secured by 41.7 percent of the members on the Post Office Committee, 23.3 percent of the members on the Natural Resources Committee, and 20 percent of the members on the Science and Technology Committee.[29]

The Senate, too, limited members' assignments, but these limitations also were routinely waived. In 1993, one senator actually had twenty-one full comittee and subcommittee assignments.[30] Sen. Robert C. Byrd (D-W.V.), the most senior Democrat in the chamber, argued that excessive committee assignments meant members were spread too thinly, creating what he called "the problem of fractured attention." The overall effect, argued Byrd, was to "marginalize the Member's participation."[31]

There were, however, important pockets of opposition to committee assignment reductions. According to the Congressional Black Caucus, the organization of African-American lawmakers, racial minorities were particularly likely to have waivers from committee assignment limits and thus would be forced to drop assignments if tighter limits were strictly enforced. In a letter to Rep. Lee Hamilton, Rep. Kweisi Mfume (D-Md.), chairman of the Black Caucus, argued that assignment limitations, in conjunction with other proposed changes to the committee system, "would diminish the presence of African-Americans within the leadership of the House of Representatives and its committee system, at a point when minorities are just beginning to qualify."[32] In addition, certain lawmakers opposed tougher assignment limits because they were not members of powerful committees, such as Energy and Commerce, and sought to compensate for that by joining more panels.

Still another aspect of committee reform concerned the impact of committee procedures and resources on the minority party. As part of their reorganization agenda, House Republicans, as noted in Chapter 2, sought the abolition of proxy voting, a larger share of committee staff, and party ratios on committees and subcommittees that reflect the party makeup of the House. Along with the incidence of restrictive amendment rules on the floor, these issues were the core of the Republican minority rights agenda. Overall, the level of sympathy for their concerns within the Democratic Caucus was not high.[33]

Floor Deliberations and Scheduling

Two categories of issues dominated this reorganization area: (1) those that touched on minority party prerogatives and (2) less partisan items relating to scheduling efficiency on the House and Senate floor. At the organizational meeting of the joint committee in January 1993, the House GOP members handed out their reform agenda, which they had offered previously as a substitute to the Democratic rules package on the first day of the 103d Congress. Prominent among the forty-eight reform recommendations were proposals to open up the amendment process on the floor.

As discussed in Chapter 2, Republicans long had complained about restrictive special rules reported by the Rules Committee, which functioned to limit amending opportunities on the House floor. In early 1993, partisan tensions about floor procedures reached new heights, as the Democratic majority on the Rules Committee issued a succession of restrictive amendment rules. Indeed, no open rules were reported until May. Minority leader Michel told Democratic members:

> We are allowed to speak certain lines at certain times, dictated by you. We are not allowed to alter one jot or title of legislation except by your capricious whim. You write us in and out of the script as if making laws were something like making movies, in which entire scenes are left on the cutting room floor.[34]

To protest the restrictive rules, Rep. Dan Burton (R-Ind.) began a campaign of parliamentary guerrilla tactics aimed at disrupting floor business. Burton repeatedly motioned for the House to adjourn, systematically objected to Democratic procedural motions, and bogged the institution down in time-consuming roll-call votes. "I intend to try and keep up the pressure on the majority until they decide they will acknowledge the minority has rights," Burton said. "Whenever there's the appearance of strong arming, I will call for votes on everything under the sun. I may call for votes on

Mondays at midnight."[35] Democrats responded with renewed efforts to curb Republican access to special orders, leading Rep. Newt Gingrich (R-Ga.) to say, "I do want to remind the majority that there are many, many things that require unanimous consent, and that if the minority's right to speak is to be strangled, other [matters] can systematically be slowed down."[36]

At the end of March, House GOP leaders asked Rep. Gerald Solomon of New York, ranking Republican on the Rules Committee and a joint committee member, to chair a task force on restrictive rules strategy, with the aim of inducing Democrats to open up the floor to more amendment opportunities. Also appointed to the task force were David Dreier and Robert Walker (R-Pa.), both key Republicans on the joint committee. The task force engaged in extensive media outreach and threatened further obstructionism on the House floor. House Republicans enlisted the support of Ross Perot, who appeared with the task force at a Washington press conference. "It's a gross imposition on democracy," charged Perot, "to have the rule system work as it does in the House."[37] In April, Speaker Foley promised House Republicans that they could "expect open rules within a matter of a very few days on major legislation."[38] By June 10, four bills were considered on the floor under open rules, but restrictive amendment procedures continued to be a central weapon in the majority leadership's arsenal.

In the Senate, floor prerogatives also were a reform issue, but there the issue was whether to curtail, not enhance, minority rights. Under Senate Rule 22, any member can filibuster a measure (block it through extended debate) unless sixty senators vote to invoke cloture and close off further discussion. Prior to the 1970s, filibusters were relatively rare and conducted mostly on major constitutional issues such as civil rights. Beginning in the 1970s, dilatory tactics became more common, and filibusters were used increasingly on minor matters. The number of attempts to invoke cloture—a rough indicator of the incidence of filibusters—increased from twenty-two during the entire period from 1917 to 1958 to almost fifty during the 102d Congress alone. Senators from both parties engaged in filibusters, but the prerogative was particularly important to minority party members, who were more likely to be on the losing side of major votes.

Not surprisingly, as use of the filibuster increased, so did support among majority party senators to curb the practice. In 1993, Sen. George Mitchell (D-Maine), the majority leader, observed:

> In the House, a common complaint is that the majority tramples on or ignores the minority. In the Senate, the complaint is often the opposite; that archaic rules permit a small minority to thwart the will of the majority. . . . The threat of a filibuster is now a regular event in the Senate, weekly at least, sometimes daily. It is invoked by minorities of as few as one or two senators and for reasons as trivial as a senator's travel schedule.[39]

Mitchell urged the joint committee to recommend restrictions on the use of the filibuster. Interestingly, as the joint committee proceeded, the main proponents of major changes in the filibuster would be House Democrats upset that the tactic was being used to derail portions of the Clinton agenda.

During the 1990s, an increasing number of lawmakers from both chambers and parties expressed frustration about the chaotic and demanding nature of the legislative schedule. Rep. Nancy Johnson (R-Conn.) remarked, "We never have enough time to let each other finish a sentence hardly. . . . It's hard to carve out time with real experts to grapple with complex issues."[40] Lawmakers also were concerned that the unpredictable floor schedule, combined with regular late-night sessions, was undermining their family lives. In May, Rep. Tim Roemer (D-Ind.) circulated a petition proposing that the House follow the Senate practice and adopt a schedule of three weeks on—one week off. Under Roemer's plan, the House would shift from conducting legislative business from Tuesday through Thursday every week to a schedule of three five-day legislative workweeks followed by one full week in the district. Almost a hundred members from both parties signed the petition.

Other House members objected to the Roemer proposal, arguing that three weeks on—one week off had not worked in the Senate and that five-day legislative weeks would make it impossible for many members to visit their districts every weekend. Although scheduling issues were highly controversial among members in both chambers, they generally were not viewed as partisan topics. Lawmakers in both parties support improving the efficiency of Congress and the family lives of individual members.

Congressional Integrity

Public skepticism about the institutional integrity of Congress triggered a rash of proposals to further "de-perk" Capitol Hill. Freshman Democrats, for example, suggested an end to lawmakers' special parking privileges at National Airport and endorsed a ban on converting frequent flier miles (resulting from official travel) to personal use. A senior member joked to a prominent freshman reformer, "I hear you guys are going to take away our telephones."[41] While lawmakers hunted for perks to abolish, the joint committee focused on broader issues related to the institutional integrity of Congress, particularly the ethics process and the application of workplace laws to the legislative branch.

In 1993, as initial publicity about Sen. Bob Packwood's (R-Oreg.) sexual harassment case focused attention on Congress's ethics process, many lawmakers argued that private citizens, rather than sitting members, should be responsible for investigating ethics complaints. Under the Constitution, members must make the final decision in such cases, but there are no constitutional barriers to involving private citizens at the investigative stage. On and off the joint committee, there was substantial support for this proposal, but the issue drew little public attention and was not viewed as a top reform priority.[42]

Of more importance to the general public was the matter of applying workplace laws to Congress. Indeed, few reform issues generated as much media attention and public anger. A *New York Times* editorial reflected the general view: "Make Congress Obey Itself. Congress is quick to impose new laws on hapless states, corporations, and just plain citizens. But it is woefully derelict in applying those laws to itself and its members."[43]

In 1993, a number of important labor and employment laws were not being fully applied on Capitol Hill. One reason was that full congressional coverage would include enforcement by the relevant executive branch agency, and many lawmakers and constitutional scholars believed that executive branch enforcement of such laws on Capitol Hill would be an unconstitutional violation of the separation of powers. A hostile president, they argued, might use the power to enforce labor laws in Congress to intimidate the legislative branch and potentially affect public policy in an illegitimate manner.

Skeptics also suggested that the drive to apply laws on Capitol Hill was primarily an effort to undermine support for these statutes rather than to protect congressional employees. Advocates of congressional compliance, however, had a different perspective. According to Rep. Christopher Shays (R-Conn.), "Bringing Congress under the law . . . will sensitize Members to the effects of the laws they pass. Congress, as a result, will write better laws when it has to live by the laws it adopts."[44]

By the early 1990s, certain labor and civil rights laws were already applied to Congress and the intent of others was reflected in House and Senate rules, but the extent of coverage varied by law and by chamber, and the enforcement procedures were lax, particularly in the House. A General Accounting Office investigation of the House process for protecting employee rights found that from 1989 through March 1993, twelve hundred inquiries were received from concerned staff, but final decisions were reached in only four cases. None of the four decisions dealt with sexual harassment. Rep. Patricia Schroeder (D-Colo.) sarcastically compared these enforcement efforts to "the Maytag repairman. . . . He has been sitting down there in that office and nothing happens."[45]

In January 1993, Shays and Rep. Dick Swett (D-N.H.) introduced legislation requiring that all relevant workplace laws be applied to Congress, without providing much detail about how that would be accomplished. But Shays and Swett, with input from the Renewing Congress project, refined their initial proposal, eventually recommending that an independent office be created within the legislative branch and provided with the power necessary to apply private-sector laws to Congress in a credible manner. Under the Shays-Swett proposal, the executive branch would not enforce laws on Capitol Hill, alleviating most constitutional concerns.

The initiative quickly drew broad support in the House, as did a similar bill introduced in the Senate by Charles Grassley (R-Iowa) and Joseph Lieberman (D-Conn.). Later in 1993, Speaker Foley asked Lee Hamilton and David Dreier, House leaders of the joint committee, to work with Shays and

Swett to refine their proposal further, with the expectation that it would be included in the reform package recommended by the panel. Both leaders recognized that the Shays-Swett initiative, because of its popularity, could improve the chances that a broader reform plan would pass.

Policy-Driven Reforms

Since the emergence of the federal budget deficit as a pressing policy problem, there has been substantial interest on Capitol Hill in budget process reform. Two budget process reforms considered during the 103d Congress—the balanced budget amendment to the Constitution and expedited presidential rescission authority over spending bills—illustrate the point.

In March 1994, the full Senate considered a balanced budget amendment authored by Sens. Paul Simon (D-Ill.) and Orrin Hatch (R-Utah). Their proposal would have required that the federal budget be balanced yearly beginning in 2001 unless three-fifths of the House and Senate voted otherwise. Almost all Senate Republicans supported the amendment, while the majority Democrats were deeply divided. Fearing that the Simon-Hatch proposal would pass, Democratic leaders worked with Sen. Harry Reid (D-Nev.) to devise a less constraining balanced budget amendment, which excluded Social Security receipts from deficit calculations.

As expected, the Reid amendment lost by a wide margin, with almost all Republican senators favoring the Simon-Hatch version. However, by first voting for the Reid alternative, wavering Democrats were able to take a public position in favor of a balanced budget amendment and then vote against the more constraining, and politically threatening, alternative offered by Sens. Simon and Hatch. As a result, the Simon-Hatch amendment fell four votes short of the necessary two-thirds supermajority. Similar political dynamics occurred in the House. In 1994, a strict version of the balanced budget amendment proposed by Rep. Charles Stenholm (D-Tex.) lost by twelve votes because sixty-four wavering Democrats were first given the opportunity to vote yes on a milder version (which lost 318 to 111) and then to vote no on the Stenholm proposal.

In both chambers, differences over the balanced budget amendment reflected substantive disagreements about budgetary policy, as well as constitutional and political concerns about the consequences of the amendments under consideration. President Clinton staunchly opposed a balanced budget amendment to the Constitution, arguing that such an amendment would require "huge increases in taxes on working families, massive reductions in Social Security benefits for middle-class Americans, and major cuts in Medicare and Medicaid that would make it impossible to pass meaningful health care reform legislation."[46] Sen. Pete Domenici, a reluctant supporter of the Simon-Hatch amendment, commented, "I have put too much of my gut into amendments on this floor to get control of this deficit. I come down that the only way to get entitlements under control is with this constitutional amendment."[47]

In addition to the balanced budget amendment, a proposal to grant the president expedited rescission authority also received congressional consideration during the Democratically controlled 103d Congress. Under the procedures established by the 1974 Budget Act, the president can propose that all or parts of a spending bill be rescinded, or dropped, after the legislation is signed. However, such rescission recommendations must be passed by the House and Senate, and Congress is under no obligation even to consider the president's requests. If Congress does nothing, the money must be spent. Under expedited rescission, the House and Senate would be required to vote on presidential rescission proposals.

Legislation providing for expedited rescission sailed through the House in 1992 by a margin of 312 to 97. The following year, however, Republicans switched positions on that proposal and instead held out for a stronger version introduced by Rep. Gerald Solomon. Rep. Newt Gingrich called the Democratic proposal "line-item voodoo" and "a silly sham that's designed to give cover to Democrats who don't want to vote for the line-item veto."[48] In 1993, the Congressional Black Caucus also raised objections, arguing that expedited rescission transferred too much congressional spending authority to the president, no matter which party controlled the White House. In April 1993, a divided House passed the expedited rescission proposal by a partisan vote of 258 to 157. The measure died in the Senate, however. There was strong opposition from Appropriations Committee chairman Robert Byrd, as well as other members of the spending panel, who viewed the proposal as reducing their power and Congress's power over the federal purse.

The joint committee also considered changes in the congressional budget process, particularly a proposal for biennial budgeting, which was championed by Vice Chairman Domenici. Under existing procedures, each year Congress passes a budget resolution, which is the blueprint for congressional budgetary policy. In addition, thirteen appropriations bills, which target money for specific programs and agencies, must be passed. Domenici argued that shifting the federal budget/appropriations process to a two-year cycle would cut down on redundant decisions, promote more long-term thinking, and free up lawmakers' time for other activities, such as oversight of the executive branch.

Other members pointed out that budget resolutions typically cover more than two years anyway and that the annual appropriations process is a critical opportunity for Congress to scrutinize program effectiveness. The 1993 joint committee survey revealed that almost 60 percent of members supported biennial budgeting and appropriations. However, intense opposition to two-year appropriations bills came from members of the House and Senate Appropriations Committees. Spending decisions are the source of their power, and the appropriators preferred to make such decisions every year rather than biennially.

Congressional Resources and Interbranch Prerogatives

The prerogatives and resources of Congress have long been on the reorganization agenda. On staffing, the lawmakers' views divided along party lines. The 1993 reform survey revealed that 80.8 percent of House Republicans felt that the chamber was overstaffed, while only 22.4 percent of the majority Democrats shared that opinion. In the Senate, 70 percent of Republicans believed that the Senate was overstaffed; just 25 percent of Democrats felt the same way.

Within the joint committee, the leading advocates for streamlining Congress, including major staff reductions, were Senator Boren and Representative Dreier. They argued that staff cuts would save money and improve the policymaking capacity of Congress. According to Boren:

> We cannot possibly function efficiently with 299 committees and subcommittees. Congress did its most efficient and effective work when there were approximately 38 committees from both Houses combined and subcommittees were unheard of. I believe our bureaucracy has become an entangling bureaucracy rather than a staff which serves our needs as it should. I think we would be more efficient and effective with a leaner staff, at least 25 percent smaller than it is now, more effectively targeted and with a committee system that works.[49]

Pointing out that House offices often lose experienced aides to the higher-paying Senate, some Democrats responded that staff budgets should be increased, not reduced. Their concerns received little attention in the 1990s.

Additional Problems

As the joint committee's hearings drew to a close in late June 1993, panel members conducted a private retreat in Annapolis, Maryland, to begin the difficult process of winnowing down the vast array of reform proposals before them. In addition to the controversial nature of congressional reorganization, other factors complicated their work. Three in particular are noteworthy: freshman ineffectiveness, hostility to Senator Boren, and bicameral tensions.

First, after three months of meetings, the House Democratic freshmen still were unable to coalesce around a package of major reform proposals. Their ambivalence toward specific reforms, which had surfaced during the December 1992 organizational sessions, continued throughout the 103d Congress. Certain first-term Democrats, such as Rep. Eric Fingerhut (D-Ohio) and Rep. Karen Shepherd (D-Utah), did favor major changes in congressional operations, but many of their classmates were reluctant to challenge the prerogatives of senior lawmakers. The GOP freshmen united behind a package of significant reform recommendations, which included abolishing the Appropriations Committees, but their reorganization plan drew little bipartisan support. In short, the large class of freshman House members, many of whom campaigned on the need to revamp Congress, did not provide a cohesive constituency for institutional change.

Second, beginning in March 1993, Senator Boren emerged as an important and highly public opponent of portions of the Clinton economic program. A House Democrat said of Boren, "The Senator seems to function on a grandstand. Sometimes a person who is loud is not always important. . . . [T]he importance may be self-appointed with the help of reporters who are willing to listen."[50] A Democratic aide remarked, "Boren could offer to double their salary, and House Democrats wouldn't take it from him."[51] A Senate Democratic leader complained about Boren's opposition to the administration: "We plead with our Members that if you can't say anything good, don't say anything at all. . . . Not all Senators have got that message."[52]

Boren responded that he was trying to keep his party from veering excessively to the left: "I think my role was appropriate, but not only that, necessary. [Liberal Democrats] are not used to moderates in the party speaking out."[53] Before the joint committee members left for Annapolis, the newspaper *Roll Call* jokingly published a list of the top ten activities panel members might engage in on their retreat. The number one suggestion: "Play 'kill the guy from Oklahoma.' "[54]

Third, the hostility of many House Democrats toward Boren was reinforced by increased resentment toward the Senate. After House Democrats cast a difficult vote in favor of a Btu energy tax proposed by the president, the provision was dropped in the Senate because of opposition from Boren and other energy-state members from oil-producing states. Next, a Senate filibuster brought down the Administration's economic stimulus package. Then, on the year's major deficit-reduction bill, President Clinton made substantial concessions to members of the Senate, leading Rep. Patricia Schroeder to complain, "We've been forced to swallow whatever the tantrum of the day turned up on the Senate side."[55] The Senate also invoked a rule against extraneous matters in budget bills, which deleted a number of House-initiated items from the deficit-reduction measure. Pointedly, Rep. Al Swift (D-Wash.) often remarked, "Republicans are the opposition, but the Senate is the enemy."[56]

DECISION MAKING

During the August 1993 recess, the four leaders of the joint committee and their staffs began preparations for a draft reform bill, which would provide the basis for amendments during a formal markup, or bill-writing session, to be conducted in the fall. The leaders recognized that the content of their draft, called the chairman's mark, would be crucial for framing the debate during succeeding stages of the reform process.

Hundreds of reform alternatives were considered for the draft. Proposals supported by all four joint committee leaders were incorporated without controversy. For example, the four agreed that all relevant workplace laws should be applied to Congress, that committee assignment limitations should be tightened and strictly enforced, and that private citizens should be included in the ethics process.

Reform ideas opposed by two or more of the joint committee leaders were dropped from consideration. The most important example was a major realignment of committee jurisdictions, which Boren and Hamilton feared would cause so much conflict that the entire reform process would be endangered. They argued instead for an indirect approach to jurisdictional reform, in which committees that lost 50 percent or more of their members because of tighter assignment limitations would automatically be considered for abolition. Dreier, however, vowed to offer an amendment to overhaul committee jurisdictions when panel members met formally to consider the legislation.

At the end of August, the joint committee leaders agreed to discuss their markup plan with their respective party leaders, as well as with the other joint committee members. The two chambers' leaders faced different circumstances, however. It was clear that Boren and Domenici were close to agreement about the content of the draft reform plan. The Senate side of the joint committee was less polarized than the House side, and the Senate chairman and vice chairman shared similar reform priorities. There was also an expectation that, regardless of what the joint committee recommended, the package would be closely scrutinized by the Senate Rules and Administration Committee, as well as on the Senate floor. And with Boren reluctant to push for major changes in the filibuster rule, minority rights issues would not undermine a bipartisan agreement on the chairman's mark.

House Conflict

In contrast to the general agreement between Boren and Domenici, Hamilton and Dreier confronted formidable obstacles in their efforts to strike a bipartisan agreement about the draft reform plan. In September, after extensive consultations with his GOP colleagues, Dreier handed Hamilton a list of his top reform priorities, which featured minority rights proposals such as the abolition of proxy voting. Hamilton supported a number of the GOP priorities. Speaker Foley also was amenable to certain of the proposed changes.

However, as Hamilton searched for possible compromises, a growing number of House Democrats argued that minority party rights concessions should not be made to House Republicans unless Senate Republicans accepted major reforms of the filibuster. Minority party rights in the House, they argued, should be directly linked to majority rule in the Senate. On October 12, 1993, an article by Rep. Barney Frank (D-Mass.) appeared in the

Washington Post, in which he argued that the filibuster should be the primary target of congressional reform.

The article was discussed the following week at a breakfast meeting of the Democratic Study Group (DSG), and within hours Frank, David Obey (D-Wis.), and DSG chairman Mike Synar (D-Okla.) were circulating a petition among House Democrats stating that "no changes extending even greater power and protection to the minority [House Republicans] should be considered until action is taken to guarantee that the decisions made by the American people at the ballot box cannot be threatened by tactics such as those permitted under current Senate rules."[57]

A meeting of the House Democratic Caucus was held on October 20 to discuss the issue. Speaker after speaker rose to criticize the Senate filibuster. According to one account, the antifilibuster effort had "as much to do with sending a message to Lee Hamilton . . . as to the Senate."[58] No votes were taken at the caucus meeting, but there was no doubt that including minority party rights concessions in the chairman's mark without major filibuster reforms would spark a revolt among House Democrats. "The filibuster is a throwback to the political stone age," Obey declared. "No congressional reformer worthy of the name can continue to stand by and allow that relic to continue. . . . This must be the focus of the Hamilton-Boren Committee changes."[59]

Later, at a press conference complete with a model Capitol Dome shrouded in chains, Frank, Obey, and Synar announced the creation of a lobbying group called Action, Not Gridlock! which would attempt to mobilize public opinion behind filibuster reform. Domenici responded that "there are some powerful Democrats who have no interest in reform who are seeking to destroy it through a smokescreen called the filibuster."[60] Boren and Domenici, it was clear, would not agree to changes in the filibuster rule of sufficient magnitude to assuage House Democrats. Absent such changes, the House Democratic Caucus would not accept any enhancements of House minority party prerogatives in the joint committee's package. And without significant minority rights provisions, Dreier and other House Republicans would not sign on to any reorganization plan.

Was this conundrum avoidable? Probably not. The conditions were not ripe in either chamber for major changes in minority party prerogatives.[61] Throughout congressional history, curtailments in the procedural prerogatives of a congressional minority have tended to occur when a highly cohesive majority party believed that the minority would use its prerogatives to obstruct the majority's legislative agenda. Conversely, the rights of a congressional minority tend to be extended when there exists a bipartisan coalition of sufficient strength to bring about change.[62]

In the Senate, the Democratic majority was divided on major policy issues and on the need for filibuster reform. According to the joint committee survey, only about half of Senate Democrats favored major filibuster reforms. Under Senate rules, altering the filibuster requires sixty-seven votes, so the likelihood of major change was remote. On the House side, the fundamental question was whether to extend minority party prerogatives. Many Democrats preferred that the Rules Committee allow more amendments to be offered on the floor, but they did not support formal rules changes granting Republicans additional prerogatives. House Democrats believed that their long majority status would continue indefinitely, further reducing their incentives to extend minority party rights. In short, coalitions capable of forcing major floor reforms were missing in both chambers.

The Joint Committee Splits

Understandably concerned that the House reform process was unraveling and incensed by House Democratic attacks on Senate procedure, Boren and Domenici decided to proceed without their House counterparts. They scheduled a markup for the Senate members of the joint committee. At a November 4 press conference, they unveiled their draft reorganization plan, which was based on the reform proposals discussed by the four joint committee leaders in August. Included, for example, were recommendations to cut subcommittees, limit committee assignments, reduce legislative branch staff, institute a two-year budget process, and make minor changes in the filibuster rule. Concrete proposals to reform the ethics process and apply employment laws to Congress were not included in the Boren-Domenici mark because they were being considered at the time by separate Senate task forces.

On November 10, after a brief and consensual markup session, the Senate members of the joint committee passed the Boren-Domenici plan with only minor changes. However, observers predicted a rocky road for the package in the Senate Rules Committee, the main panel of jurisdiction, and on the Senate floor. An aide to majority leader George Mitchell remarked, "This is only the beginning. Obviously it's going to be changed."[63]

The House markup began on November 16 and continued, on and off, for an arduous five days. As expected, an agreement between Hamilton and Dreier on a draft markup measure was not attainable. Instead, Chairman Hamilton presented panel members with a stripped-down mark that included only reform proposals with broad bipartisan backing. The Indiana Democrat explained:

> The membership of this committee is equally divided between the two political parties. Even if all of the Republicans or all of the Democrats on [the] committee objected to a provision, they would not be able to delete it from the bill without the support of Members of the other party. For this reason we have decided only to include in the markup draft proposals that are supported by a majority of the House Members on the Joint Committee.[64]

Included in Hamilton's base bill were proposals to apply workplace laws to Congress, involve private citizens in the ethics process, require two-year budgets (but not appropriations), clamp down on committee assignments, reduce subcommittees, and decrease legislative branch staff. Hamilton acknowledged that the initial draft was not as substantial as he had hoped but said, "At this point, we should primarily focus on keeping the reform process going."[65] He promised to work to strengthen the package during the markup and at succeeding stages in the reform process.

Republican members of the panel expressed deep disappointment about the content of the draft reform plan. Vice Chairman Dreier described the mark as "neither bipartisan nor comprehensive. . . . Basically, from my perspective, we're back to ground zero."[66] Gerald Solomon called the plan "a minimalist approach to tinkering. . . . We are making a mockery out of our name. . . . We no longer are joint, and we no longer are really organized."[67]

During the markup sessions that followed, almost fifty amendments to the Hamilton draft were considered. Fifteen amendments passed, eight offered by Republicans and seven by Democrats. Approximately thirty GOP proposals, however, were defeated on straight party-line votes. Included were a comprehensive realignment of committee jurisdictions offered by Dreier, as well as proposals to abolish proxy voting and to increase the minority party's share of committee slots and staff resources. A number of Democratic amendments also were rejected.

The House reform plan, as amended, resembled the package reported by the Senate members of the joint committee two weeks earlier.[68] Still, Republicans criticized the outcome. Dreier and Rep. Bill Emerson (R-Mo.) voted with the six Democrats to report the reform package, but only to keep the reorganization process going. Dreier remarked:

> [Although] there are some significant elements in the base bill, there are several very important elements to comprehensive congressional reform that don't appear. [The] only reason I am voting for this is that I hold out a little hope that under an open amendment process, we will be able to allow the membership to work its will."[69]

THE CHAMBERS RESPOND

When Congress reconvened for the second session of the 103d Congress, Boren and Domenici introduced the Senate reform package as the Legislative Reorganization Act of 1994. As expected, the measure was referred to the Committee on Rules and Administration. The same day, Hamilton introduced the House reform plan, also titled the Legislative Reorganization Act of 1994, which was referred to three committees, although the Rules Committee was expected to take the lead in considering the package. Dreier declined to cosponsor the legislation with Hamilton because the Californian could not secure a commitment from Speaker Foley that reform would be considered on the floor under a generous amendment rule.

The year 1994 began auspiciously for the House and Senate reorganization plans. By spring, a succession of hearings were conducted in the two main committees of jurisdiction, the House and Senate Rules Committees. As the summer months approached, however, it became clear that neither reform package had much support from Democratic congressional leaders, especially majority leader Mitchell and Speaker Foley. Still, Hamilton continued to pressure Democratic leaders to bring the bill to the floor and allow a reasonable range of amendments. From his position on the Rules Committee, Dreier also urged committee Democrats to expedite consideration of the measure. In the Senate, Boren and Domenici likewise lobbied their colleagues to proceed with the reorganization process.

THE DENOUEMENT

In June, the Senate Rules Committee divided the Boren-Domenici bill, weakened key provisions, and reported to the floor three separate reform measures. Deleted were two-year appropriations and the recommendation that committees losing more than 50 percent of their members be considered for abolition. Boren called the result "about two-thirds of what I hoped it would be."[70] But Domenici remarked, "After all the work the Joint Committee did, I'm very disappointed with the outcome."[71]

For the next three months, the three reform measures reported by the Senate Rules Committee were not scheduled by the leadership for consideration on the floor. In late September, Boren and Domenici offered the joint committee's original reform package as a floor amendment to an unrelated appropriations bill. Boren told his colleagues, "We have been unable to bring . . . these important recommendations to this body for consideration. Out of frustration, the Senator from New Mexico . . . and I decided we should not allow this Congress to adjourn without giving the Members of the Senate an opportunity to vote on these reform recommendations."[72]

For the Boren-Domenici package to be so considered, certain Senate rules had to be waived, which required sixty votes. The joint committee leaders fell two votes short. A few days later, majority leader Mitchell attempted to bring up a revised version of the Shays-Swett proposal to apply workplace laws to Congress, but a parliamentary objection derailed that effort, effectively ending the reorganization process in the Senate for the 103d Congress. None of the joint committee's recommendations were considered by the full Senate.

On the other side of Capitol Hill, the House reform package met a similar fate. In June, Rules Committee chairman Joseph Moakley (D-Mass.) warned that the House plan also might be divided, with the popular proposal applying labor laws to Congress split off and brought separately to the floor. The reform bill was "too much to grasp at one time," Moakley said.[73] A Democratic aide commented, "We're not sure that the voting blocs are united on passage of the full package."[74] Hamilton opposed the division. "If the reform package is divided," he wrote to Speaker Foley, "it will be harder to concentrate the attention of Members and the public on institutional reform. Also, if the Joint Committee's package is divided, the application of laws section will no longer function as a valuable sweetener for reforms that are less popular, but still necessary."[75]

The same month, Representatives Shays and Swett, original sponsors of the proposal to apply workplace laws to Congress, threatened to file a discharge petition, aimed at extracting their bill from committee and bringing it directly to the floor, unless Foley scheduled a vote on the congressional compliance issue before the August recess. One impact of their threat was to increase the pressure on House Democratic leaders to separate the application of laws section from the rest of the reform package.

On July 13, Foley indicated to reporters that the package would be divided. The following week, Hamilton met with the Speaker, majority leader Richard Gephardt, and Rules Committee chairman Moakley. In exchange for an explicit promise from the Speaker that the rest of the package would receive floor consideration in September, Hamilton accepted Foley's decision to break off the congressional compliance section of the reform bill. "My preference was not to break it up," Hamilton said. "But I was forced to face reality."[76] Dreier strongly opposed the decision: "I'm very disappointed. Breaking it up is little more than a divide-and-conquer strategy. It's a great disservice to a year of effort."[77]

On August 10, the House passed an amended version of the Shays-Swett bill by an overwhelming margin of 427 to 4. Rep. Barney Frank remarked, "We are daring today to do the right thing. We are changing hundreds of years of tradition."[78] Earlier that day, Dreier had argued unsuccessfully that the rule governing floor debate on the application of laws bill should be amended to allow consideration of the full joint committee package. "Adoption of this rule," Dreier said, "will mark the death of congressional reform. There is no way the Democratic leadership will allow an effective reform bill on this floor."[79]

The Shays-Swett bill, even with its broad base of popular and legislative support, did not become law during the 103d Congress. As mentioned, efforts to bring up a companion measure in the Senate failed. Instead, before adjourning for the November elections, the House adopted a chamber-specific resolution to apply ten labor laws to its employees.

Dreier was right about the rest of the joint committee reform package. Two days of markup on the remainder of the reorganization bill did occur in the House Rules Committee, one in August and the other in mid-September, with partisan strife dominating the proceedings. Rep. Anthony Beilenson of California, a Rules Committee Democrat, planned to offer an amendment to abolish proxy voting, and it appeared that at least two other Democrats on the panel might vote for the proposal. Along with the four Rules Committee

Republicans, the three Democratic votes would give the proxy ban majority support within the panel.

During the second day of markup, on September 21, as it became apparent that the Beilenson proposal to abolish proxies might pass, the Democrats on the Rules Committee left the meeting room to caucus privately with the Speaker. Foley urged them not to vote for the proxy ban, as well as another Beilenson amendment that would have made modest changes in committee jurisdictions.

Late in the afternoon, Moakley stepped back into the meeting room and told the assembled audience and staff that the markup was over. Although the joint committee's package remained on the floor schedule for the last few weeks of the session, the Rules Committee never returned to the reform plan, and the Legislative Reorganization Act of 1994 died at the end of the 103d Congress.

ORGANIZATIONAL RATIONALES

Postmortems of the 103d Congress tend to blame Democratic leaders, particularly in the House, for the demise of comprehensive reform. Speaker Foley, for example, was reluctant to support the creation of the Joint Committee on the Organization of Congress until public furor over the House bank scandal in 1992 made it imperative for Democrats to cast a preelection vote for reform. Then, as Lee Hamilton and other reformers attempted to build support for major changes in 1993, Democratic leaders largely backed away from the reform process. The next year, the Speaker did not follow through on his commitment to Hamilton to bring the joint committee's recommendations to the full House.

Senator Mitchell likewise lacked enthusiasm for the reform process. The majority leader did not consider congressional reorganization a major priority for the Senate. By most accounts, he viewed David Boren, the leading Senate reformer, as an independent-minded party maverick. Like Foley, Mitchell chose not to schedule the reorganization plan for floor action.

However, congressional reorganization failed during the 103d Congress for reasons more fundamental than leadership indifference or opposition. A mix of partisan, clientele, and other incentives led lawmakers to embrace the institutional status quo. All five organizational rationales are relevant to reform politics under the Democratic majority, although the importance of each factor varied by reorganization area. Overall, conditions within the congressional parties played a decisive role in the demise of reform.

Partisan rationales are evident when majority party members seek to enhance leadership prerogatives. Strengthening party leaders can enhance the ability of the majority party to achieve its legislative agenda. However, in 1993–1994, fractious conditions within the majority caucus inhibited any significant expansion of leadership powers. In fact, the Speaker resisted attempts to augment his authority.

Another organizational rationale—the personal power agendas of individual lawmakers—also was apparent in the leadership reform area. Committee chairs and other influential lawmakers were concerned that they might lose clout under an empowered majority leadership. The Democratic rank and file, deeply divided on policy issues, lacked the incentives to support initiatives strengthening the party leadership. Accordingly, the House Democratic Caucus chose not to substantially increase party leadership powers at the beginning of the 103d Congress.

What factors were behind the lack of major change in the area of committee reform? In contrast to the Republican reforms following the 1994 elections, there was little indication that the majority Democrats sought significant changes in the committee system to promote their party's agenda. After the Democratic Party's four decades of predominance on Capitol Hill, its policy priorities were already embodied in the House and Senate committee systems. Most Democrats also did not relish the prospect of a divisive intraparty fight over committee jurisdictions at a time when they wanted to unite behind their new president's program.

Broader institutional concerns played a limited role in committee reform politics in 1993–1994. Reorganization advocates on the Joint Committee on the Organization of Congress argued that the committee system was outdated and inefficient, and thus in need of a major overhaul. Public opinion also provided some incentive (saving taxpayers' money, for example) to reduce the number of panels and otherwise trim the congressional bureaucracy.

However, the incentives favoring committee reform were overridden by other factors, particularly the personal power agendas of individual members. The House committee chairs, for instance, were a cohesive and organized force against realignment. Clientele factors also worked against major change, as interest groups fought jurisdictional reforms that might reduce the value of their relationships with influential lawmakers and committee staff aides.

Prominent on the reorganization agendas of both chambers were proposals to alter the procedures for floor deliberations, particularly as they relate to minority party prerogatives. Partisan considerations propelled such proposals onto the reorganization agenda. The impact of partisan factors, however, was conditioned by the overall level of agreement (or disagreement) on policy matters within the two congressional parties. The result: In neither chamber did there emerge a cross-party coalition of sufficient strength to expand (House) or restrict (Senate) minority party rights on the floor. In the Senate, the personal agendas of individual lawmakers helped preclude a major curtailment of their procedural powers.

Lawmakers also considered recommendations to make the scheduling of floor business less chaotic, reflecting institutional concerns for greater certainty and predictability and a simple desire to improve the quality of life for members and their families. Lawmakers disagreed, however, about the best way to improve scheduling practices, and little progress was made in this reform area.

Policy-driven reforms, mostly relating to the budget process, also were on the reform agenda during the 103d Congress. A range of organizational rationales shed light on reform politics in this area. Democrats and Republicans disagree about budgetary issues, and major changes in the budget process can affect the ability of the two political parties to advance their spending and taxing priorities. Although strongly endorsed in public opinion polls, the balanced budget amendment divided members along partisan and institutional (Congress versus the president) lines. In both chambers, constitutional balanced budget amendments failed to garner the necessary two-thirds support for passage.

After the House adopted a measure to provide the president with expedited rescission authority (another budgetary reform), lawmakers concerned about their personal power agendas, as well as protecting congressional spending prerogatives, defeated it in the Senate. For similar personal and institutional reasons, many members opposed the organizational changes to the budget process recommended by the joint committee.

Partisan incentives and public opinion were central in the area of congressional resources and interbranch prerogatives; institutional considerations played a limited role. In previous decades, lawmakers periodically increased the staff and analytical support available to Congress. The emphasis in the 1990s, however, has been on staff reductions and funding cuts. Public opinion surveys indicate that voters want to scale back what they perceive to be a bloated congressional bureaucracy. Under the Democratic majority, lawmakers differed by party in their reactions to proposals to slash congressional resources. Democrats argued that significant reductions, typically promoted by Republicans, would weaken Congress and undermine their ability to advance the majority party's agenda. Consequently, they blocked GOP initiatives to slash legislative branch personnel and funding. However, Democrats did back incremental reductions in legislative branch resources.

Perhaps the main impetus for reform in 1993–1994 was highly negative public opinion about the integrity of Congress. Lawmakers from both political parties continued to hunt for perks and privileges to abolish. Partisan considerations led many Republican members to emphasize this reform area, as part of their concerted efforts to further undermine public confidence in the Democratic majority. Many lawmakers in both parties continued to run for Congress by running against it.

However, members from both parties also were concerned about the impact of public dissatisfaction with Congress on the long-term legitimacy of the legislative branch. Concerns about the institution led them to support certain proposals aimed at restoring public confidence in the integrity of

Congress. In both chambers, legislation applying laws to Congress gathered significant bipartisan support before becoming entangled in the controversy surrounding the recommendations of the joint committee.

Although public opinion was pivotal in the emergence of institutional reform as a major issue in the early 1990s, the impact of public attitudes on the content of the reorganization agenda in 1993–1994 was less pronounced. This is a key reason reform failed under the Democratic majority.

Clientele and institutional considerations did not create strong momentum for organizational change in the 103d Congress. Similarly, the personal power agendas of key players in the reform game were not conducive to major change. And most important, in neither chamber was there sufficient partisan incentive to pass comprehensive reform. For significant reorganization to occur, it was critical that public opinion be mobilized behind a package of concrete reform proposals.

However, from leadership prerogatives and committee restructuring to the budget process and minority party rights, the reorganization proposals that dominated the reform process during the 103d Congress did not resonate with public concerns about the institution, which mostly focused on perks, pork, term limits, and perceived ethical lapses. Democratic leaders believed that for all the conflict that reform would create, it could do little to improve public opinion about the Democratic Congress. In the end, the Democratic majority rejected reform because reform did not appear to be worth the trouble. Following the November 1994 elections, a new majority made a different calculation.

Notes

1. *Congressional Quarterly Weekly Report,* January 23, 1993, 192.

2. Hearings before the Joint Committee on the Organization of Congress, S. Hrg. 103–74, 103d Cong., 1st sess., 776.

3. Robert Byrd, *The Senate, 1789–1989* (Washington, D.C.: U.S. Government Printing Office, 1988), p. 539.

4. William H. Riker, *Liberalism Against Populism* (San Francisco: W. H. Freeman and Company, 1982), p. 222.

5. Sometimes this meant amending House rules to prohibit irritating dilatory practices used by the minority party during the previous Congress.

6. Thomas E. Mann and Norman J. Ornstein, *Renewing Congress: A First Report* (Washington, D.C.: American Enterprise Institute and Brookings Institution, 1992). A second report of the Renewing Congress project, published in 1993, provided numerous recommendations for the Joint Committee on the Organization of Congress. Many of these proposals ended up in the House and Senate packages reported by the panel. A third report, published the following year, evaluated the joint committee's recommendations. Matt Pinkus ably assisted the Mann-Ornstein project.

7. Karen Foerstel, "Chairmen Worry Changes in Rules Will Erode Power," *Roll Call,* September 17, 1992, 14.

8. Editorial, *Roll Call,* December 10, 1992, 4.

9. Mary Jacoby, "Capitol Greets Frosh," *Roll Call,* December 3, 1992, 22.

10. Kenneth J. Cooper, "House Democratic Leaders Travel to Freshman Class," *Washington Post,* November 9, 1992, A8.

11. Richard Blow, "Foley Flexes," *Mother Jones,* July/August 1993, 41, 40.

12. Cooper, "House Democratic Leaders," A8.

13. Kenneth J. Cooper, "14 of 110 Freshmen Attend 'Revolution,' " *Washington Post,* November 24, 1992, A13.

14. David W. Rohde, *Parties and Leaders in the Postreform House* (Chicago: University of Chicago Press, 1991). See also John H. Aldrich, *Why Parties?* (Chicago: University of Chicago Press, 1995). The classic study in this area is Joseph Cooper and David W. Brady, "Institutional Context and Leadership Style: The House from Cannon to Rayburn," *American Political Science Review,* 75 (1981), 411–25.

15. American Samoa, the District of Columbia, Guam, and the Virgin Islands are represented in the House by delegates. Puerto Rico is represented by a resident commissioner, who has the same formal prerogatives as the four delegates. Prior to the 103d Congress, the delegates and resident commissioner were not allowed to vote on the House floor. In December 1992, the Democratic Caucus endorsed a proposal to allow them to vote on floor amendments but not on the final passage of legislation (for constitutional reasons). The next month, a scaled-down proposal was offered by Rep. David Skaggs (D-Colo.), in which delegate votes on floor amendments would be counted only when they did not affect the final outcome. House Republicans filed suit in federal court, claiming that this awkward compromise was unconstitutional, but the court declined to overturn the delegate voting rule. This rule was deleted by the GOP-controlled 104th Congress.

16. Kenneth J. Cooper, "House GOP Warns on Rules Changes," *Washington Post,* December 10, 1992, A11.

17. Karen Foerstel, "Democrats Back Down on Special-Order Limits," *Roll Call,* December 14, 1992, 24.

18. The panel received testimony from almost 250 witnesses, including more than 150 members of Congress. Almost 500 distinct recommendations for reforming Congress were proposed.

19. Hearing before the Joint Committee on the Organization of Congress, S. Hrg. 103–10, 103d Cong., 1st sess., January 26, 1993, 2.

20. Ibid., p. 1.

21. Richard E. Cohen, "Capitol Hill Watch," *National Journal,* March 13, 1993, 637.

22. Scholarly analyses of the evolution and maintenance of jurisdictional boundaries include David King, "The Nature of Congressional Committee Jurisdictions," *American Political Science Review,* 88 (1994), 48–62; and Bryan D. Jones, Frank R. Baumgartner, and Jeffrey C. Talbert, "The Destruction of Issue Monopolies in Congress," *American Political Science Review,* 87 (1993), 657–71.

23. Hearings before the Joint Committee on the Organization of Congress, S. Hrg. 103–74, 103d Cong., 1st sess., April 20, 22, 27, 29; May 4, 6, 11, 13, 1993, 64.

24. In February 1993, however, the House did abolish its four select committees. These panels had no legislative jurisdiction but held hearings and distributed information about certain issues—child welfare, hunger, narcotics, and the elderly.

25. Part of the problem also was disagreement about the principles that should guide committee reorganization. At various points, lawmakers emphasized (1) making House and Senate jurisdictions parallel, (2) consolidating major issues within the jurisdiction of a single committee, (3) structuring jurisdictions so that they match up with executive branch agencies, (4) creating more equitable workloads across panels, and (5) devising committee boundaries that evoke a balance of competing interests. When concrete realignment plans were discussed, however, it was clear that these principles were fundamentally inconsistent.

26. "Foley on Congress and the Executive," *National Journal,* April 29, 1989, 1037.

27. Hearings, April 20, 22, 27, 29; May 4, 6, 11, 13, 1993, 613–15.

28. Republicans also treated the Energy and Commerce Committee as an exclusive committee.

29. Background materials: Supplemental Information Provided to Members of the Joint Committee on the Organization of Congress, S. Prt. 103–55, 103d Cong., 1st sess., 489.

30. Ibid., p. 485.

31. Hearing before the Joint Committee on the Organization of Congress, S. Hrg. 103–26, 103d Cong., 1st sess., February 2, 1993, 8.

32. *Final Report of the House Members of the Joint Committee on the Organization of Congress,* 103d Cong., 1st sess., 1993, Rept. 103–413, vol. 1, 151.

33. Democratic leaders responded that proxy voting was necessary for lawmakers to juggle the scheduling conflicts they faced and that, present or not at the relevant committee meeting, members typically know how they are going to vote. Committee ratios, Democrats argued, seldom diverged from the partisan makeup of the full House by more than a few percentage points, with the exception of the leadership-dominated Rules Committee. On the matter of committee staff allocations, Democrats responded that the majority party was responsible for running the House and should have the lion's share of committee resources.

34. Hearing before the Joint Committee on the Organization of Congress, S. Hrg. 103–10, 103d Cong., 1st sess., January 26, 1993, 33.

35. Karen Foerstel, "Guerrilla Warfare Ahead as Republicans, Democrats Spar Over Floor Proceedings," *Roll Call,* April 1, 1993, 12.

36. Ibid.

37. Karen Foerstel, "Perot Backs GOP in Fight on Closed House Rules," *Roll Call,* June 14, 1993, 5.

38. Karen Foerstel, "Rules Will Soon Open, Says Foley," *Roll Call,* April 26, 1993, 1.

39. Hearing, January 26, 1993, 47–50.

40. Kevin Merida, "Racing the Clock on Capitol Hill—and Losing," *Washington Post,* May 16, 1993, A1.

41. Maureen Dowd, "New Lawmakers See Reform Where Veterans See Self-Piety," *New York Times,* March 16, 1993, A17.

42. An in-depth analysis of the ethics process as it relates to institutional integrity is provided in Dennis F. Thompson, *Ethics in Congress: From Individual to Institutional Corruption* (Washington, D.C.: Brookings Institution, 1995).

43. Editorials/Letters, *New York Times,* April 12, 1993.

44. Hearings before the Joint Committee on the Organization of Congress, S. Hrg. 103–15, 103d Cong., 1st sess., May 27, June 8, 17, 1993, 38.

45. Ibid., 3.

46. *Congressional Quarterly Almanac 1993,* 145.

47. David Cloud, "Politically Influential Issue Settled As Budget Amendment Fails," *Congressional Quarterly Weekly Report,* March 5, 1994, 528.

48. *Congressional Quarterly Almanac 1993,* 147.

49. Hearing before the Joint Committee on the Organization of Congress, S. Hrg. 103–10, 103d Cong., 1st sess., January 26, 1993, 3.

50. Richard E. Cohen, "Dismal Reviews for Sen. Boren's Show," *National Journal,* May 29, 1993, 1308.

51. States News Service wire, June 25, 1993.

52. Ibid.

53. *National Journal's Congress Daily,* July 2, 1993.

54. Craig Winneker, "Heard on the Hill," *Roll Call,* June 24, 1993, 25.

55. Janet Hook, "Bad Blood Clouds Effort to 'Reform' Congress," *Congressional Quarterly Weekly Report,* September 18, 1993, 2514.

56. Rep. Swift made this remark a number of times in the Joint Committee on the Organization of Congress.

57. Letter from Rep. Mike Synar and others to Rep. Lee Hamilton, October 12, 1993.

58. *CQ's Congressional Monitor,* October 21, 1993, 7.

59. "News from Congressman Dave Obey," October 20, 1993.

60. "Domenici Statement on Democratic News Conference on Congressional Reform," news release, October 20, 1993.

61. See Sarah A. Binder and Steven S. Smith, "Acquired Procedural Tendencies and Congressional Reform," in *Remaking Congress,* ed. Roger H. Davidson and James A. Thurber (Washington, D.C.: Congressional Quarterly, 1994).

62. Ibid.; Sarah A. Binder, "Partisanship and Procedural Choice: Institutional Change in the Early Congress, 1789–1823," paper presented at the Annual Meeting of the Midwest Political Science Association, Chicago, April 6–8, 1995. See also Douglas Dion, "Majority Rule, Minority Rights, and the Politics of Procedural Change," paper presented at the Annual Meeting of the American Political Science Association, San Francisco, August 30–September 2, 1990.

63. Mary Jacoby, "Hell of a Fight Still Lies Ahead," *Roll Call,* November 11, 1993, 1.

64. Business meetings of the Joint Committee on the Organization of Congress, S. Hrg. 103–320, 103d Cong., 1st sess., November 1993, 75.

65. Ibid.

66. Ibid., p. 78.

67. Ibid., p. 80.

68. Unlike the Senate bill, the House package included proposals to apply labor laws to Congress and involve citizens in the ethics process. The committee reforms in the Senate plan were stronger than those included in the House bill.

69. Business meetings, November 1993, 500–501.

70. Karen Foerstel, "Senate Reformers Face Floor Battle," *Roll Call,* June 20, 1994, 30.

71. Karen Foerstel, "One-Third of Reform Heads to Senate Floor," *Roll Call,* June 13, 1994, 24.

72. *Congressional Record,* September 29, 1994, S13665.

73. Karen Foerstel, "In a Letter to Moakley, Hamilton Fights Move to Divide Reform Plan," *Roll Call,* May 16, 1994, 3.

74. Karen Foerstel, "Reform Plan May Be Split in Pieces," *Roll Call,* April 25, 1994, 30.

75. Letter from Rep. Lee H. Hamilton to Speaker Thomas S. Foley, June 30, 1994.

76. Karen Foerstel, "Foley, Hamilton Strike Deal to Vote in Fall on Internal Reform Package," *Roll Call,* July 25, 1994, 26.

77. Ibid.

78. Karen Foerstel, "House Approves, 427–4, Compliance with Sweeping Private-Sector Laws," *Roll Call,* August 11, 1994, 26.

79. Ibid.

4

Taking Charge
of the House

O N ELECTION night 1994, as national television networks announced that the GOP was winning majorities in both chambers of Congress, Rep. Newt Gingrich (R-Ga.) stepped before an Atlanta victory audience and declared, "This is truly a wildly historic night." The stunning electoral outcome meant that Republicans would control the Senate, as the party had from 1981 to 1987. The implications for the House were significantly more profound. An unprecedented forty years in the minority wilderness was ending for the House GOP, and Gingrich, whose remarkable climb to power often featured strident attacks on Congress, would be the next Speaker.

In the days that followed, Gingrich and other House Republican leaders planned the transition to GOP control. Shortly after the election, the incoming Speaker asked Rep. Jim Nussle (R-Iowa) to head the official transition team. Three years previously, Nussle had drawn the ridicule of House Democrats by appearing on the floor with a bag over his head, as part of an effort to publicize the House bank scandal. About his appointment, Nussle observed, "It's almost like sticking a finger in the eye of the [old] Democratic majority who resisted reform . . . by putting the guy who put the bag on his head in charge [of the transition]."[1] But Gingrich argued that his goal was constructive change: "We're saying to the Democratic leadership, we want to establish a different style and a different tone . . . rather than simply replacing the Democratic machine with a Republican machine."[2]

Much of the groundwork had been laid for the GOP transition months before election day. The Contract with America, for instance, pledged that eight congressional reforms would be passed on the first day of the 104th Congress. More concretely, the contract promised that a Republican House would (1) apply all workplace laws to Congress, (2) provide for an independent audit of House finances, (3) reduce the number of House committees and cut the number of committee staff by one-third, (4) limit the terms of committee chairs, (5) abolish proxy voting, (6) require that committee meetings be open to the public, (7) require a three-fifths vote in the House to pass tax increases, and (8) adopt base-line budgeting (a budget accounting reform).

The morning after the election, Gingrich spoke with Rep. David Dreier (R-Calif.), who was at home in California. During the 103d Congress, Dreier served as vice chair of the Joint Committee on the Organization of Congress, emerging as a leader among House Republicans on congressional reform issues. He recalled his postelection telephone conversation with Gingrich:

> I got an early-morning call on November 9th, very early California time, from Newt Gingrich, and he asked me to craft some proposals to overhaul the committee system. And I was very honored to be offered a chance to take part in what I believe is very historic change in the leadership here in the House of Representatives, really an effort to bring this institution out of the dark ages.[3]

In the fall of 1994, as the prospects for a GOP takeover improved, aides to House Republicans also drafted blueprints for restructuring the House committee system, reforming management practices in the chamber, and achieving other reorganization goals. These efforts continued after November 8, with Republican staff of the Rules Committee devising a list of possible rules changes for the 104th Congress, mostly derived from the GOP reform plans offered as substitutes to previous Democratic rules packages. Included were a diverse range of recommendations, from committee assignment limitations to the partisan distribution of committee staff to automatic roll-call votes on tax and spending measures. This list of procedural and related reforms was forwarded to Republican leaders and transition team members for possible inclusion in the rules package to be adopted on the opening day of the 104th Congress.

When the Nussle transition team and key Republican leaders began formal meetings the week after the election, they were able to draw on a wide range of reorganization ideas and background materials. Most aspects of House operations were considered for change. For instance, the agenda items for a pivotal meeting on November 16 included leadership prerogatives, the selection of committee chairs, committee restructuring, personnel issues, and the development of a scheduling plan for implementing the Contract with America.

After three weeks of intense and often controversial effort, transition leaders in early December announced the most sweeping overhaul of House operations in almost fifty years. Their reorganization recommendations were ratified by the full Republican Conference, with minor changes, the following week and adopted by the House on the first day of the 104th Congress.

The purpose of this chapter is to analyze the content of and the goals behind the institutional reforms adopted in January 1995. Our focus here is on the House Republican transition. The Senate Republican majority also considered major institutional changes, but reform deliberations in that chamber mostly occurred after the 104th Congress began and thus are explored in Chapter 5. The reforms considered during the House Republican transition shed additional light on the organizational rationales that shape congressional procedures and structures. In the concluding section of this chapter, we evaluate the relative importance of these factors in understanding the GOP reorganization that followed the 1994 elections.

LEADERSHIP PREROGATIVES

In the 103d Congress, Democrats declined to strengthen significantly the prerogatives of the House Speaker. Members of the majority party, divided on key policy issues, lacked a cohesive legislative agenda for their party leaders to promote or enact. They preferred to center power in the committee system. Yet, as Gingrich realized, several advantages may be derived from reforms that empower the Speaker's office.[4]

Advantages of a Powerful Speaker

Discourage Defections

Even relatively unified majority parties have potentially serious disagreements about specific policy objectives. The rank and file may mostly agree about the general direction of policy change, but on specific issues a subset of the party caucus can be pressured by other interests, particularly constituency concerns, and thus be inclined to vote against or not actively work for the party's position. As a result, the majority caucus may choose to provide its leadership with the resources and sanctions necessary to enforce loyalty. The potential costs to the majority party of defections within its ranks are particularly high the smaller the size of the majority caucus.

Reduce Bargaining Costs

On Capitol Hill, the legislative process is fundamentally an exchange process, with coalitions typically glued together through bargaining and compromise. The disagreements about policy that characterize even relatively unified partisan majorities usually require concessions and logrolling if legislation is to move and party cohesion is to be maintained. Legislative bargains, however, are costly in the sense that time, effort, and resources are required to make them happen.

When bargaining is centered in committees, agreements tend to develop discretely, on an issue-by-issue basis, and between members of relatively equal stature (fellow committee members, for example). Under such conditions, the coalition-building process can be cumbersome and time-consuming. Shifting groups of lawmakers have a seat at the bargaining table, and no one individual may have the power to whip reluctant members into line. In contrast, strong party leaders can forge agreements that reach across diverse issues and committee jurisdictions, reducing the negotiating costs of legislative work (delay, dilution of policy objectives, jurisdictional feuds, and the like). The larger and more complex the majority party's agenda, the greater the advantages of delegating substantial prerogatives to the Speaker. Similarly, if the views of important committee chairs diverge from the party's program, partisan incentives will exist to strengthen the party leadership.

Focus the Agenda

If the overall legislative agenda of the House is not set by the Speaker, it tends to emerge piecemeal from the various standing committees. Individual committee chairs respond, to varying degrees, to party leaders and the party rank and file. But they also respond to cross-partisan coalitions within their panels, the interest groups activated by their jurisdictions, and their own personal agendas. If the House's policy priorities emerge primarily from the various standing committees, the legislative agenda will tend to be fragmented and lacking in coordination and cohesion. Thus, reforms that increase the role of the majority party leadership in institutional agenda setting make it more likely that the policy priorities of the majority caucus as a whole will structure the legislative agenda. The more ambitious and wide-ranging a majority's agenda, and the more committed rank-and-file members are to that agenda, the greater the importance that party leaders, and not committee leaders, dominate the agenda-setting process.

Publicize the Agenda

The media can more easily cover and the public more easily comprehend the policy priorities advanced by an individual or small set of party leaders rather than by a larger group of committee and subcommittee chairs. Thus, when the House majority party speaks with one or a few voices, it can better focus public debate on its policy priorities and perhaps challenge the president's influence over the national political agenda. Elevating the Speaker's role, particularly in setting the legislative agenda, enhances the bully pulpit capacities of the position and of the majority party more generally. Clearly, the advantages to the majority party of using the bully pulpit capacities of the Speaker are higher when the other party controls the executive branch.

Empowering the Speaker

Following the 1994 elections, House Republicans adopted a number of reforms that significantly strengthened the Speaker. Gingrich explained that the GOP had changed "from a party focused on opposition to a majority party with responsibilities for governing. That requires greater assets in the leader's office."[5] Departing Republican leader Robert Michel of Illinois observed, "Newt knows what he's doing. I didn't crave power when I was leader—I don't know if it would have changed if I were Speaker. I just hope it doesn't go to our newly elected leaders' heads."[6]

Unlike conditions under previous Democratic majorities, the climate was ripe within the Republican Conference for substantially enhancing leadership prerogatives. Most important, a united Republican majority was concerned that key committee leaders might be insufficiently committed to the party's agenda. House Republicans long have been more cohesive than their Democratic counterparts. And in 1994, more than three hundred GOP incumbents and challengers appeared on the Capitol steps to sign the Contract with America. After the election, GOP lawmakers believed that their new majority would be judged by its ability to pass most of the contract items within the promised one hundred days.

Although House Republicans were cohesive, the emergence of some intraparty cleavages was inevitable. The small size of the Republican majority meant that a coalition of twenty to thirty moderate conservatives might be pivotal when considering certain contract measures, such as welfare and regulatory reform. There were also concerns about the commitment of certain senior committee leaders to the party's agenda, providing further incentives for rank-and-file Republicans to strengthen the Speaker relative to the incoming chairs.

Consider the case of Rep. John Myers (R-Ind.), who was the most senior member of the Appropriations Committee eligible to chair that panel.[7] First elected in 1966, Myers has been described as "the kind of middle-American, moderate-mannered Republican who once composed the inner circle of the House GOP leadership, but now is relegated to the fringes."[8] Gingrich and other Republican leaders were concerned that Myers, steeped in the bipartisan norms of the old-style appropriator, might not be aggressive or partisan enough to slash federal spending. Similar questions were raised about other potential committee chairs.

The scope and complexity of the House Republican policy program also created incentives for GOP lawmakers to enhance the Speaker's prerogatives. By all accounts, the immediate legislative demands facing the new Republican majority were extraordinary: move the entire Contract with America to the floor before May, devise a plan to balance the federal budget over seven years, process the annual appropriations bills, and deal with the myriad conservative policy initiatives that had gathered dust under Democratic rule.

As the inevitable policy disagreements emerged, House Republicans believed that they would need an empowered leadership to facilitate the legislative bargaining so central to coalition building on Capitol Hill. Republicans also needed to rely on their leaders to keep the legislative agenda focused on party priorities rather than the interests of individual committee chairs. And the presence of a hostile administration, controlled by the other party, elevated the importance of the Speaker as a national spokesman for House Republicans.

A summary of the GOP organizational changes aimed at enhancing the Speaker's prerogatives is provided in Table 4.1. Most were proposed by the transition team, adopted by the Republican Conference in December, and passed by the full House in January. Other changes occurred more informally, as a result of Gingrich's efforts to consolidate power after the election.

First, Speaker Gingrich assumed the authority to name (and remove, implicitly) all the leaders of the standing committees, and he exercised this authority especially for committees deemed crucial to the fulfillment of GOP policy objectives. Rather than appoint Myers to chair the Appropriations Committee, Gingrich selected Rep. Bob Livingston (R-La.), who was viewed as more committed to major spending reductions.[9] Also bypassing the seniority system, Gingrich named ideological loyalists and strong-willed partisans to chair the Commerce (Thomas Bliley [R-Va.]) and Judiciary (Henry Hyde [R-Ill.]) Committees. An eleven-term GOP veteran, Carlos Moorhead of California, who had the seniority to head either Commerce or Judiciary, was passed over for both chairmanships because of his conciliatory approach to lawmaking. "They tell me that I'm not mean enough," Moorhead said.[10] However, seniority was observed in naming most of the other committee chairs. As an aide to Gingrich noted, "[Y]ou can't have an ideological purge and build a team."[11]

Gingrich also reconstituted his party's "committee on committees," the panel responsible for assigning GOP members to the various standing committees. Shortly after the election, aides to the incoming Speaker drafted a

TABLE 4.1 Leadership Prerogatives

- Allow incoming Speaker Gingrich to appoint committee chairs (no rules change)

- Increase leadership influence over GOP committee assignments

- Allow the Republican leader to appoint members and the Republican leader of the Committee on House Oversight

- Reorganize House administrative offices and place them under the Speaker's authority

- Abolish joint referral of legislation (referring entire bills to two or more committees simultaneously) but authorize the Speaker to designate a primary committee of jurisdiction

- Facilitate the consideration of limitation amendments to appropriations bills by allowing only the majority leader to offer a preferential motion to rise

- Limit the Speaker's term to eight years

memorandum titled "System for Selecting Chairmen and Members to Standing Committees." The memorandum stated, "The current Republican structure [for selecting committee members] is dominated by regional influences and intricate personal relationships. The leadership has little voting influence even if their voting bloc is enlarged substantially. The committee would be dominated by the current cult of personalities, many of whom are from the nonactivist wing."[12]

Gingrich substantially increased the Republican leader's control over the committee assignment process. Under the old system, members of the assignment panel cast votes in proportion to their state's Republican representation in the House. Under the new process, the Speaker would control one-fourth of the votes on the panel through his own votes as well as the votes of appointed leaders.[13] The Rules Committee chair sits on the Steering Committee (the GOP panel that assigns Republicans to the standing committees), for example, and since 1989 the GOP leader has appointed the Republican leader and other GOP members of the Rules Committee.

With his expanded appointment powers, Gingrich set out deliberately to ensure that aggressive and energetic junior lawmakers—his major political base of support in the party—received good assignments, even if that meant enlarging committee sizes beyond the levels preferred by the chairs. For example, one freshman and four sophomores were named to the Rules Committee. Of eleven open GOP positions on Appropriations, freshmen received seven; of ten open slots on Ways and Means, freshmen got three; and of ten vacancies on Commerce, freshmen won eight.[14] Republican Conference rules also were amended to permit the Speaker, and not the Steering Committee, to name the chair and GOP members of the House Oversight Committee, which is responsible for monitoring the internal administrative operations of the chamber.

The Contract with America called for six-year term limitations for committee and subcommittee chairs, which reduced the likelihood that individual chairs would accumulate enough power to challenge the Speaker's authority, a common occurrence during the years of Democratic control. Rotating the chairs was intended to diminish the potency of seniority in committee leadership selection, increase the number of lawmakers who gain insight and expertise from serving as committee leaders, and reduce the informational and other advantages that can accrue to long-serving chairs. The change codified in House rules a previous Republican Conference requirement that GOP committee leaders step down after six years. According to Rep. Robert Walker (R-Pa.), the purpose of limiting the terms of chairs is "to not create little fiefdoms of power. Members will have to think more broadly, instead of simply rising and carving their legislative niche."[15]

In another move that strengthened Gingrich's prerogatives, on December 1 Nussle announced a major overhaul of the administrative management of the House, placing these functions squarely under the Speaker's authority. House administration had become a reform issue in 1991 when systematic mismanagement of the House bank was publicized, leading to the check-kiting scandal. At that time, Republicans urged that the purely administrative aspects of the House (payroll, parking, computer services, the restaurants, and so on) be removed from partisan control and placed under the direction of a professional administrative officer. In 1992, the chamber created a nonpartisan House administrator, but the majority Democrats were slow to transfer all nonlegislative functions to that official. The Nussle blueprint, labeled "The GOP's Open House," proposed that a new chief administrative officer take over all nonlegislative, purely administrative responsibilities for the chamber.

In contrast to prior GOP arguments, the chief administrative officer would report directly to the Speaker rather than to a bipartisan panel or the bipartisan leadership.[16] Democrats criticized the Nussle recommendations. Handed a copy of the plan, Rep. Ben Cardin (D-Md.), leader of the Democratic transition team, remarked, "They're going to hand the day to day operations to a partisan operation with no Democratic participation at all? . . . That's exactly what the Republicans were screaming about in the last Congress."[17] Nussle responded, "This post [House administrative officer] has never really been non-partisan, and it is inappropriate for the Democrats to now claim that it ever was."[18] Politicized or not, transferring control over these administrative functions to the Speaker further consolidated Gingrich's power within the institution.

The House Republican reforms also included the abolition of joint referrals, the practice of referring entire bills to two or more committees simultaneously. GOP members had supported the abolition of joint referrals for decades, arguing that the practice mired Democratic Speakers in intramural turf fights between and among competing committee chairs. Under the new rule, the Speaker must designate a primary committee of jurisdiction upon initial reference of a measure to committee, but he also has significant flexibility in determining whether, when, and how long additional panels will receive the legislation.

Another leadership reform allowed only the majority leader to cut off debate on amendments to appropriations bills that would limit spending. Previously, committee chairs typically had exercised that prerogative. One account described the change as "part of Gingrich's overall accumulation of power in the leadership—this time at the expense of committee and subcommittee chairmen, whose bills can be more easily amended on the floor."[19]

As House Republicans began their organizational sessions in December 1994, it was apparent that Gingrich would be a far more influential Speaker than his Democratic predecessors. The incoming Speaker himself drew parallels to Sam Rayburn (D-Tex.), the masterful House leader of the 1940s and 1950s. But many congressional observers believed that a more appropriate comparison was to the "czar rule" speakers of the 1890–1910 period.

As the magnitude of Gingrich's formal and informal prerogatives became clear, freshman Republicans led a drive to limit the term of the House

Speaker to eight years. The informal leader of the effort was incoming representative Lindsey Graham (R-S.C.), who remarked, "I trust Newt Gingrich to lead us to the promised land, but the good Lord never let Moses go. We'll do to him what the good Lord did to Moses."[20] As support for the proposal grew among the incoming freshmen, at a leadership meeting on December 14 Gingrich accepted an eight-year term limit for the Speaker, which the House adopted on January 4. On the whole, however, the Republican reforms constituted a remarkable consolidation of power in the Speaker's office. In the next chapter, we explore the consequences of this consolidation for decision making during the 104th Congress.

THE COMMITTEE SYSTEM

The reforms adopted by House Republicans at the beginning of the 104th Congress touched most aspects of committee politics: decision-making autonomy, internal procedures and structures, and committee jurisdictions. These changes reinforced the increased delegation of power to party leaders and were intended to make the committee system more accountable to the Republican Conference. A list of the major committee reforms adopted by the Republican House is provided in Table 4.2.

Although the GOP limited the terms of committee chairs to six years, certain prerogatives of chairs were strengthened at the beginning of the 104th Congress. According to a leadership aide, Gingrich "wanted to give the chairmen the same kind of power and authority to run their committee that he has to run the House."[21]

In this regard, the Republican majority repealed practices associated with the Subcommittee Bill of Rights, keystone of the 1970s committee reforms.[22] House Democrats had passed the Subcommittee Bill of Rights (which provided subcommittees with fixed jurisdictions, staffs, and budgetary resources) as part of their effort to reduce the power of full committee chairs and make the committee system more accountable to the Democratic Caucus.

Under the Republican reforms, standing committee chairs are allowed to (1) name their subcommittee leaders; (2) assign members to subcommittees; (3) hire all majority staff, who work for subcommittees only as directed by the full committee chair; and (4) control the committee's budget, effectively reversing the previous Democratic reforms aimed at empowering subcommittees. Commerce Committee chairman Thomas Bliley explained that now the "chairman controls the staff, the chairman has the right to name subcommittee chairmen and has much more power than the . . . Democratic chairmen [had] when they were in the majority."[23] Don Young (R-Alaska), chairman of the Committee on Resources, highlighted his prerogatives more bluntly: "If I was really nasty, there wouldn't be any subcommittees. There's

TABLE 4.2 Committee System Reforms

- Limit full and subcommittee chairs to six-year terms
- Give full committee chairs the power to appoint subcommittee chairs on their panels
- Abolish independent subcommittee staffs and otherwise consolidate committee funding procedures
- Abolish proxy voting in committee
- Limit members to two full committee assignments and four subcommittee assignments; exceptions must be approved by the relevant party caucus
- Limit the number of subcommittees to five for most standing committees
- Restructure the committee system by abolishing the District of Columbia, Merchant Marine, and Post Office Committees and shifting their jurisdictions to other panels; transferring certain items from the jurisdiction of Energy and Commerce to other committees; and renaming many existing committees to reflect Republican policy priorities
- Allow members to chair only one full committee or subcommittee
- Prohibit rolling quorums (the practice by which committee roll calls can be "held open," allowing absent members to arrive and cast their votes)
- Change the size, composition, and term length for the Intelligence Committee
- Require more systematic committee oversight plans

no rule about having subcommittees. I run the committee, period. I keep what I want under my jurisdiction [at the full committee]."[24]

Members and staff, however, emphasize that the new prerogatives granted to full committee chairs are not intended primarily to buttress the policy-making role of committee leaders. Instead, the changes should be considered in conjunction with reforms that increased the Speaker's power relative to the chairs.[25] The new prerogatives that Republicans granted to committee chairs are hedged by the Speaker's ability to appoint or remove them. Further, the chairs' authority to name subcommittee leaders means that the Speaker indirectly influences a committee's subcommittee organization and direction. Finally, the rules of the GOP Conference provide a mechanism for reining in committee chairs who might misuse their prerogatives. The selection of subcommittee chairs and the assignment of members to subcommittees is lodged in the full committee chair, according to Republican Conference Rule 19, "unless a majority of the Republican Members of the full Committee disapprove the action of the Chairman." Another Republican Conference rule states that the Speaker may designate certain issues as "leadership" issues, which require that there is "early and ongoing cooperation between the relevant committees and the Leadership as the issue evolves."

In short, Gingrich, acting as the agent of the Republican Conference, sought the power necessary to coordinate the actions of the full committee chairs, who in turn would be expected to use their new authority to coordinate decision making within their subcommittees. The repeal of the Subcommittee Bill of Rights was part of a general strategy to make the committee system more responsive to the majority leadership and the party rank and file. Previous Democratic Speakers had lacked Gingrich's leverage over committee chairs, and, as a result, Democrats had strengthened subcommittees to constrain the discretion of full committee leaders. In the Republican House, with its more influential Speakership, the Subcommittee Bill of Rights was instead viewed as an impediment to committee accountability because it potentially fragmented decision making by creating disparate subcommittee power centers. Thus, the Republican majority reduced subcommittee prerogatives for the same reason the Democratic majority had increased them— to make the committee system more accountable to the House majority party.

At the beginning of the 104th Congress, House Republicans also abolished proxy voting in committee. For years, GOP lawmakers had chafed under a system in which their members faithfully attended committee markups but were often outvoted by the smaller number of Democrats present at the meeting. Except on those few panels that banned proxy voting (Appropriations, Ethics, Rules, and Veterans' Affairs), the chairs could vote the proxies of missing Democratic members and carry the day. Upon achieving majority status, House Republicans abolished proxy voting to promote greater participation in committees and to improve the quality of committee deliberations. Rep. Robert Walker cited the reform "as perhaps the single most important change we [made]."[26]

The Republican majority also embraced a recommendation of the 1993 Joint Committee on the Organization of Congress limiting House members to no more than two full committee assignments and four subcommittee assignments. The goals of the change were to induce lawmakers to focus more closely on fewer committee responsibilities and to curtail scheduling conflicts, making the abolition of proxy voting logistically feasible. The GOP rules changes also limited most House committees to no more than five subcommittees, which, in conjunction with the abolition of three full committees, reduced the number of subcommittees by about thirty.

The Jurisdiction Minefield

As with past reorganization efforts, the matter of realigning committee jurisdictions was the most difficult topic addressed by Republican reformers following the November 1994 elections. Indeed, GOP efforts to alter House committee boundaries demonstrate how important aspects of reorganization politics can transcend partisan majorities.

During the summer of 1994, as Democratic leaders in both chambers resisted efforts to bring to the floor the reform package of the Joint Committee on the Organization of Congress, a group of House Republicans prepared the Contract with America and planned for what they hoped would be a GOP majority in the next Congress. As part of these preparations, Republican staff discussed a range of approaches to committee jurisdictional reform.

Newt Gingrich, then the minority whip, was highly skeptical about comprehensively realigning committee boundaries. One Republican aide recalled:

> The Speaker doesn't believe that changing jurisdictions matters very much. At the end of the day, he doesn't think it's make or break. To move legislation along, you can always appoint a task force or some ad hoc group. . . . He views [jurisdictional reform] in a political context. The Republicans promised change and you have to do something. But what's in the "Contract" is gospel. What's outside that box is peripheral.[27]

Another Republican staffer said,

> From the beginning, Newt didn't want to do jurisdictions and I think he was right. His primary concern was consolidating power with the chairmen. He wanted unanimous Republican support for everything on the opening day reforms and a dirty fight within the transition would mess that up. . . . Newt isn't a nuts and bolts guy. He wants to know how [realigning committees] will affect his goals. Will it help elect a dozen new Republicans? Will it help win the White House?[28]

Consequently, the Contract with America contained a provision calling for a reduction in the number of committees and subcommittees, but no specific jurisdictional alternatives were included.

During his postelection conference call with Gingrich and other transition leaders, David Dreier urged that major changes in committee jurisdictions be considered in the overhaul of House operations. There was substantial support among the participants for considering such reforms, and Gingrich asked Dreier to prepare four committee realignment plans for consideration by the Republican transition group. Absent clear instructions from Gingrich not to consider major realignment, Dreier quickly developed the four options, which ranged from incremental alterations to a comprehensive reshuffling of committee boundaries. At the time, Dreier predicted major change: "We're going to have a bold reform plan, which is going to allow us to implement the mandate we got last week at the polls." But he also acknowledged the likely opposition to major jurisdictional change within the Republican Conference, observing that "there is a high level of concern all the way around."[29]

This "high level of concern" was apparent on November 16, when Dreier met with the Republican leadership and members of the transition group to present his recommendations for realigning committees. Of the four options, the first and last were the main alternatives. Option 1 was viewed as the incremental plan, abolishing four standing committees and transferring their jurisdictions to other panels. Dreier pointed out that his first option satisfied the Contract with America provision for a reduction in the number of House committees, but it fell short of a comprehensive jurisdictional realignment.

Instead, Dreier urged the transition team to support Option 4, which can be referred to as the Dreier plan. At the November 16 meeting, Dreier told Republican leaders and transition team members that his plan would promote a number of objectives important to the new Republican majority, illustrating how partisan concerns can shape proposals to restructure the House. Dreier's plan included the creation of new panels, such as a Committee on Empowerment, that would reflect the policy priorities and governing principles of the Republican Party. In addition, certain committees, which had become Democratic Party power centers under the previous majority, would be dismantled. Dreier also argued that his plan would facilitate the Republican majority's ability to enact the Contract with America and the more long-term aspects of their legislative agenda by consolidating control over key GOP initiatives in single committees. The reduction in the number of committees from twenty-two to seventeen also would demonstrate to the public that House Republicans were serious about streamlining the congressional bureaucracy.

The response to Dreier's plan was swift and intense, with key elements of the proposal drawing strong opposition from incoming committee chairs and affected outside groups. The chairs and other committee members who stood to lose jurisdiction fought what they viewed as an encroachment on their personal power agendas. Important clientele groups also preferred the jurisdictional status quo because a realignment would reduce the value of their existing contacts in the committee system, forcing them to develop new alliances with different members and staff.

After a copy of the Dreier plan was reportedly found in a wastebasket and leaked to the press, conflict over the proposal quickly spread to the House as a whole and the lobbying community. Most of the key decisions and negotiations occurred behind the scenes among Republican leaders, transition group members, and incoming committee chairs and their staffs. The focus of this jurisdictional infighting varied by committee and by issue, illustrating the byzantine nature of turf politics on Capitol Hill.

Agriculture

Under the Dreier plan, the Agriculture Committee's jurisdiction over the food stamp program would have shifted to a proposed new Committee on Empowerment, consolidating control over the Republican welfare reform proposal in a single panel. However, Agriculture Committee members value their jurisdiction over food stamps in part because the program, linked with agricultural subsidies, substantially broadens support for the farm bill.[30] As a welfare initiative, the food stamp program appeals to urban lawmakers, who otherwise might have little incentive to support farm subsidies that benefit rural constituencies. Shifting food stamp jurisdiction from the Agriculture Committee might narrow support for agricultural legislation. Incoming Agriculture Committee chairman Pat Roberts (R-Kans.) was a member of the House Republican transition team, and he and other farm state representatives strongly opposed the transfer.

Banking

Dreier's plan would have transferred jurisdiction over securities issues from the Commerce Committee to the Banking Committee. As the services produced by banks, insurance companies, and other financial institutions have become more intertwined, it has become increasingly difficult to distinguish banking issues from securities issues. Under the Democratic majority, the result was bitter turf battles between the two committees, conflict that was cited as one reason for the failure of major banking reform legislation in 1991.[31] But Energy and Commerce, under Democratic chairman John Dingell of Michigan, opposed ceding control over securities issues because of policy differences with the Banking Committee, Dingell's long-standing interest in securities issues, and his reputed personal dislike for Banking Committee chairman Henry Gonzalez (D-Tex.). This turf war was mediated by the Speaker, other Democratic leaders, and the House parliamentarians, but it consumed valuable time and political capital—an outcome the new Republican majority sought to avoid.

Following the November 1994 elections, reformers believed it might be possible to shift securities matters from Commerce to Banking, a transfer sought by Rep. James Leach (R-Iowa), incoming chairman of the Banking Committee.[32] Dreier argued that the consolidation of financial services issues in the panel would facilitate the reform of what many Republicans view as outdated regulatory barriers between commercial and investment banks. However, as with his Democratic predecessor, the prospective chairman of the Commerce Committee, Thomas Bliley, opposed giving up securities jurisdiction. Both Leach and Bliley spoke at the November 16 transition meeting on behalf of their panels.

In his efforts to block the transfer, Bliley was supported by lobbyists for the securities industry, which had contributed almost $12 million to members of the Commerce Committee over the previous twelve years.[33] One GOP official remarked, "You make an investment in certain members over time, and obviously there's going to be resistance to change."[34] An industry lobbyist observed, "You're saying to [Commerce] that you are taking away one of their crown jewels. [Securities jurisdiction] is a big money maker for members."[35] On substantive grounds, opponents of the shift argued that the sources of the Dingell-Gonzalez rift would be less problematic in a GOP-controlled House and that the Commerce Committee had the expertise necessary to reform the financial services market.

Education and Labor

Renamed the Committee on Empowerment under the Dreier plan, the old Committee on Education and Labor stood to gain substantial jurisdiction. In addition to transferring jurisdiction over food stamps from the Agriculture Committee to the Empowerment Committee, Dreier sought to transfer welfare and family policy from the Ways and Means Committee to the new panel, giving it sole jurisdiction over the welfare reform plank in the Contract with America. Both the Agriculture and Ways and Means Committees opposed these shifts, and Rep. Bill Goodling (R-Pa.), likely chairman of the proposed Empowerment Committee, did not seek these policy areas, so as not to be perceived as raiding the jurisdiction of other panels. Dreier's plan also would have shifted housing issues from the Banking Committee to the Empowerment Committee, but acceptance of that transfer by incoming Banking Committee chairman Leach was contingent upon securities issues being transferred to his panel from Commerce, a move that Bliley opposed.

Energy and Commerce

This panel would have been the biggest jurisdictional loser under the Dreier plan, reflecting the breadth of its turf at the end of the Dingell years and the desire of reformers to distribute committee workloads more equitably. Slashing the Energy and Commerce Committee's jurisdiction also would provide GOP lawmakers with an opportunity to settle old scores with Dingell, whom they viewed as one of the most partisan Democrats in the House. Under the Dreier plan, in addition to securities issues, Energy and Commerce would have lost jurisdiction over energy policy, railroads, and the many environmental programs within its domain.

The panel would have picked up Medicare jurisdiction from Ways and Means, partially compensating it for the turf reductions and also separating health care benefits from the Medicare funding mechanism, which would remain with Ways and Means. This change, argued Dreier, would promote a more pro-market approach to health care reform. Overall, however, Energy and Commerce was the major loser under Dreier's plan.

During the transition period, incoming Commerce Committee chairman Bliley fought major reductions in the panel's jurisdiction, evoking comparisons with his Democratic predecessor. One staffer commented, "If Tom Bliley wants to be John Dingell, he should become a Democrat." But a Bliley aide remarked, "Mr. Bliley has not spent 14 years toiling in the vineyards trying to uphold the Republican principle against the best the Democrats had to offer so that we could be robbed of the opportunity of enacting the Republican agenda." The aide warned that the proposed committee realignment would be fought "at every level."[36] Bliley quickly emerged as the key opponent of the Dreier plan.

Ethics and House Administration

Under the Democratic majority, the Ethics Committee was responsible primarily for implementing the chamber's ethics code. The House Administration Committee had jurisdiction over the internal managerial functions of the House. Drawing on ideas previously considered by the 1993 Joint Committee on the Organization of Congress, Dreier recommended that the two committees be combined into a new Committee on Ethics and Administration. Under Democratic control, there were certain redundancies in the two jurisdictions. House Administration, for example, was responsible for developing regulations dealing with financial management and personnel within House offices—regulations that were in turn interpreted by the Ethics Committee. The objective of Dreier's proposal was to create a one-stop shop where members could receive advice on such matters. Ethics complaints against individual members would be handled by a bipartisan subcommittee of the new panel and reported directly to the House, maintaining the bipartisan structure of the ethics process.

However, after the Dreier plan was leaked, House Democrats, as well as a number of outside observers, strongly criticized the proposed merger, with Democratic leaders attempting to tie it to an impending ethics investigation of Newt Gingrich. Democratic whip David Bonior of Michigan charged, "Newt Gingrich trying to do away with the House ethics committee is kind of like Howard Stern trying to do away with the FCC. . . . This is the height of arrogance and stupidity."[37] In a press release, Dreier responded, "There was never any intention to move ethics investigations into the kind of politically charged House Administration Committee which the Democratic leadership used to run the House through patronage and partisanship." Republican leaders downplayed Bonior's criticism, but the proposed merger of the two panels was quickly and publicly dropped.

Public Works and Transportation

The Public Works Committee stood to gain significant jurisdiction from Dreier's plan, picking up railroad, merchant marine, and emergency management issues. Public Works had particularly sought a transfer of railroads from Energy and Commerce to consolidate its jurisdiction over transportation policy.

Dreier also proposed shifting jurisdiction over the Clean Water Act, a major environmental program, from Public Works to the new Committee on Environment and Natural Resources, where environmental issues would be consolidated with the natural resources issues of particular interest to western lawmakers. The change, Dreier argued, would reduce the points of access environmental groups have into the committee system and force them to confront (in committee) western members less enamored with the environmental movement. However, Bud Shuster (R-Pa.), incoming chairman of the Public Works Committee, resisted losing jurisdiction over clean water issues, and a number of House Republicans were wary about concentrating environmental jurisdiction in a single panel.

Ways and Means

Another big loser under the Dreier plan was the Committee on Ways and Means. Dreier's proposal would have stripped Ways and Means of its jurisdiction over major entitlement programs such as Medicare and welfare policy, and the panel would have been renamed the Committee on Revenues. Committee members opposed the transfers, arguing that jurisdiction over entitlement benefits should not be separated from jurisdiction over the special taxes used to fund them, which the Revenue panel would have retained. Bowing to intense pressure against these changes, within two days of the November 16 meeting House Republican leaders were reporting that the Ways and Means jurisdiction would not be substantially reduced.

The Chopping Block

Dreier's preferred jurisdictional reform plan, Option 4, recommended the abolition of the Small Business Committee, but Option 1, his incremental alternative, retained the panel. Rep. Jan Meyers (R-Kans.), incoming chairwoman of the Small Business Committee, urged Gingrich not to abolish the panel, and transition team members were aware that the small business community was largely a GOP constituency. Republican leaders also were hesitant to abolish the one committee likely to be chaired by a woman in the 104th Congress. Gingrich decided to keep the Small Business Committee.

In contrast, all of Dreier's jurisdictional plans called for the abolition of the District of Columbia Committee and the Post Office and Civil Service Committee, which were to be merged into a new Committee on Reform and Government Oversight.[38] These changes were viewed as all but inevitable from early in the transition process. There was little GOP support for maintaining the two panels, both of which appealed primarily to traditional Democratic constituencies.

All of Dreier's jurisdictional plans also proposed that the Committee on Merchant Marine and Fisheries be eliminated, with its jurisdiction divided among three panels. In 1974, jurisdictional reformers had targeted this panel for abolition, but the resulting mobilization of industry and union groups ensured its survival. Unlike the District of Columbia and Post Office Committees, there was some Republican opposition to abolishing the Merchant Marine Committee.[39] Within days of the election, however, participants in the transition process reported that the Merchant Marine panel also would go.

Half a Loaf?

The November 16 transition meeting and the release of the Dreier plan generated a flurry of meetings, telephone conversations, letters, and memos. Incoming chairs spoke with their members and with the leadership about the proposed changes. The private nature of these communications and the short duration of the transition process should not mask the intensity of the turf fights that developed as Republican committee leaders lobbied the House leadership to maintain or expand their jurisdictions. A bidding war erupted between panels over the jurisdiction of the soon-to-be-abolished Merchant Marine Committee, with one staffer likening the dispute to "a Middle Eastern Bazaar."[40]

As Republican members feuded, Gingrich and other GOP leaders decided, within days of the November 16 meeting, that a major realignment of committee jurisdictions would not be included in their reform package. Instead, they settled on a modified version of the first, mostly incremental jurisdictional reform option that Dreier presented. Three standing committees (District of Columbia, Merchant Marine, and Post Office) were eliminated, thus fulfilling the Contract with America pledge to reduce the number of committees. In addition, according to Republican estimates, approximately 20 percent of the huge Energy and Commerce jurisdiction would be transferred to other panels. Bliley and other committee members viewed the loss as a small price to pay for keeping their turf largely intact.

The Republican package also included a number of changes in committee names to reflect GOP priorities. For example, the Committee on Banking, Finance, and Urban Affairs was renamed Banking and Financial Services to de-emphasize the Democratic focus on housing and urban issues. The Education and Labor Committee was first renamed Economic Opportunities and then Economic and Educational Opportunities, dropping the reference to organized labor. The Foreign Affairs Committee became the Committee on International Relations because the old name struck some Republicans as too insular. Government Operations was renamed Government Reform and Oversight, highlighting the GOP's reform agenda. Public Works and Transportation became Transportation and Infrastructure because Republicans believe that whereas *public works* evokes visions of the pork barrel, *infrastructure* constitutes an investment opportunity. And so on.

Interestingly, some of the name changes were controversial, and Dreier encountered substantial difficulties in negotiating the necessary semantic compromises. For example, in a December 2 press release, the old Natural Resources Committee was listed as the Committee on Public Lands and Resources, underscoring that natural resources belong to people and not to nature. But some members of the committee objected to inclusion of the word *public* because it evoked visions of excessive federal management of natural resources. The solution to this dilemma? The panel is now known simply as the Committee on Resources. The battle over committee titles also reflected intraparty divisions over how to handle environmental and resources issues.

Dreier announced the committee reforms accepted by the leadership at a press conference on December 2, stating that the proposals "represent the kind of comprehensive internal reform that was simply not conceivable under prior management." Asked why more sweeping jurisdictional changes were not included, he responded, "This is a very strong package which goes a long way toward addressing our need and the mandate of the American people. [Such a] reduction in the number of panels is something that cannot be overlooked; and since [the Legislative Reorganization Act of 1946] we haven't had any kind of change like this."

The Republican jurisdictional reforms, as well as the committee name changes, were adopted with the rest of the reorganization package on January 4, 1995, with substantial bipartisan support. The jurisdictional changes were not comprehensive, but they also were not trivial. Since 1946, only one House standing committee had been abolished; the opening-day reforms of 1995 abolished three. Many GOP lawmakers, however, particularly David Dreier, had hoped that the jurisdictional changes would go much further. As a result, the Republican Conference established the Task Force on Committee Review (chaired by Dreier with freshman Sam Brownback of Kansas as vice-chair) to "further reduce the number of committees of the House and clarify questions of multi-committee jurisdiction." The task force began its work in the summer of 1995 and continues to function throughout 1996.

The consideration of jurisdictional reform during the Republican transition resembled previous Democratic experiences with the issue, particularly the internal divisions within the majority caucus, the opposition of GOP committee leaders (many who had been waiting years for the gavel) to turf losses, and lobbying by outside interests against the proposed changes. Further, many majority members argued that comprehensive jurisdictional reform would impede the party's ability to enact the Contract with America, echoing concerns raised by Democratic leaders in previous years that a jurisdictional upheaval would stymie action on their agenda. Gingrich, like former Speaker Thomas Foley (D-Wash.), was skeptical about the value of committee realignment. Republicans, like the Democrats before them, have been buffeted by many of the same political forces that affected past reorganization efforts.

FLOOR DELIBERATIONS AND SCHEDULING

Open Rules

During their decades in the minority, House Republicans often complained that the Democratic leadership was unfairly constraining their ability to participate in floor deliberations. The GOP leader of the Rules Committee, Rep. Gerald Solomon of New York, was a leading advocate of greater openness on the House floor. During the 103d Congress, after minority leader Robert Michel's announcement that he would retire at the end of that Congress, Solomon briefly offered himself as an alternative to Gingrich as Republican leader. But Gingrich had locked up the position, and Solomon soon withdrew from the race. After the 1994 election, rumors surfaced that Gingrich might retaliate and appoint another lawmaker as Rules Committee chair. Solomon, however, had been a staunch party loyalist on the panel, and the incoming Speaker named him chair on November 16.

Following the appointment, both leaders promised to open up floor deliberations to more amendments and participation. Solomon pledged, "We're going to have fair rules . . . free and open debate. . . . We're going to let the House work its will." The new Rules chairman also pointed out that floor amendments likely would be less threatening to the Republican majority, which was more cohesive than previous Democratic majorities: "We don't have a fractionalized situation as they do in the Democratic party. I can afford to be even more fair than . . . under normal circumstances. . . . The difference will be that the one with the most votes wins. That way you're not trying to shaft the House."[41]

The GOP commitment to open rules would be complicated by the press of business, particularly the pledge to consider the entire Contract with America during the first one hundred days of the 104th Congress. Allowing individual lawmakers to offer on the floor a large and diverse array of amendments would make it more difficult, if not impossible, to process all of the legislation included in the contract within that period.

Also at odds with the desire for open rules was Gingrich's pledge to make the floor schedule more family friendly. On November 14, Rep. Frank Wolf (R-Va.) was appointed to chair a bipartisan Family Friendly Advisory Committee. Wolf's task force was asked to report back to the House with recommendations to improve the existing House schedule, which, according to Gingrich, "brutalizes and damages families by its intensity and its pace."[42] But incoming majority leader Richard Armey (R-Tex.) also stated, "We would be prepared to work seven days a week if necessary, even 20 hours a day if necessary," to meet the one-hundred-day deadline.[43]

The tension among the goals of openness, legislative efficiency, and family-friendly scheduling was apparent on the opening day of the 104th Congress, when the House adopted the Republican reforms. On the first day of previous Congresses, Democrats had allowed only a single up or down vote on their rules packages, with strict limits on debate. The special rule used by the GOP majority on January 4, 1995, allowed for more participation. After a period of general debate, divided equally between the parties, the eight Contract with America reforms were considered sequentially, with a separate vote on each item. Next came debate and a vote on the remainder of the reform package. As Rules Committee chairman Solomon pointed out, three and one-half hours of debate were permitted on the 1995 rules package, compared to the one hour allowed in previous years. And instead of providing for just one vote on the rules, there were nine such votes at the beginning of the 104th Congress. Solomon said, "We have designed in this procedure the fairest and most open process on a House rules resolution in over a century in this House."[44]

Still, no amendments to the 1995 rules package were allowed, meaning that the Republican reforms were considered under the equivalent of a closed rule. Minority whip David Bonior remarked, "After the years of whining and complaining on the Republican side about the damages to democracy [from] closed rules, what is the first thing they offer us? A closed rule."[45]

In the Contract with America, the House GOP had promised to pass a number of major reforms on the opening day of the 104th Congress. Even with the closed rule, the House was in session until well past midnight (a fourteen-hour session, the longest opening day ever) to fulfill that promise. Republicans realized that allowing amendments to their rules package would make it more difficult, if not impossible, to pass all the reforms on opening day. GOP leaders also recognized that permitting Democratic amendments might create opportunities for the minority to divide or embarrass Republican lawmakers. Democrats, for example, sought to offer a lobbying reform proposal that was potentially controversial within the Republican Conference. Faced with these competing demands, the Republican majority opted for a closed rule.

Minority Party Prerogatives

The GOP reform package also included concrete rules changes in the area of floor deliberations and scheduling, which are summarized in Table 4.3. While in the minority, Republicans had sought a guarantee to the minority party of the right to offer a motion to recommit (return a bill to committee) with instructions on all measures. This motion allows the minority party to offer a policy alternative immediately before the vote on final passage. The majority Democrats had occasionally denied the GOP the opportunity to offer a recommittal motion with instructions, and guaranteeing in House rules the right to offer such a motion had been a key minority party rights priority for House Republicans. On the first day of the 104th Congress, they extended this right to the minority Democrats, specifically the minority leader or his designee.

The opening-day reforms included other extensions of minority party prerogatives, particularly the abolition of proxy voting. Also, Republican leaders regularly pledged during the transition that three-quarters of legislation considered on the floor would be under open rules. Why did House Republicans take certain steps to enhance minority party rights?

TABLE 4.3. Selected Changes Related to Floor Deliberations and Scheduling

- Pledge to use open rules on approximately three-quarters of the bills considered on the floor (no change to standing rules of House)
- Guarantee the minority party the right to make a motion to recommit with instructions
- Eliminate the right of delegates to vote on the floor
- Require the Rules Committee to explain, to the maximum extent feasible, all waivers of House rules included in special rules
- Ban commemorative measures
- Promise to establish a family-friendly schedule

As discussed in Chapter 3, political scientists suggest that the procedural prerogatives of the minority party are restricted when a cohesive majority party fears that the minority will use its prerogatives to block the majority's agenda. In contrast, enhancement of minority party rights tends to occur when a bipartisan coalition strong enough to force such changes exists. The coalitional structure of the House may have been a factor behind the GOP majority's decision to strengthen certain minority party rights. The Republican Conference included a pivotal coalition of twenty to thirty moderates capable of coalescing with conservative Democrats. However, our analysis reveals that the decision to strengthen minority party rights resulted far more from three other factors: (1) the GOP's long public commitment to open up the House, (2) the personal preferences of key Republicans about these issues, and (3) GOP awareness that they might again be in the minority and thus in need of such protections.

First, Republicans had made a public issue out of allegedly autocratic behavior by Democratic House leaders. Although the prerogatives of the minority party were not (and are not) a major public concern, the Washington media was aware of the long history of Republican complaints in this area and would have accused the new majority of hypocrisy if the GOP, having won majority status, simply walked away from its minority party rights agenda. These charges would have undermined the House Republicans' attempt to portray themselves as the party of reform.[46]

Second, Republican members such as David Dreier, Gerald Solomon, and Robert Walker have a strong personal preference for broad-based participation and full and open floor debate. Their preference is shared by many of the freshman members, as well as other House Republicans, who also want ample opportunities to participate on the House floor.

Third, the specter that the GOP might again be in the minority created incentives for Republicans to ensure that the House minority have certain procedural protections. In previous Congresses, the possibility that Democrats would lose their majority status seemed small, and thus the incentives for Democrats to protect the rights of the minority party were limited.

An exploration of the GOP commitment to minority party rights should examine the floor amendment rules they used during the 104th Congress. We address this topic in Chapter 5.

Several other floor reforms were included in the GOP reform package. As expected, the limited floor voting rights that Democrats had granted to the delegates from U.S. territories and the District of Columbia were revoked on January 4. Another GOP rules change required the Rules Committee to provide as much information as possible about waivers of House rules included in the special rules it crafts to regulate floor debate. And, at the request of the incoming freshmen, the GOP banned commemorative bills—measures that designate specific time periods (days, weeks) after particular commercial interests. In previous Congresses, more than 25 percent of public laws had been commemorative designations, such as Tap Dance Day, National Dairy Goat Awareness Week, Country Music Month, and the Decade of the Brain. GOP reformers and many Democrats viewed commemoratives as a waste of time and of minimal symbolic or electoral value.

OTHER REFORM AREAS

The new Republican majority also adopted rules changes related to other reorganization areas—congressional integrity, policy-driven reforms, and congressional resources and interbranch prerogatives. These reforms are listed in Table 4.4.

Congressional Integrity

To a certain extent, most of the reorganization items passed on January 4, 1995, were intended to address public concerns about the institutional integrity of Congress. This was particularly the case for the reorganization items included in the Contract with America, which were systematically tested for public popularity. Term limitations for House members and senators were a key contract provision that tapped public concerns about the integrity of Congress, and both chambers would consider the issue in 1995. Other contract reforms addressing congressional integrity included proposals that all relevant private-sector laws be applied to Congress, that an independent audit be conducted of House administrative and financial records, and that committee meetings be as open as possible to the public.

In the early-morning hours of January 5, the House passed the Congressional Accountability Act, which ended congressional exemptions from labor and workplace safety laws. The same legislation had passed the chamber in

TABLE 4.4 Other House Changes

Congressional Integrity

- Apply relevant private sector workplace laws to Congress (statutory change)

- Conduct an independent audit of House administrative and financial records

- Open all public committee meetings to radio/TV coverage as a matter of right unless deliberations would expose sensitive information (e.g., classified material)

- Require that the *Congressional Record* be a substantially verbatim account of floor deliberations and that committee meeting transcripts be a verbatim account

- Include committee voting records in committee reports

Policy-Driven Reforms

- Adopt base-line budgeting

- Require a three-fifths supermajority to pass income tax rate increases and prohibit retroactive tax increases

- Prohibit nonemergency provisions in emergency funding bills

Congressional Resources and Interbranch Prerogatives

- Reduce committee staffing by one-third

- Abolish legislative service organizations (LSOs)

- Make the *Congressional Record* and other House documents available to the public via the Internet (no rules change)

August 1994 by an overwhelming margin but had been blocked in the Senate. A somewhat different version of the measure passed the Senate on January 11, 1995. The House accepted the Senate-passed bill, and the president signed the legislation on January 23.

On opening day, the House also passed the contract provisions calling for an outside audit and enhanced committee openness. In addition, the House adopted new rules providing that the *Congressional Record* and committee transcripts be substantively verbatim accounts of congressional debate and that records of committee votes be made accessible to the public. The aim of such openness reforms was to address voter perceptions that Congress is excessively insular and secretive.

Policy-Driven Reforms

Certain policy-driven reforms also were on the reorganization agenda in January 1995, particularly those relating to budgetary decision making. The Contract with America called for House consideration of a balanced budget amendment to the Constitution and the line-item veto. Both measures would be major issues later in the 104th Congress and are discussed in Chapter 5.

On January 4, the House passed three rules changes that dealt with spending and taxing. First, by an overwhelming margin, the House adopted baseline budgeting, a reform addressing conservative concerns that budget information was biased toward increased spending.[47] More controversial was a GOP proposal that any legislation increasing income tax rates must have three fifths support (rather than a simple majority) to pass.[48] Republicans embraced the proposal as embodying their party's commitment to hold the line on tax increases. Democrats, in contrast, argued that the supermajority requirement singled out one form of taxation for special protection and also that the provision was inconsistent with the core constitutional principle of majority rule. Nevertheless, the change was adopted on January 4 by a vote of 279 to 152, with conservative Democrats joining GOP lawmakers in support of it. The final policy-driven reform was a ban on the inclusion of non-emergency items in emergency funding bills (disaster relief legislation, for example). The goal here was to keep emergency funding measures from turning into "Christmas tree" bills, laden with unrelated projects. This rules change was not controversial.

Congressional Resources and Interbranch Prerogatives

In this final reorganization area, the House GOP also made certain changes. Most important, the Contract with America provided that the number of House committee staff would be reduced by one-third. As House Oversight chairman Bill Thomas (R-Calif.) stated, "Under Democratic control, the number of committee staff averaged 1,854. We have now set a strict ceiling of 1,233 positions—a reduction of 621 congressional jobs."[49] Since the Republicans were moving to majority status, the number of committee staff they hired would increase significantly in 1995. As a result, the impact of the staff cut fell mainly on the minority Democrats, who were forced to fire large numbers of committee aides. On the other hand, the Republicans provided the committee minority with more staff and resources than they had received during their own years in the minority.

Another January 1995 rules change abolished the legislative service organizations (LSOs)—member organizations funded by contributions from the office accounts of participating lawmakers. In the 103d Congress, a wide range of LSOs existed within the House, from the Congressional Black Caucus to regional and issue-specific groups such as the Steel Caucus. The Democratic Study Group (DSG) also was an LSO. In addition to serving as a reform catalyst within the Democratic Caucus, the DSG provided members with daily reports about upcoming floor issues. Democrats argued that LSOs fulfilled important functions and that abolishing them would not save money since their budgets would simply revert back to the office accounts of contributing members. According to Rep. David Skaggs (D-Colo.), incoming chairman of the DSG, "Closing down DSG seems to be part of an effort to centralize information and to stifle debate on legislation that the new Republican majority produces."[50]

Republicans countered that LSO budgets were not being properly monitored and that public money should not be funding special-interest organizations within the House. Incoming House Oversight Committee chairman Bill Thomas remarked, "The key concern over [the LSOs] was they could literally stand alone—hire staff, occupy space, buy equipment."[51] Republican Conference chairman John Boehner of Ohio suggested that the daily analysis of floor legislation provided by the DSG could instead be supplied by the Democratic leadership.

During the transition period, the incoming Speaker also pledged to bring the House more fully into the modern information age. Significantly enhancing public access to committees and the House in general, Gingrich put Congress on the Internet by launching a computer system in the Library of Congress called THOMAS (after Thomas Jefferson).

The consequences of putting Congress on the information highway are still unclear, but they are potentially significant and reflect long-term efforts by Gingrich to involve the public more in legislative decision making. From early in his House career, Gingrich regularly argued that the mood of the electorate was increasingly favorable to the GOP but that the Democratic House was insulated from public sentiment. In a 1984 floor statement, Gingrich said, "The House remains in a sense the cap over the cauldron. While the country, the pressure cooker of the Nation is changing, the House with a liberal Democratic establishment tries to hold on to an old order, an old establishment, an old way of doing things."[52] He emphasized the importance of television and other information technologies for opening up the institution to enhanced public participation. Gingrich argued, "I would say that technology expands the chance for self-government, just as the printing press allowed us to reach out far beyond handwritten manuscripts, so television allows us to reach out further."[53]

Ten years later, incoming Speaker Gingrich embraced more advanced technology to communicate more effectively with the public. Speaking to a Washington audience three days after the November 1994 elections, he said, "We will change the rules of the House to require that all documents . . . be filed electronically as well as in writing . . . so that information is available to every citizen in the country at the same moment that it is available to the highest paid Washington lobbyist."[54]

It is tempting to discount Gingrich's ruminations about the impact of the information highway on congressional decision making—just as it was tempting in the early 1980s to dismiss Gingrich's argument that a more confrontational House GOP could win majority status. Over the years, he has argued repeatedly that improving the information technology available to Congress will make the institution more responsive to a public mood that, in his mind, increasingly favors the Republican Party. The informational reforms adopted by the new Republican majority should be considered from that perspective.

ORGANIZATIONAL RATIONALES

Why did the new Republican majority embrace substantial organizational changes, while the Democratically controlled 103d Congress was unable to pass a comprehensive reform bill? Which organizational rationales help explain their different responses to the reform agenda? The answers to these questions vary somewhat depending on the reorganization area. The most significant changes adopted by House Republicans following their 1994 election victory were in the areas of leadership prerogatives, the committee system, and, to a lesser extent, floor deliberations and scheduling. In evaluating the overall relevance of the various rationales, we focus on these topics.

In the area of leadership prerogatives, many of the changes implemented by the GOP majority had been considered, at least informally, and rejected two years earlier by the then majority Democrats. Partisan rationales for organizational change help explain the two sets of outcomes. The incentives for rank-and-file majority party members to accept a consolidation of party leadership power are strongest when the majority party is relatively unified on major policy issues. Whereas the divided Democrats would not accept a fundamental enhancement of Speaker Thomas Foley's formal prerogatives (nor did Foley want additional authority), the more unified GOP majority was willing, if not eager, to increase Speaker Gingrich's leverage over the committee chairs and chamber proceedings. Gingrich's personal power agenda also played a role, as he moved aggressively to consolidate his influence within the House.

The major losers in the enhancement of Gingrich's office were the incoming chairs and other influential Republicans. New to majority status, however, the committee leaders were not fully entrenched in their positions. Thus, they had somewhat less to lose from strengthening the Speakership than had their Democratic predecessors, who were used to exercising considerable autonomy.

In short, the 1990s reform experience supports the assertion that an increase in *preference homogeneity* (agreement on policy issues) within the majority party, particularly when accompanied by a change in partisan majorities, will make the centralization of power more likely. Conversely, an increasingly fragmented majority of long duration probably will be associated with the weakening of party leadership prerogatives.

The Republican majority embraced nontrivial committee changes, whereas the majority Democrats had mostly rejected such proposals. Why? The answer is complex because all five organizational rationales are evident in committee reform politics. Congressional committees are often called little legislatures. To a certain extent, the committee system can be viewed as a microcosm of Congress as a whole. It makes sense, then, that the entire range of organizational rationales should be relevant to this area of reform.

Based in part on public opinion polls, GOP leaders included in the Contract with America a promised reduction in the number of panels. Partisan concerns were partially behind the selection of the three committees targeted for abolition, as they represented primarily Democratic constituencies. David Dreier sought simultaneously to devise a committee structure that would modernize the committee system for the twenty-first century (institutional rationales) and to advance GOP goals and policy priorities (partisan rationales). Partisan considerations also helped convince Speaker Gingrich and other Republican leaders to reject Dreier's preferred committee reform plan, as they feared it would divide the majority party and imperil passage of the contract.

When House Republicans considered Dreier's proposals, clientele concerns and the personal power agendas of the incoming chairs clearly dominated partisan or broader institutional pressures for comprehensive change. Why were the incoming chairs and other influential Republicans able to block comprehensive jurisdictional reform but not the aggrandizement of the Speaker's formal powers? The answer lies in the consequences of change for the majority party in each reform area. With committee reform, the benefits from a complete realignment to the Republican Conference were ambiguous, but the costs, in terms of intraparty conflict and policy delay, were substantial. Gingrich also had little to gain personally from a comprehensive reshuffling of committee boundaries. In contrast, in the area of leadership prerogatives, the benefits to the majority party, and to Gingrich personally, from constraining GOP committee leaders were clear-cut and significant, and thus well worth the trouble. Recall that the nonjurisdictional committee reforms adopted by the Republicans strengthened the new Speaker's hand, and the actions taken early in the transition to buttress Gingrich's prerogatives also reduced the potential gains from jurisdictional reform. From the beginning, it was clear that committees in general would be less autonomous in the 104th Congress.

Based on the 1990s reorganization experience, what can we infer about the conditions that promote a major reshuffling of the committee system? It is apparent that committee structures and procedures on Capitol Hill reflect a complex mix of organizational rationales. Hence, comprehensive committee reform is as difficult to predict as it is to accomplish. Under both the Democratic and the Republican majorities, clientele demands and the personal power agendas of individual members blocked a fundamental realignment.

The key change following the 1994 elections was that the new House majority had publicly pledged to abolish some committees, and that the clientele groups affected by certain perennial targets for abolition were less important to Republicans. Thus, three committees ended up on the chopping block.

Partisan rationales typically are critical in the area of floor deliberations and scheduling. Unlike leadership prerogatives, where a key condition is preference homogeneity within the majority party, the distribution of preferences in both parties usually plays a role in decisions to extend or restrict minority party rights. A strong cross-party coalition is usually necessary to alter minority prerogatives. Such a coalition was absent during Democratic control of the House, and the 103d Congress did not adopt extensions of minority rights. However, a strong cross-party coalition was not significantly more apparent in the GOP-controlled 104th Congress, which did make selected changes in this area. Why were they adopted? Partisan rationales are relevant here, but so are public opinion and the institutional concerns of certain Republican reform leaders.

Most important, minority party rights provisions were included in the Contract with America, and Republicans had spoken long and often about the need for more participation on the House floor. For them to discard these proposals after winning majority control would have drawn charges of hypocrisy from the media and possibly in the court of public opinion. The extension of minority rights was also a form of partisan self-protection because the longevity of the Republican majority was unclear. Institutional motivations, too, led GOP reformers to support changes in this reform area, out of a belief that full and open debate would improve the deliberative capacity of Congress. Thus, factors other than the coalitional makeup of Congress influence decisions to change minority party prerogatives.

In the three remaining reform areas (congressional integrity, policy-driven reforms, and congressional resources and interbranch prerogatives), the January 1995 changes likewise were shaped by partisan and public concerns. The opening-day budgetary reforms were in part an attempt to alter House procedure to promote the Republican agenda, and the brunt of the committee staff and funding cuts fell on Democrats. Still, most of the transition proposals in these three reform areas were from the Contract with America and were thus intended to mobilize public opinion behind GOP candidates. Partisan concerns were relevant, but they mostly surfaced as position taking for electoral gain rather than an attempt to reorganize the House to facilitate the passage of Republican legislation.

Although all five organizational rationales explain aspects of the House Republican transition, partisan incentives were the overriding factor behind the changes that were adopted immediately following the November 1994 elections. In the next chapter, we turn our attention to institutional developments in the remarkable 104th Congress, as the House and Senate confronted the most sweeping policy agenda in a generation.

Notes

1. Richard Wolf, "'Bulldog' Nussle Says Status Quo Won't Do," *USA Today*, November 17, 1994, 5.

2. Jeffrey Katz, "Republicans Dust Off Blueprints for Changing House Operations," *Congressional Quarterly Weekly Report*, November 12, 1994, 3220.

3. News conference with Rep. David Dreier, U.S. Capitol, December 2, 1994.

4. On the features of strong majority party leadership, consult especially Barbara Sinclair, *Legislators, Leaders, and Lawmaking* (Baltimore: Johns Hopkins University Press, 1995). See also David W. Rohde, *Parties and Leaders in the Postreform House* (Chicago: University of Chicago Press, 1991); John H. Aldrich, *Why Parties?* (Chicago: University of Chicago Press, 1995). The classic study in this area is Joseph Cooper and David W. Brady, "Institutional Context and Leadership Style: The House from Cannon to Rayburn," *American Political Science Review*, 75 (1981), 411–25.

5. David S. Cloud, "Gingrich Clears the Path for Republican Advance," *Congressional Quarterly Weekly Report*, November 19, 1994, 3319.

6. "On Way Out, Michel Stops to Warn GOP," *Washington Times*, November 26, 1994, A2.

7. The most senior Republican on the panel was Rep. Joseph McDade (R-Pa.). But McDade was under federal indictment on corruption charges and, by general agreement, would not be considered for the chairmanship until those charges were resolved.

8. Philip D. Duncan and Christine C. Lawrence, *Politics in America, 1996: The 104th Congress* (Washington, D.C.: Congressional Quarterly, 1995), 471.

9. Myers reportedly threatened to challenge the decision in the full Republican Conference but quickly backed off when Republican leaders threatened to deny him a subcommittee chairmanship on Appropriations.

10. *Los Angeles Times*, November 18, 1994, A6. See also Marc Lacey, "Moorhead Bypassed for Committee Post," *Los Angeles Times*, November 18, 1994, B1.

11. Cloud, "Gingrich Clears the Path," 3322.

12. Robert D. Novak, "Putting Old Bulls Out to Pasture," *Washington Post*, November 21, 1994, A25.

13. Mary Jacoby, "Big States Big Losers in Gingrich's Plan for Committee on Committees," *Roll Call*, December 1, 1994, 3. See also Mary Jacoby, "Conference Adopts Gingrich's Steering Panel Setup," *Roll Call*, December 8, 1994, 22.

14. Laurie Kellman, "GOP Freshmen Fill Key House Posts," *Washington Times*, December 10, 1994, A4.

15. Guy Gugliotta, "In New House, Barons Yield to the Boss," *Washington Post*, December 1, 1994, A38.

16. Nussle's plan included an enhanced inspector general's office, also reporting to the Speaker, which would audit House financial records.

17. Mary Jacoby, "GOP 'Reinvents' House," *Roll Call*, December 5, 1994, 45.

18. Report from Jim Nussle (R-Iowa) to Newt Gingrich and the members of Congress for the 104th Congress, December 1, 1994.

19. "Power Play, Cont.," *Roll Call,* December 12, 1994, 4.

20. David S. Cloud, "GOP's House-Cleaning Sweep Changes Rules, Cuts Groups," *Congressional Quarterly Weekly Report,* December 10, 1994, 3487.

21. Richard Cohen, "The New Regime," *National Journal,* June 17, 1995, 1439.

22. The Subcommittee Bill of Rights was formally included in the rules of the Democratic Caucus.

23. Kirk Victor, "Mr. Smooth," *National Journal,* July 8, 1995, 1759.

24. Benjamin Sheffner, "Young: GOP's Old Bull," *Roll Call,* February 27, 1995, 18.

25. On this point, among others, we have benefited from conversations with congressional scholar Thomas Mann.

26. Gugliotta, "In the House," A38.

27. Personal interview with anonymous staff member, 1995.

28. Personal interview with anonymous staff member, 1995.

29. Richard Wolf and William M. Welch, "GOP Puts Its House in Order," *USA Today,* November 17, 1994, 11A.

30. John Ferejohn, "Logrolling in an Institutional Context: A Case Study of Food Stamp Legislation," in *Congress and Policy Change,* ed. Gerald C. Wright, Jr., Leroy N. Rieselbach, and Lawrence C. Dodd (New York: Agathon, 1986).

31. Martin Gold et al., *The Book on Congress: Process, Procedure and Structure* (Washington, D.C.: Big Eagle, 1992).

32. In the Senate, securities issues fall within the jurisdiction of the Banking Committee.

33. Jim Drinkard, "Securities Industry Battling to Protect Investment in Congress," Associated Press, November 21, 1994.

34. Ibid.

35. Ibid.

36. Nancy E. Roman, "Dingell Panel Cuts Would Anger Heir to Chairmanship," *Washington Times,* November 16, 1994, A3.

37. Nancy E. Roman, "Bonior Launches Attack on Gingrich," *Washington Times,* November 18, 1994, A3.

38. The change combined the jurisdictions of the District of Columbia, Government Operations, and Post Office Committees.

39. For example, on November 15 eight senior Republican members of the committee, including prospective chairman Jack Fields (R-Tex.), wrote Gingrich, urging that the Merchant Marine Committee be maintained.

40. "D.C., Marine, Post Office Committees on Chopping Block," *National Journal's Congress Daily,* November 15, 1994, 2.

41. Pat Towell, "GOP's Drive for a More Open House Reflects Pragmatism and Resentment," *Congressional Quarterly Weekly Report,* November 19, 1994, 3320–21.

42. Ibid.

43. Kenneth J. Cooper, "GOP Vows Quick Action to Change Housekeeping," *Washington Post,* November 15, 1994, A4.

44. *Congressional Record,* January 4, 1995, H11.

45. Ibid.

46. See Sarah A. Binder and Steven S. Smith, "Acquired Procedural Tendencies and Congressional Reform," in *Remaking Congress,* ed. James A. Thurber and Roger H. Davidson (Washington, D.C.: Congressional Quarterly, 1995).

47. Base-line budgeting provides that for any legislation proposing expenditures, the new funding level must be compared to the current level of spending for the program, rather than an estimate of how much it would cost to continue providing the current level of services into the future (the so-called current services estimate). Prior to the 104th Congress, committee documents focused on the current services estimate rather than actual base-year spending levels. According to conservatives, because of factors such as inflation, using the current services estimate as the base for calculating changes in funding levels led to a bias in favor of increased expenditures.

48. The version included in the Contract with America referred to all tax hikes. However, as concerns mounted about the scope of the initial proposal, Republican leaders narrowed it to cover only income tax rate increases.

49. Bill Thomas, "Putting Our Own House in Order," *Washington Times,* March 31, 1995, A23.

50. *Congressional Record,* January 4, 1995, H84.

51. Kenneth J. Cooper, "Cut Back, Caucuses Struggle to Go Forward," *Washington Post,* March 23, 1995, A25.

52. *Congressional Record,* May 15, 1984, 12300–12301.

53. Ibid., p. 12299.

54. "New House Speaker Envisions Cooperation, Cuts, Hard Work," *Congressional Quarterly Weekly Report,* November 12, 1994, 3296.

5

Reform and the
Republican Majority

O N JANUARY 4, 1995, House members began the 104th Congress by formally selecting Newt Gingrich (R-Ga.) as Speaker. Richard Gephardt (D-Mo.), who had replaced the defeated Thomas Foley (D-Wash.) as Democratic leader, addressed a House chamber packed with incoming members, their families, and visiting senators. A solemn Gephardt handed the gavel to the first Republican Speaker since 1955. "With resignation, but with resolve," he said, "I hereby end 40 years of Democratic rule of this House." The new minority leader told Gingrich, "You are now my Speaker, and let the great debate begin."[1]

On the Senate side of the Capitol, power also was shifting to a new Republican majority, but there the emphasis was as much on continuity as on change. Sen. Strom Thurmond (R-S.C.), ninety-two years old and a forty-year veteran of the institution, was elected president pro tempore. And while House members were passing major reforms of their rules, senators focused on a single reorganization proposal—an initiative by Thomas Harkin (D-Iowa) and Joseph Lieberman (D-Conn.) aimed at substantially altering the filibuster rule. As expected, the Harkin-Lieberman proposal failed by a wide margin.

By most accounts, the legislative agenda of the 104th Congress has been remarkable. From the Contract with America to major deficit-reduction and balanced-budget proposals to efforts to overhaul Medicare and the welfare system, lawmakers considered legislation intended to fundamentally revamp federal policy and the role and reach of the national government. The impact of this wide-ranging agenda remains unclear. Well into 1996, only selected portions of the GOP policy program had become law. However, certain changes in the process of legislative decision making were apparent early in the Republican Congress, and a preliminary assessment of these trends is both feasible and useful. How have the decision-making processes of the Republican Congress differed from those that characterized Democratic control? How has the nature of institutional change differed in the House relative to the Senate? And to what extent have the structural and procedural reforms implemented by the Republican majority affected substantive policy-making on Capitol Hill? The purpose of this chapter is to explore the institutional developments that have occurred during the 104th Congress.

Once again, our focus is primarily on the House because institutional change in that chamber has been more pronounced relative to the more informal, bipartisan, and tradition-oriented Senate. The first section of this chapter outlines the remarkable policymaking activities of Speaker Gingrich during the 104th Congress. In the second section, we assess the role of standing committees in the Republican House. The third section deals with changes in floor deliberations and scheduling. Fourth is a discussion of the remaining reorganization areas—congressional integrity, policy-driven reforms, and congressional resources and interbranch prerogatives. Fifth is an examination of reform politics in the Senate. We close by exploring how the various organizational incentives influenced institutional developments in the 104th Congress.

LEADERS AND FOLLOWERS

The Democratic Speakers of the 1980s and 1990s were actively involved in the legislative process and exerted a significant influence on policy outcomes. The level of policy agreement among House Democrats grew during this period, as southern Democrats became less conservative and the Reagan domestic agenda polarized the House along ideological lines. In addition, the reforms of the 1970s enhanced the Speaker's ability to influence the timing and content of legislation. The result, according to political scientist Barbara Sinclair, was the emergence of a House Democratic leadership that "significantly influences the course of legislation and the probability of legislative success."[2]

However, the policy activism of recent Democratic Speakers is heightened only in comparison with the relatively weak Speakers of the post–World War II Congress. Throughout his Speakership (1989–1995), Thomas Foley was significantly constrained by the preferences and prerogatives of House committee chairs, such as Jack Brooks (D-Tex., Judiciary), John Dingell (D-Mich., Energy and Commerce), and Dan Rostenkowski (D-Ill., Ways and Means). Although House Democrats grew more cohesive on key policy issues during their last two decades of majority status, important divisions remained, precluding a major centralization of power in the Speaker's office.

As we have shown, the election of a more unified and aggressive Republican majority in November 1994 led to a substantial strengthening of the Speaker's formal powers. To characterize the 104th House as a return to the "czar rule" of the early twentieth century would be an exaggeration. Long-term changes in congressional rules and the broader political system make the reemergence of autocratic party leaders unlikely in the modern Congress. Yet it is plain that Newt Gingrich plays a pivotal policymaking role in the mid-1990s House. Indeed, the scope and impact of his Speakership have been without precedent in recent congressional history.

As we discussed in Chapter 4, an empowered party leadership can fulfill four key functions for rank-and-file members of the majority party: publicize the agenda, focus the agenda, reduce bargaining costs, and discourage defections. During 1995, Speaker Gingrich fulfilled all four leadership functions to a greater extent than his Democratic predecessors.

Publicize the Agenda

Gingrich has been the key public spokesman for the new Republican majority, often upstaging Senate majority leader Robert Dole (R-Kans.), the presumptive 1996 Republican presidential nominee. Throughout his congressional career, Gingrich has emphasized the importance of using the media to shape public opinion. As a backbench minority firebrand during the 1980s, he used C-SPAN coverage of special order speeches to publicize GOP complaints about the Democratic House. In the late 1980s, as Gingrich sought to focus media attention on the ethics of Speaker James Wright (D-Tex.), the Georgian remarked, "We are engaged in reshaping a whole nation through the news media."[3] In 1988, Gingrich became head of GOPAC, a political action committee aimed at financing and electing a farm team of Republican candidates in state and local races. GOPAC provided candidates with tapes emphasizing the importance of rhetoric and ideological themes for shaping the public mood. The tapes even suggested key phrases and derogatory terms (such as *sick, corrupt, self-serving,* and *decay*) that Republicans could use to characterize Democrats.

In 1994, Gingrich, Richard Armey (R-Tex.), and other House GOP leaders devised the Contract with America, which was pretested through polls and focus groups to ensure that its language would resonate with public concerns about government—hence the catchy titles of the separate bills, such as the American Dream Restoration Act, the Taking Back Our Streets Act, and the Job Creation/Wage Enhancement Act. At Gingrich's urging, the contract was advertised in *TV Guide* because he knew subscribers would repeatedly open the magazine and see the GOP initiatives.

Gingrich's emphasis on public relations continued throughout the 104th Congress. To help focus media attention on the contract, every day the House was in session during the first one hundred days a GOP lawmaker read the contract provisions on the floor. According to one adviser, "Gingrich understands the power of repetition better than anyone."[4]

Early in 1995, the Speaker allowed television coverage of his daily press conferences with congressional correspondents. Under previous Democratic

Speakers, television coverage of these briefings was not permitted. By allowing cameras into the room, Gingrich provided television producers with a daily source of footage spotlighting the Speaker, ensuring that he would be a regular feature on the nightly news. Faced with complaints from other GOP lawmakers about the quantity of his coverage, which was beginning to overshadow the Republican agenda, as well as negative publicity resulting from flare-ups with reporters, Gingrich discontinued the daily briefings in the spring of 1995. (In April 1996 the daily press briefings resumed, but they were now untelevised and conducted by Majority Leader Dick Armey.)

Then, in an unprecedented event that mirrored presidential communications strategies, on April 12 the Speaker delivered a prime-time, nationally televised address in which he highlighted the legislation passed by the Republican House and outlined his views of the country's future. A few months later, President Bill Clinton and the Speaker shared a stage in New Hampshire and discussed the need for bipartisan cooperation and political reform. Media interest in the event was intense.

No House Speaker has so systematically tried to influence public opinion. Indeed, Gingrich's media tactics often parallel presidential communications strategies more than they do the public roles adopted by previous Speakers. *Time* magazine even chose the Speaker as its "Man of the Year." Gingrich uses this tactic of "going public" to promote the GOP's accomplishments and to attempt to frame the terms of public discourse to benefit Republicans.[5] It should come as no surprise that he uses an extensive array of communications strategies—focus groups, polls, image consultants, and more— as part of an ongoing effort to ensure that the GOP's message resonates with the public.

Consider the example of Medicare reform. Shortly after the 1994 election, incoming Budget Committee chairman John Kasich (R-Ohio) told Gingrich that the GOP's pledge to balance the budget within seven years while passing a major tax cut would require large reductions in the growth of Medicare. Medicare, the nation's second-largest entitlement program, is highly popular with voters. Republican pollsters warned Gingrich that the public would not support balancing the budget through Medicare cuts. On April 4, however, the trustees of the Medicare trust fund, who included top Clinton administration officials, reported that program costs would exceed revenues by the year 2002. This impending insolvency was not new information. However, Gingrich and other Republican leaders decided to use the trustees' report to frame the proposed reductions in Medicare not as a means toward deficit reduction, but as necessary to save the Medicare system.

The GOP leadership coordinated the public utterances and written statements of lawmakers about Medicare reform. Never were Republicans to utter the word *cut*. Instead, House Republicans began emphasizing the same themes. Medicare expenditures, they said, "will continue to grow, only the rate of increase will be cut." Their goal was to "preserve, protect, and strengthen" Medicare. "Repeat it until you vomit," advised Haley Barbour, chairman of the Republican National Committee and a close adviser to the Speaker. Republicans also argued that "the President's own trustees say that changes are needed to protect Medicare."[6] Democratic leaders responded with their own organized message campaign, with minority lawmakers arguing that the GOP's Medicare cuts were draconian and primarily intended to finance a $245 billion tax cut for the wealthy.

Gingrich also assigned GOP Conference chairman John Boehner (R-Ohio) responsibility for coordinating outreach with major constituent groups. Every Thursday morning, Boehner meets with key lobbyists to coordinate plans and strategies. He recommended that, on every major bill, committee chairs "prepare a battle plan for public relations, lobbying efforts and vote mobilization."[7] Communications aides to Gingrich and other Republican leaders also met weekly with the press secretaries of House Republicans to develop a coordinated party message. The Speaker, in sum, clearly functioned as the chief public spokesman for the party. He remarked, "I see the speakership [as] somebody who [can] somehow combine grassroots organizations, mass media, and legislative detail into one synergistic pattern."[8] In 1996 Gingrich asked House Budget chairman John Kasich (R-Ohio) to devise a national public relations strategy for the November elections.

In November 1995, the House and Senate passed comprehensive deficit-control legislation aimed at balancing the federal budget by 2002. The measure also included large portions of the broader GOP policy agenda, from an overhaul of agricultural subsidy programs to Medicare and welfare reform. Arguing that many of the cuts were excessive and unnecessary, President Clinton vetoed two different versions of the legislation. That fall, most of the annual appropriations bills also were either bottled up in Congress or opposed by the president.

The impasse over the deficit-reduction bill and the annual spending measures led to two partial shutdowns of the federal government. As many federal facilities were temporarily closed and public employees furloughed, popular opinion swung sharply against Gingrich and the GOP majority. Interbranch conflict over legislation to increase the federal debt ceiling also fed public perceptions that congressional Republicans were inflexible. By the end of the year, the consensus view was that the Speaker had lost the public relations battle over the budget to President Clinton. Gingrich temporarily scaled back his public profile. In February 1996, however, the Speaker and other Republicans leaders decided that he should focus more, not less, on developing and communicating their party's message.[9]

Focus the Agenda

If the Speaker does not determine the overall legislative agenda of the House, policy priorities tend to bubble up from the committee system, often in a piecemeal fashion. Recent Democratic Speakers played a leading role in setting the floor schedule, but Gingrich's influence over the House agenda has been more pervasive and all-encompassing, typically extending into committee deliberations on Republican priorities. Policy and political direction on items important to the party have been managed from the top down. Gingrich's ability to control the House legislative agenda derived from his overwhelming support among the GOP freshman and sophomore classes (they constitute more than half the Republican membership), as well as general perceptions that Gingrich, in contrast to the Democratic Speakers, could appoint and remove committee chairs.

For example, during the first one hundred days, Gingrich took steps to ensure that the committees of jurisdiction moved quickly on the Contract with America. After one chairman informed Gingrich that his committee was having trouble meeting the contract timetable, the Speaker responded, "If you can't do it, I will find somebody who will."[10] When Barney Frank (D-Mass.) complained to Judiciary Committee chairman Henry Hyde (R-Ill.) that the panel was processing legislation too quickly, Hyde remarked that he lacked discretion over legislative timing. "I'm really a subchairman," he said.[11] Hyde, a staunch opponent of term limitations for members of Congress, quickly shepherded a term limits proposal through his committee because the item was in the contract. He acknowledged that "there has not been time to implement items of my personal agenda. But they are small potatoes. I'm fully in accord with the priorities of this leadership."[12]

From 1981 to 1995, the House Committee on Ways and Means was chaired by Democrat Dan Rostenkowski, who exercised significant personal control over his panel's agenda. In contrast to Rostenkowski, Bill Archer (R-Tex.), the Republican chairman of Ways and Means, has mostly responded to leadership directions in selecting his panel's legislative priorities. "In the end," said Archer, "you have to be part of the process. You don't run out there like the Lone Ranger and do whatever you want to do."[13]

The enhanced agenda control exerted by Republican House leaders extended beyond the one-hundred-day contract period, as the chamber's attention turned to the thirteen annual appropriations bills. Decision making within the House Appropriations Committee traditionally has been bipartisan, with substantial cooperation occurring between committee and subcommittee leaders across the two political parties. In previous years, the appropriators also had substantial discretion about how their bills were managed on the floor. In 1995, Republican leaders harnessed the panel behind the GOP agenda. The speaker required each GOP Appropriations member to sign a "letter of fidelity," stating that they would cut the federal budget as much as the party wanted.[14] And throughout 1995, GOP leaders, particularly majority leader Richard Armey, were integrally involved in the appropriations process.

On July 13, for example, as the full House considered the Interior appropriations bill, Republican committee leaders approached Rep. David Obey of Wisconsin, ranking Democrat on the committee, in an attempt to devise an agreement establishing a time limit for further amendments. Obey and the GOP Appropriations leaders agreed on a process that would have allowed the House to adjourn by 9:00 P.M. Under Democratic control, such agreements among the bipartisan floor managers were embraced by the Speaker and the majority leader. Armey, however, rejected the deal with Obey. He wanted the House to work beyond 9:00 P.M. A visibly angry Obey complained about the decision on the floor, saying:

> What is at issue here, in my view, is whether or not this House is going to be able to conduct its business at reasonable times in public view or whether we are going to be reduced to making virtually every major decision in subcommittees and on the floor at near midnight, with minimal public attention and minimal public understanding.

Obey characterized the leadership's action as "willfulness" and retaliated with a series of dilatory motions that tied up the chamber for almost an hour.[15]

Reduce Bargaining Costs

When Democrats controlled the House, key legislative agreements typically were devised in the committees of jurisdiction. In the 104th Congress, House standing committees continue to function as important legislative arenas, but party leaders have been highly active in the nuts and bolts of crafting policy and political coalitions. An Appropriations subcommittee chairman observed that party leaders have special resources for building majorities within the GOP Conference on potentially divisive measures, facilitating the bargaining and exchange necessary to hold Republicans in line. Gingrich, he said, "brings an awful lot to the table, so you may have resources, financial and otherwise, that you didn't know you had."[16]

Republican leadership strategies are devised and implemented via a more centralized and elaborate party structure than had been employed by the Democrats. A GOP leadership aide described the basic division of labor: "Newt is the strategist and overseer. Armey runs things day to day. [Majority whip Tom] Delay's job is growing the vote and counting the vote. [GOP Conference chairman John] Boehner deals with [outside] coalitions, communications, and member services."[17] A core group, called the Speaker's Advisory Group, meets once or more each week the House is in session to discuss legislative strategy.[18]

In contrast to Democratic Speaker Foley, Gingrich also meets weekly with the committee chairs as a group to discuss legislative and political developments. Particularly on hot issues, Gingrich is in regular contact with the relevant chairs. During the spring of 1995, according to a Gingrich aide, the Speaker met "with Armey, Kasich (Budget Chair), Archer (Ways and Means Chair), and Livingston (Appropriations Chair) in group settings two to three times per week."[19]

Health policy provides a useful point of comparison between leadership behavior in the Republican and Democratic Houses. When the Clinton administration's massive bill to reform the health care system was introduced in November 1993, many Democrats warned Speaker Foley not to rely on the committees of jurisdiction to refine the plan and assemble a supporting coalition. Jurisdiction over health policy was dispersed across many standing committees, with three panels (Commerce, Education and Labor, and Ways and Means) claiming jurisdiction over all or most of the Clinton bill. Commerce chairman John Dingell informed Foley that moving the measure through the normal committee process would guarantee "a Tower of Babel approach in which conflicting claims and provisions yield a health care system even more irrational than today's."[20]

Foley, however, ignored Dingell's predictions. He referred the legislation, in whole or in part, to ten different committees. As the three leading health care panels encountered difficulties forming majorities behind comprehensive reform, the Democratic leadership continued to defer to the committees of jurisdiction. It was not until the summer of 1994 that majority leader Richard Gephardt took formal control of the coalition-building process, at which point insufficient time and political capital remained to craft and pass a Democratic package. In the end, neither the House nor the Senate acted on Clinton's health reform proposal.

Republican leaders recognized that they, too, would have to confront health care reform in order to devise a plan that would balance the budget in seven years. Early in 1995, as the House focused on the Contract with America, Gingrich took personal control over efforts to craft a proposal for overhauling Medicare. He hoped to minimize opposition from the interest groups and other forces that had defeated the Clinton plan. Unlike Foley, Gingrich circumvented the normal committee process, explaining that "Medicare is the most difficult and delicate issue that we're dealing with" and not a matter only for the committees of jurisdiction.[21]

The Speaker assigned chief deputy whip Dennis Hastert (R-Ill.) to oversee the work of two GOP health study groups. One included the chairs of the committees and subcommittees with principal health jurisdiction and was called the Speaker's steering committee; the other was a resource group of about thirty Republican members who conveyed ideas and issues to the health steering group. "It's more than centralization," Gingrich noted. "It's an effort to pull together a task force, to hear the whole Conference. You can't let [Medicare] be an isolated effort."[22]

Throughout the summer of 1995, Gingrich took the lead in devising the House Republican Medicare proposal, meeting regularly with representatives of key interest groups, such as the American Medical Association (AMA), hospital associations, and the insurance industry. The chairmen of the two primary committees of jurisdiction, Bill Archer (Ways and Means) and Thomas Bliley (R-Va., Commerce), played significant but secondary roles. The two health subcommittees played no formal role in the process. According to one industry official, "The Speaker has done a superb job figuring out what was important to all of the health care groups and what it would take for them to support [the proposal] given some of the less attractive parts of the plan."[23]

In October 1995, following a private meeting with Gingrich, the AMA endorsed the GOP Medicare plan, leading President Clinton and other Democrats to charge that "the Republican leadership cut a deal with the AMA."[24] Commerce Committee chairman Bliley summed up Gingrich's Medicare role: "This bill, right from the start, was written in the Speaker's office."[25]

Republican leaders also used the appropriations process to facilitate their legislative agenda by including extensive legislative riders (extraneous policy provisos) in appropriations bills. These riders were aimed at downsizing government, reversing federal policy, and eliminating funds to enforce federal regulations in certain areas such as environmental policy.

Under House rules, the regular order for appropriations is for the authorizing panels to suggest policy and the Appropriations Committee to recommend how much money should be made available to implement that policy. However, the House rule against advocating policy change in appropriations bills is often waived by the Rules Committee. Under Democratic control, substantive riders to spending bills were common, but they were seldom intended to make so many major changes in policy.

By contrast, the Republican majority systematically included significant policy departures from the status quo in its appropriations measures, leading Democrats to charge that GOP riders circumvented normal procedure and subverted federal programs supported by most Americans. GOP leaders recognized that relying on the authorizations process was not viable because of time constraints and the breadth of the Republican agenda. They also knew that it would be more difficult for the administration to block Republican policy changes if they were included in appropriations bills, which fund large portions of the federal government. Appropriations Committee chairman Bob Livingston (R-La.) did not support the systematic inclusion of legislative riders in spending measures, but he bowed to pressure from the leadership and the Republican Conference. He remarked, "It has been a leadership decision to move forward on this initiative."[26]

During the summer of 1995, majority leader Armey played a key role in deciding which riders to include in the various spending bills. On July 19, he sent a letter to all Republican members outlining the leadership's approach to dealing with policy matters in the appropriations process.

> With the knowledge that President Clinton will have to sign the 13 appropriations bills, it is in our best interest to use these bills to further policies that reflect our party's goals and priorities. The Leadership hopes to use this approach on policies that enjoy support from both the authorizers and appropriators, or when the Leadership agrees a certain policy serves to advance our party's overall agenda.

The strategy articulated by Armey includes early planning by committee and leadership staff and appearances by the relevant full and subcommittee chairs before the Republican Policy Committee to discuss potential floor amendments. According to Armey's letter, if authorizers and appropriators "are unable to reach an agreement, any authorizing language in an appropriations bill would be subject to a point of order if it does not reflect a leadership position."

The large number of controversial riders was partially responsible for the slow pace of the appropriations process in 1995, which in turn led to the partial government shutdowns. By March 1996, however, some of the riders had been codified in statute, as compromise spending measures were passed to fund federal programs for the rest of the fiscal year. The collective consequences of these riders, particularly in the regulatory area, has been significant. Funding was zeroed out entirely for certain regulatory activities. A range of riders limited the enforcement efforts of the Environmental Protection Agency. A House appropriations bill prohibited the promulgation of new federal rules covering repetitive motion injuries in the workplace. According to some, the impact of the Republican riders was "de facto deregulation."[27] To minimize the chances for any further government shutdowns, in spring 1996 GOP leaders decided to limit somewhat the use of controversial riders on appropriations bills.

Discourage Defections

The extensive legislative involvement of GOP leaders was apparent in efforts to maintain Republican unity on key policy matters. Compared to previous Democratic majorities, Republicans are highly cohesive. Most GOP members signed the Contract with America in September 1994, and they realized that the fate of their majority depended on successful consideration, if not passage, of the contract items.

Early in 1995, certain organized coalitions emerged within the Republican Conference, reflecting the differences among GOP lawmakers. About twenty-five to thirty GOP moderates formed the Tuesday Lunch Bunch, meeting weekly to plan legislative strategy. Organized factions also emerged among Republican conservatives, including the Family Caucus, the Conservative Action Team, the New Federalists, and the Pro-life Caucus. At various points, these Republican factions, as well as the change-oriented freshman class, threatened to defect from the party's position on major issues unless their policy goals were met. With a narrow GOP majority of less than 240, including 5 southern Democratic defectors, and 218 votes needed to win on the floor, every GOP vote was important to Gingrich.

Republican leaders, however, were remarkably successful at maintaining party unity throughout 1995. On 73.2 percent of the roll-call votes conducted during 1995, a majority of House Republicans voted against a majority of their Democratic counterparts. If the trend continues, this would be the highest level of partisan polarization on House floor votes since the 61st Congress (1909–1911). On these party unity votes, 91 percent of GOP lawmakers supported their leadership.[28] For the 33 votes on final passage of bills included in the Contract with America, an average of just 4.73 Republicans voted against the party's position.[29] House GOP support was unanimous on 16 of the contract bills. On only 3 of the measures did Republican defections exceed 10, and on only the term limits amendment did the GOP lose. Indeed, a majority of Democrats voted for final passage on 17 of the 33 contract bills.

Although Republicans were united behind their party's overall agenda, there was a large potential for significant defections on certain amendments offered to contract legislation. For instance, on February 16 the House voted 218 to 212 to delete a GOP-backed provision for an antimissile defense system in the National Security Revitalization Act, the contract's defense plank. Still, the leadership was usually successful at whipping Republicans into line.

On the contract proposal for a $500 per child tax credit, more than one hundred Republicans, including Rules Committee chairman Gerald Solomon (R-N.Y.), signed a letter to the leadership urging that the family income ceiling be reduced from $200,000 to $95,000. Just days before House consideration of the tax-reduction package, it appeared that thirty moderate Republicans might break with their party on the measure. In the end, an extensive lobbying campaign by Gingrich and other GOP leaders, who enlisted grassroots organizations to lobby wavering members, held Republican defections on the tax bill to just eleven, keeping the $200,000 ceiling intact.

Republican cohesion continued after the contract period, although defections increased as the chamber considered the annual appropriations bills. On July 12, for instance, the Republican leadership lost its first vote on a special rule from the House Rules Committee when 61 Republicans joined 176 Democrats to kill the procedure for considering the Interior appropriations bill. The leadership quickly compromised with the rebellious Republicans, and a second rule was adopted. On September 29, for a variety of reasons, the House rejected the House-Senate compromise on the spending bill, with substantial GOP defections. Just hours later, 130 Republicans joined 136 Democrats to defeat the conference report on the Defense Department appropriations bill.

These defeats, however, were exceptions. For the most part, Gingrich and company were able to maintain sufficient party unity to pass their ambitious and controversial agenda through the House. Majority leader Armey managed legislative operations for the party on a day-to-day basis, but Gingrich played a key role in striking bargains among warring GOP factions.[30] On the Labor–Health and Human Services (HHS) appropriations bill, the Speaker met repeatedly with different GOP coalitions, eventually brokering a deal between reproductive rights supporters and pro-life lawmakers on abortion and family planning issues.

Gingrich occasionally threatened to punish potential defectors from the party's position, although the GOP leadership's ability to penalize lawmakers was sharply constrained by the mood of the Republican Conference and various factions within it. For example, in December 1994 GOP leaders appointed freshman Mark Neumann (R-Wis.) to the Appropriations Committee, a plum assignment for a freshman member.

On the committee, the independent-minded freshman voted against a defense supplemental bill that was supported by Chairman Livingston and the Republican leadership. Gingrich reportedly threatened to remove Neumann from the committee if the action was repeated. Neumann recalled, "Three freshmen specifically came to me at the direction of the leadership and said, 'You can't do this.'. . . They said I would be off the committee. They said, 'Your future in Congress is done.' "[31]

Still, Neumann's independent streak continued to surface. In September 1995, he voted against the conference report on the Defense Department appropriations bill. Then, on October 4, Livingston, with the Speaker's knowledge, sent Neumann a letter notifying him of his removal from the National Security Appropriations Subcommittee and reassignment to the less important Military Construction Subcommittee. Livingston said, "We have tried very hard to address Mr. Neumann's concerns, yet he has refused to support the National Security bill. We need conferees who can get the committee's work done."[32] Other GOP freshmen, however, rallied to Neumann's support. To mollify the freshmen and save face for Livingston, the GOP leadership kept Neumann on the Military Construction panel but granted him an additional plum assignment on the Budget Committee. (To create a vacancy for Neumann to fill, Gingrich persuaded Peter Hoekstra [R-Mich.] to resign from the Budget panel by making him chair of a GOP task force on campaign finance reform.)

Republican leaders also demonstrated their willingness to circumvent committees that do not support leadership aims. Consider the case of the House Agriculture Committee, which was instructed to slash the nation's farm program by $13.4 billion as part of the 1995 deficit-reduction process. The Agriculture panel long has been a classic constituency-oriented committee, highly responsive to the needs of America's farmers. The free-market orientation of the Republican majority, as well as the need for steep budgetary reductions, did not bode well for agricultural price supports and the crop subsidy programs. Majority leader Armey, a former economics professor and a leading critic of agricultural subsidies, once wrote an article titled "Moscow on the Mississippi: America's Soviet-Style Farm Policy." GOP leaders had even considered abolishing the Agriculture Committee when the 104th Congress began, merging its jurisdiction with energy and natural resources issues, but dropped the idea when rural lawmakers strenuously objected.

In September 1995, the Agriculture Committee considered legislation, written by Chairman Pat Roberts (R-Kans.), to implement $13.4 billion in spending cuts by ending incentives for farmers to let land lie idle and by scaling back existing subsidies. Gingrich and other Republican leaders endorsed the Roberts draft. Prior to the markup, they sent the Agriculture chairman a letter warning that the leadership would circumvent his panel if the legislation was not passed without major modifications. GOP Conference chairman Boehner, a member of the Agriculture Committee, was quoted in the media as saying, "If this committee can't do it [make the $13.4 billion in cuts], the future of this committee is seriously in doubt."[33] As Roberts told his committee colleagues, "It is a decision of whether we do this in committee or . . . others will do it for us, or to us."[34]

At the September 20 markup, the committee voted 22 (yea) to 27 (no) against the Roberts draft, with four Republicans voting with the twenty-two Democrats to defeat the plan. (A fifth Republican changed his vote from yes to no to be eligible under House rules to offer a motion to reconsider the bill at a future markup; this changed the no vote from 26 to 27.) Responsibility for devising the $13.4 billion in agricultural cuts shifted to the Budget and Rules Committees and to top GOP leaders.

At a meeting of these leaders, Gingrich raised a number of retaliatory measures that could be taken against the Agriculture Committee Republicans who had opposed Roberts. According to a staff memo that described the meeting, Bill Emerson (R-Mo.), second in seniority among committee Republicans, could be denied the chairmanship if Roberts was elected to the Senate. Larry Combest (R-Tex.) could be stripped of his chairmanship of the Intelligence Committee. And Richard Baker (R-La.) could be transferred from the Agriculture panel to the Committee on Transportation and Infrastructure. The memo did not mention sanctions against the fourth Republican, Saxby Chambliss of Georgia. After the staff memo was mistakenly E-mailed to a Democratic staff office and promptly dispersed to the media, Gingrich assured the three members that such retaliatory measures were not forthcoming. But Republican leaders clearly had little patience for the independence of the Agriculture Committee, and the panel was stripped of its control over the 1995 reductions. After Clinton vetoed the GOP deficit-reduction package, which included the agricultural policy changes and cuts, the House and Senate stripped off the so-called Freedom to Farm bill and passed it again as a separate measure in February 1996. The president signed the landmark measure in April.

At the start of 1996, as Gingrich and other Republican leaders negotiated with the Clinton administration to keep the federal government fully operating, the House Republican freshmen were reluctant to make any significant concessions to the president and Democratic congressional leaders on budgetary matters. Indeed, the freshmen were pivotal in convincing an initially reluctant Gingrich to adopt government shutdowns as a bargaining tactic. However, after telling one member to "sit down and shut up" at a key party meeting in January, Gingrich informed the assembled Republican Conference, "I'm here to tell you what the team's going to do. Now some of you wanted to have a shutdown forever. And that's unsustainable for 30 or 40 of our members. So we can't do that."[35] The lawmakers then walked to the floor and passed legislation to begin paying federal workers who had been affected by the second shutdown. Only fifteen Republicans voted against the Speaker. Gingrich asked for and received a list of their names.

In the aftermath of the two federal government shutdowns and a threatened government default on the payment of its financial obligations (legislation to raise the legal debt limit had been temporarily held up in the overall budgetary impasse), Gingrich and Senate majority leader Bob Dole became concerned that Republicans had gotten off message. The public was focusing more on the shutdowns and interbranch conflicts than on what they viewed as the GOP's agenda of downsizing government and balancing the budget. In public opinion polls, support for the Speaker plummeted. Democratic incumbents and congressional candidates railed against the "Gingrich Republi-

TABLE 5.1 House GOP Strategic Plan for 1996: Responsibilities of Leadership

Gingrich's New Role

• Create team plan for 1996

• Ensure training necessary to implement the [strategic] plan

• Modify the plan as reality changes and then ensure retraining, etc.

• Get our messages through to the public (winning the communications contest)

• Ensure resources at every level

• Monitor indicators of achievement so that the plan is implemented

• Speak—fundraise—arouse public to our cause

• Help in potential crises in the House

• Play a role in developing the following issue areas: disabilities, environment, education, military reform, campaign reform, ethnic groups, and women (reporting to Armey)

Armey's New Role

• Manager of legislative schedule

• Legislative problem solver (with [Speaker's] advisory group)

• Coordinate committees

• Coordinate with the Senate (focus on legislation)

• Assist with communications

• Assist with coalitions

• Fundraise, energize base voters

• Lead the leadership

Source: "House GOP Conference Strategic & Operational Plan for 1996," February 1996, 4.

cans." Accordingly, the Speaker unveiled plans for a new division of labor within the House Republican leadership.

The Speaker said that in the lead-up to the 1996 election he would relinquish to majority leader Armey his responsibilities for setting the House's daily schedule, forging winning coalitions, managing the GOP leadership and standing committee agendas, and coordinating legislative action with the Senate. Instead, the Speaker would focus more on formulating and articulating the House Republican message to the public. "I have been totally immersed in things like the details of Medicaid and Medicare reform," Gingrich observed. That approach "is basically over until 1997."[36] The House GOP strategic plan for 1996 summarized the intended new division of duties between Gingrich and Armey (Table 5.1). Whether the highly active Speaker will follow through on this pledge is unclear, but the GOP leadership as a whole remains integrally involved in the nuts and bolts of coalition building.

COMMITTEE DEVELOPMENTS

The Republican reforms affected most aspects of the House committee system—chairs' prerogatives, decision-making autonomy, jurisdictions, internal procedures and structures, and openness to the public. These changes were part of the overall delegation of authority to party leaders and were intended to make the committee system more accountable to the Republican Conference. Although certain 1970s innovations, such as the Subcommittee Bill of Rights and the joint referral of legislation, were repealed in 1995, the goals of the GOP committee reforms (consolidation of jurisdictions, greater openness, party accountability, and the like) were mostly consistent with the underlying goals of the 1970s changes.

Declining Autonomy

The decision-making autonomy of House and Senate committees has declined in recent decades. Beginning in the 1960s, significant floor challenges to committee recommendations became more common. The introduction of multiple referrals in the House further undermined the jurisdictional control of individual panels. More generally, lawmakers are no longer expected to focus only on the issues considered by their own committees and to defer to the committee of jurisdiction on other matters. The use of extra-committee mechanisms such as leadership task forces also increased during this period, further undermining the power of congressional committees. As the 104th Congress began, a long-term trend away from the insular legislative fiefdoms of the pre-1970s committee system existed.

This trend continued, at an accelerated pace, during the 104th Congress. As mentioned, House GOP leaders were integrally involved in the nuts and bolts of legislative work on a wide range of policy initiatives. The early legislative agenda was set by the Contract with America, which had been devised by leadership task forces. And throughout the 104th Congress, Republican leaders demonstrated a willingness, if not an eagerness, to override or circumvent standing committees that diverged from the party line. In addition to the agricultural cuts, Gingrich and other GOP leaders made the key decisions on major telecommunications legislation, pension reform, the Defense Department appropriations bill, Medicare and Medicaid reform, and other significant measures. When Republicans used the appropriations process to pass major policy changes, the leadership coordinated which legislative riders would be incorporated, drawing complaints from Appropriations Committee chairman Livingston.

In short, although the procedural prerogatives of House committee chairs were enhanced at the beginning of the 104th Congress (see Chapter 4), power shifted primarily from the chairs to the party leadership—and to the Republican Conference as a whole. More generally, hard-line conservatives, particularly among the freshmen, constrained the chairs and GOP leaders throughout 1995. When committee or leadership decisions diverged from the ideological mood of the rank and file, backbench Republicans voted against their party, as on the Interior and Defense Department appropriations bills.

The declining power of the committee chairs was particularly apparent in the procedures Republicans adopted to prepare for conference committee deliberations with the Senate. Although chamber rules give the Speaker the power to appoint conferees, the chair and ranking minority member of the committee of jurisdiction traditionally exert significant control over which lawmakers are assigned to conference committees (the temporary panels that reconcile differences between the House- and Senate-passed versions of a bill). Scholars suggest that the role of the chair and other committee members at the conference stage is an important source of committee power in the legislative process.[37] As the overall legislative activity of the Democratic Speakers increased during the 1980s and 1990s, however, party leaders began playing a more significant and independent role in the appointment of conferees.[38] This trend increased markedly in the Republican House.

In a memo to committee and subcommittee chairs, majority leader Armey outlined the steps for conference preparation, emphasizing the role of the leadership in what had been a mostly committee-dominated process. First, wrote Armey, party leaders and the committee chair meet to identify goals and priorities for the conference. Then the Speaker identifies a list of potential conferees, after consultation with the chair. Next, the Speaker, majority leader, and prospective conferees meet to make sure that the conferees support the party's policy priorities. The majority leader and whip also make sure that the conferees consult with other interested House Republicans.

The conferees are given latitude to settle policy details with their Senate counterparts but must stay within the parameters set by Republican leaders. Indeed, when subcommittee chairman Bill Young (R-Fla.) closed conference deliberations on the 1996 Defense Department appropriations bill without consulting GOP leaders, the leadership did not lobby Republicans to support the conference agreement, allowing it to lose 240 to 176.[39] Speaker Gingrich, in unprecedented actions and as part of the GOP's effort to woo conservative Democrats to switch parties, on several occasions named a number of right-leaning Democrats to serve on the GOP's contingent of House conferees.

Jurisdictions

Yet another indicator of declining committee importance in the Republican House is the relative absence of jurisdictional infighting between panels. As the prospects for an immediate overhaul of committee boundaries dimmed during the Republican transition, the GOP Conference created, as noted in Chapter 4, the Task Force on Committee Review.

Compared to previous Democratic Congresses, however, there were few jurisdictional battles between and among committees during the 104th Congress, in part because committees in general were less important. Chairs regularly waived their rights to sequential referral of measures in the interest of expediting legislative action. They also worked in private to settle their jurisdictional differences, and the GOP leadership stepped in quickly to help resolve any controversies.

GOP leaders also were less tolerant than their Democratic predecessors about turf fights. One Republican aide observed, "Jurisdictional problems have not occurred because the chairmen know there are 73 freshmen ready to take their heads off if they do." According to a staffer of majority leader Armey, "At the leadership level, if you see some potential strain, the immediate response is to have the two chairmen come in for a meeting."[40]

Binding time constraints were another factor muting jurisdictional strife in the Republican House. Within the space of several months, Republicans considered the Contract with America and moved aggressively to cut federal spending and to eliminate scores of federal programs. As noted earlier, they used the appropriations rather than the authorizations process to achieve many of their goals. Traditionally, the two sets of committees have jealously protected their prerogatives, but in 1995 appropriators and authorizers worked together under the leadership to include more policy language in the must-pass appropriations bills. Reflecting on the use of the appropriations process to carry policy riders, Speaker Gingrich said, "The amount of change [appropriators] are managing this year is, I think, without precedent going back to 1933."[41]

Task Forces

During the 104th Congress, not only was the role of the authorizing panels in substantive policymaking bypassed in some respects by the Appropriations Committee, but virtually all committees faced competition from ad hoc task forces. Earlier Speakers used task forces to forge consensus, draft legislation, involve noncommittee and junior members in issue areas, coordinate strategy, and promote intraparty communication.[42] Under Gingrich, however, task forces have been increasingly important "because the Speaker," according to Rep. Bob Barr (R-Ga.), "is much more active than other Speakers have been in putting together members with a particular interest."[43]

For example, Gingrich established five task forces (in the areas of crime, regulatory reform, term limits, legal reforms, and welfare reform) to expedite action on the Contract with America, facilitating communication among the leadership, the relevant committees, and interested members. A complete listing of all the task forces created by the majority leadership does not exist. But setting aside working groups, steering groups, staff gatherings, and task forces formed to mobilize support for the Contract with America, the House Republican leadership has created at least fifteen other task forces.[44] Some of the task forces are more active and organized than others. Some work closely with the committees of jurisdiction; others do not. Most are partisan, but a few are bipartisan, such as the Task Force on Immigration Reform.

The leadership uses these task forces for diverse purposes. The traditional goals behind the creation of such ad hoc groups—moving high-priority legislation to enactment and involving a cross section of lawmakers in policy formulation—still apply, but additional objectives also are evident in the 104th Congress. One involves outreach. Rep. Sonny Bono (R-Calif.), for instance, heads an entertainment task force "to improve relations between the GOP and traditionally liberal Hollywood."[45] Another motivation for the task forces is electoral. The Speaker created the California Task Force, composed of the state's entire twenty-five-member GOP delegation, in part because of the state's electoral importance and its economic and social impact on the nation.[46] Still another motivation is to devise Republican policy solutions and generate GOP consensus before the Democrats do so.

Another goal may be to dilute the authority of committee chairs and, on certain overlapping issues, circumvent the committee process. Task forces, said a Gingrich aide, are devices for "finessing some institutional obstacles to decisionmaking." The staffer added, "We envision using task forces a lot."[47] Sometimes committee chairs use task forces to reach out to the Republican Conference. Freshman George Nethercutt (R-Wash.) put together the twenty-eight-member Agriculture Task Force at the request of Agriculture Committee chairman Pat Roberts. Composed of GOP members who are not on the Agriculture Committee, the group's objective, according to Roberts, was to educate "other legislators on the consequences of severe budget cuts on rural America."[48]

Interestingly, during the 104th Congress the minority Democrats also relied on task forces to draft alternatives to GOP proposals and to communicate their views to the public. A Democratic drafting group, for instance, bypassed Democrats on the Ways and Means Committee and devised a comprehensive welfare reform bill that was endorsed by the Democratic Caucus. This approach to policymaking would not have succeeded when Democrats were in the majority, according to Democratic Caucus chairman Vic Fazio of California: "We were deathly afraid of interfering with committee chairmen. . . . But with Republican control, we need to broaden the base on every issue in the Caucus. Our goal is to empower our Members."[49]

The shift in power from the standing committee system to the leadership and various ad hoc groups was partially due to the extraordinary policy agenda considered in 1995. Members and staff predicted that the committees and subcommittees would become more important arenas for legislative work in the second session of the 104th Congress. Gingrich remained committed to ad hoc mechanisms for overcoming jurisdictional and other committee-related impediments to the GOP program. But the role of task forces was expected to decline somewhat. A Gingrich aide observed, "When we first came in [and] there was a lot of excitement, we said, 'Oh, let's create a task force.' Now we're more sophisticated and know how to better use the committees."[50]

Committee Procedures

House Republicans also adopted certain changes in committee procedures at the beginning of the 104th Congress. Most important of these was the ban on proxy voting. Given the frenetic legislative pace and the narrow GOP majority on the standing committees, the ban on proxy voting has made life difficult for committees and their members. As a result of the proxy ban, lawmakers often must sprint to cast votes in committees that are marking up bills concurrently. In addition, they must run back and forth between committee sessions and the floor to cast votes, because Republicans often waive the House rule prohibiting committee meetings while the House floor is operating under the five-minute rule (the floor amending phase). At a meeting of the Economic and Educational Opportunities Committee, George Miller (D-Calif.) asked Chairman William Goodling (R-Pa.), "What if we have to go to the bathroom?" Goodling's response: "Well, just put up one finger or two."[51]

In May 1995, thirteen members of the Banking Committee missed an important committee vote because they were casting roll-call votes on the floor. Two days later, Banking Committee chairman Jim Leach (R-Iowa) repeated the committee vote, which this time a number of Democratic members missed.[52] The Science Committee also repeated a committee vote because sixteen members were absent casting floor votes on the legislative branch appropriations bill.[53]

Some Republican chairs have expressed dismay with the ban on proxy voting. According to Judiciary Committee chairman Henry Hyde, "If they are going to let people serve on more than one committee and if they are going to simultaneously debate and vote on amendments on the floor [and in committee], then they should allow proxies."[54] Republican reformers such as Robert Walker, however, continue to regard the abolition of proxy voting as a centerpiece of the 1995 reorganization.

Committee Partisanship

As House committees have become less autonomous, they also have become increasingly vulnerable to the intense partisanship that characterizes the 104th Congress. Congressional committees differ from one another in many ways, one of which is the level of partisanship in committee deliberations.[55] Some panels, such as those dealing with explosive social issues or high-stakes procedural matters (Economic and Educational Opportunities, Judiciary, Rules), have traditionally been partisan, but others (Appropriations, Ethics, National Security) have regularly generated cross-party coalitions. Although systematic data are necessary to address fully changing trends in committee partisanship, it is apparent that the sharp partisanship often characterizing floor deliberations in the 104th Congress also has seeped into panels that heretofore operated in a largely bipartisan manner. Few committees appear to be immune from this heightened partisanship.

Consider two panels that, under Democratic control, functioned in a relatively bipartisan fashion: Appropriations and Ethics. In previous Congresses, Appropriations was generally free of party infighting, in part because it is easier for members to reconcile numbers than qualitative differences over policy. However, with budget balancing and deep spending cuts a key goal for House Republicans, and with these cuts targeting social programs long supported by Democrats, decision making within the Appropriations Committee was intensely partisan in the mid-1990s.

According to David Obey, ranking Democrat on the panel, some new members "are acting like drunken sailors with their new power."[56] During the appropriations markup for the Veterans Administration (VA) and for Housing and Urban Development (HUD), the former Appropriations subcommittee chairman Louis Stokes (D-Ohio) called the GOP spending cuts "unconscionable," "reprehensible," "appalling," and a "prescription for disaster."[57] Democrats on the Appropriations Committee even boycotted meetings to frustrate committee actions. Tom Delay (R-Tex.), majority whip and an appropriator, lauded the inclusion of pro-business policy riders in appropriations bills, saying, "Our pork is freedom. Their pork is projects."[58]

The House Ethics Committee became embroiled in partisan controversies during the 104th Congress (as did the Senate Ethics Committee over the Packwood sexual harassment case). The House Committee, unlike other standing committees, is divided evenly between Republicans and Democrats. Reminiscent of the ethics charges previously leveled by Gingrich at then Speaker James Wright (which led to Wright's resignation), House Democrats made numerous ethical charges against Gingrich.[59] Democrats also called for the appointment of an outside counsel to investigate these charges. Jim McDermott (D-Wash.), the panel's previous chair and now ranking member, severely criticized the way the committee handled the Gingrich case. Any further delay, he said, "exposes the panel and the full House to the charge of a coverup."[60] Ethics Committee chairwoman Nancy Johnson (R-Conn.) rejected McDermott's criticisms. In December 1995, a special counsel was appointed for the investigation.

On traditionally partisan committees, the level of partisan infighting increased under the Republican majority. For example, when it came time for the Ways and Means Committee to vote on a welfare reform bill, a Democrat raised a point of order (parliamentary objection) against the proposed action because he wanted to see the bill's legal language. When Chairman Bill Archer overruled the point of order, tempers quickly flared. As Archer attempted to gavel the meeting to order, Democrats raised their voices so that they could be heard over the banging of the gavel. One Republican threatened to summon the sergeant at arms. A Democrat retorted, "That would be great . . . just like Nazi Germany."[61] Subsequently, Archer and committee Democrats agreed to a new procedure for reporting out legislation.[62]

Such squabbling continued as the Ways and Means Committee's attention turned to reductions in Medicare spending, with ranking Democrat Sam Gibbons (D-Fla.) at one point yanking on the tie of Rep. Bill Thomas (R-Calif.). Indeed, in committee after committee, nerves frayed as the various portions of the Republican deficit-reduction plan were reported along near-party-line votes.

FLOOR DELIBERATIONS AND SCHEDULING

During the postelection transition, House Republicans passed some reforms aimed at opening up floor deliberations. But their key initiative in this area was a pledge to provide a more open amendment process than had characterized the Democratic House. On opening day of the 104th Congress, Rules Committee chairman Gerald Solomon said, "Speaker Gingrich has asked me to be as open and fair as we possibly can, and to reverse the fact that 70 percent of all the rules [regulating the offering of amendments] that came to the floor last year were closed or structured or restricted rules."[63] Has the new Republican majority followed through on this commitment? To a certain extent, yes.

For one thing, the GOP leadership discontinued use of "King of the Hill" rules, which they had criticized during their minority status. Under such rules, a number of substitute proposals are considered, with the last alternative getting majority support emerging as the winner. The outcome of this procedure is highly sensitive to the order of consideration, with alternatives voted on later in the process having a substantial advantage. By most accounts, the Democratic leadership exploited the strategic potential inherent in these rules to promote their policy agenda. Instead, the Republican majority has opted for "Queen of the Hill" rules, in which a succession of comprehensive alternatives are voted on. The alternative receiving the most support is considered again for final passage. With these rules, the order in which policy alternatives are considered is less directly determinative of the outcome.

More generally, House Republicans have had to balance their commitment to openness with their desire to advance an ambitious legislative agenda. Procedures that provide ample opportunities for amendment and debate also make it more difficult to process legislation in an efficient, timely, and predictable manner. This tradeoff is unavoidable on Capitol Hill, no matter which political party is in control.

The first open rule of the 104th Congress, for instance, was for legislation limiting federal unfunded mandates on state and local governments. The House began consideration of the legislation on January 20, with more than 150 amendments pending. During the first ten hours of debate, the chamber dealt with just nine of the proposals. Republicans charged, and Democrats denied, that many of the amendments were aimed at slowing action on the Contract with America rather than making substantive changes in the unfunded mandates bill. Rules Committee chairman Solomon remarked, "It looks like we're going to have to increasingly restrict rules if the Democrats don't cooperate."[64]

On January 20, the House voted to limit debate on amendments to the legislation. Ten days later, Democratic members withdrew many of their remaining proposals and allowed others to be settled by voice votes rather than more time-consuming roll calls. But the unfunded mandates bill underscored for GOP leaders the downside of an open amendment process. Consequently, House Republicans have not been reluctant to employ structured rules during the 104th Congress.

The degree to which House Republicans have reversed the Democratic practice of restrictive amendment procedures is a subject of partisan dispute. Democrats, trying to hold the GOP to their openness pledge as well as embarrass the majority, have regularly chastised Republicans for providing anything less than a completely open and unrestricted amendment process. Republicans have returned the rhetorical fire, repeatedly telling Democrats that a House minority "never had it so good." Echoing earlier Democratic charges, GOP members have periodically suggested that some Democratic amendments are not intended to improve legislation but are dilatory and aimed at foiling prompt action on Republican legislation.

Throughout the 104th Congress, Republicans and Democrats have prepared "dueling statistics" on the number of open versus restrictive rules.[65]

For instance, during the period when the House was considering the Contract with America, Republicans said that they reported open rules 72 percent of the time; Democrats claimed that the proportion was only 26 percent. The differences stemmed from how each party defined an open rule.

To balance their pledge for relatively open rules with the need to act quickly on priority measures, the Republicans have employed *time-structured rules*. Such rules establish debate limits on the entire amendment process but do not necessarily delineate the amendments to be offered. H.Res. 155, considered by the House on May 23, 1995, is an example of a time-structured rule. The resolution provided for the consideration of H.R. 1561, a bill to authorize appropriations for the State Department and various foreign assistance programs. The rule permitted two hours of general debate and a ten-hour open amendment process, including the time necessary to conduct roll-call votes. All amendments were required to be preprinted in the *Congressional Record*. After completion of the ten-hour open amendment period, additional preprinted amendments could be considered until 2:30 P.M. on May 25, at which point the amending process would cease. In addition, the rule waived the three-day availability period for committee reports, the prohibition of appropriations on a legislative bill, and several sections of the Congressional Budget Act.

Under the rules categorization previously used by House Republicans during their minority years, H.Res. 155 would have been characterized as a restrictive rule because the ten-hour time constraint implicitly limited the number of amendments to be offered. However, under the rules categorization used by House Republicans in the 104th Congress, a distinction is drawn between restrictive rules that are modified open or modified closed. With modified open rules, any member can offer a germane amendment subject to an overall time cap. Modified closed rules, in contrast, specify the amendments that can be offered or preclude amendments to parts of the bill. As Republicans note, during the 104th Congress most rules have been open or modified open. In the periodic exchanges about the openness of GOP rules, Democrats use the old Republican categorization of special rules and count modified open rules as restrictive amendment procedures.

H.Res. 155, the special rule proposed for the State Department authorization, was opposed by Lee Hamilton (D-Ind.), now ranking Democrat on the International Relations Committee. Hamilton observed that it was not unusual for one hundred amendments to be offered on a foreign aid bill and that many amendments could not be considered with a ten-hour time constraint. More generally, Hamilton argued that time-structured rules undermine the quality of congressional deliberation.

This is really not an open rule, and it should not be so described. As an institution, the Committee on Rules in the House needs a rational mechanism to ensure that major questions are debated on this bill or any other bill. That outcome depends not on how we describe the rule, open or modified, or whatever, but on whether

the Committee on Rules makes sure that there is a process for thorough consideration of all of the major issues in the bill. . . . You have a 10-hour time cap, you
throw the bill open for amendment at any point, and you create a kind of free-for-
all, making the foreign policy of the United States, under this rule, dependent on
who gets recognized first.[66]

Democrats also have argued that because the time for voting on amendments is counted against the cap, a ten-hour restriction may leave only seven
hours for offering and debating amendments. Such limits, they say, encourage dilatory tactics. Recorded votes might be called on amendments that
could pass by voice vote "in order to consume time allotted for considering
amendments."[67] On some occasions, GOP lawmakers also have been upset
with the cap because of their being foreclosed from offering amendments.

Republican leaders note that Democrats and other members should consult with their leaders in advance to identify priority amendments that need
to be offered inside the cap. David Dreier, vice chairman of the Rules Committee, acknowledged that any restrictions on debate, including time limits,
have the potential to preclude consideration of important amendments, but
he said that the leaders of the committee of jurisdiction can focus the institution on critical issues.

The [GOP] majority . . . on the Committee on Rules has reported a large number
of rules in which a time cap has been used. The reason is very simple, Mr. Speaker.
After years in the minority, during which time the 9 to 4 [Democratic] majority
structured rules to stack the deck politically for the majority, we learned how unfair structured rules can be. Time limits, I acknowledge, are not perfect. However,
it is possible with time limits for the chairman and ranking member of a bill's committee of jurisdiction to minimize the drawbacks of those time limits. They are recognized for amendments before other Members [and they can] largely set the
course of debate.[68]

Of course, some rules generate bipartisan support even when the two parties disagree on the substance of the underlying legislation. In August 1995,
for example, David Obey urged Democrats to support the rule for consideration of the Labor-HHS appropriations bill but to vote against the spending
bill itself, which he adamantly opposed. On the controversial GOP policy of
having appropriations bills rewrite laws in various policy areas, Anthony
Beilenson of California, a Rules Committee Democrat, remarked, "We have
generally been supportive of the majority's stated intention to provide open,
unrestricted rules for as many of the appropriations bills as possible, and for
its policy of providing waivers of House rules only when the authorizing
committees agree to those waivers."[69]

Partisan disagreements about the fairness or openness of floor deliberations are unlikely to be resolved on Capitol Hill. Absent agreed-upon evalua-
tive criteria, each party will continue to count, chart, and characterize rules
in a manner that corresponds to its partisan interest. But Republican and
Democratic statistics and the private comments of members and staff suggest

that the Republican majority has been somewhat more protective of minority party prerogatives on the House floor. Democrats have prefiled many more amendments than Republicans, but the percentage of prefiled amendments considered by the House (in some form) is relatively similar for both parties.[70] Definitional disputes aside, the floor amendment process in the Republican House has been generally more open than during the years leading up to the 104th Congress.

Family-Friendly Scheduling

During the postelection transition period, Speaker Gingrich also promised to make the floor schedule more predictable and family friendly, and he asked Rep. Frank Wolf (R-Va.) to chair a task force to consider scheduling reforms. The Speaker's pledge, however, quickly fell by the wayside during the hectic period when the House considered the Contract with America, and it continued to be unobserved because of the press of priority business and the controversial nature of the GOP's agenda. The large quantity of work conducted by the chamber during January through June 1995 is apparent in Table 5.2, which compares the period with the analogous time span in 1993. In 1995, activity levels in both the House and the Senate substantially exceeded the corresponding levels for 1993.

In the House, the legislative pace did not slacken after the one-hundred-day period. After March, late nights remained commonplace, and several

TABLE 5.2 Congressional Workload, January–June 1993 and 1995

	1993	1995
House		
Days in session	78	90
Hours in session	454	774
Pages in *Congressional Record*	4,409	6,699
Recorded votes	164	338
Measures introduced	3,124	2,358
Senate		
Days in session	85	108
Hours in session	587	950
Pages in *Congressional Record*	8,381	9,596
Yea-and-nay votes	192	296
Measures introduced	1,452	1,218

Source: *Roll Call,* July 13, 1995, 4.

around-the-clock sessions were conducted. "The schedule is atrocious," Wolf said. "We cannot continue to go night after night after night like this. We are frankly going at breakneck speed and that is eventually going to destroy families."[71] Indeed, 54 percent of the time between January and the August recess, the House adjourned after 9 P.M. Some younger lawmakers hinted that they might retire from the House because of the late nights, hectic pace, and stress that was placed on their families. Others worried about the capacity of members to make intelligent decisions when they are plagued by overwork and little sleep. Still others suggested kiddy sit-ins on the House floor as a way to demonstrate the need for more family friendliness.

The Speaker and other party leaders expressed sympathy about the frenetic schedule, but family-friendly scheduling clearly took a back seat to the need to move an ambitious, even path-breaking, legislative agenda. Processing that agenda "has taken a lot longer than we would have expected," GOP Conference chairman John Boehner said. Still, Wolf's advisory committee continued to survey members and staff about ways to improve the House schedule. "Maybe this body can never be truly family friendly," he wrote in a letter distributed to members. "But if we don't work at it, it can surely become even more family unfriendly."[72] The second session of the 104th Congress witnessed a slower-paced and more normal level of activity in part to accommodate the GOP freshmen's re-election efforts.

Abolition of Joint Referrals

The Republican House has implemented other reforms in the area of floor deliberations and scheduling. The most important of these is the abolition of joint referrals. Under Democratic control, entire bills often were referred simultaneously to two or more committees. But in 1995, the new Republican majority abolished joint referrals as part of an effort to reduce the turf fights that often erupted between competing chairs during the Democratic years. Entire bills can no longer be referred upon introduction to more than one committee, although other, more structured forms of multiple referral still occur frequently. Now the Speaker must designate a primary committee of jurisdiction upon initial reference of a measure. The Speaker retains significant flexibility in determining whether, when, and how long additional panels will receive legislation.[73] A fundamental objective of the primary designation is to achieve greater committee accountability for legislation.

The House parliamentarians, who refer measures on behalf of the Speaker, called this new form of multiple referral an additional initial referral. The standard parliamentary language for designating a primary committee and identifying the *additional initial referrals* is provided in the following example, involving a 1995 bill to abolish the Department of Commerce. It was sent to eleven standing committees when it was introduced on June 7, a record number of referrals for a bill in the 104th Congress.

Referred to the Committee on Commerce, and in addition to the Committees on Transportation and Infrastructure, Banking and Financial Services, International Relations, National Security, Agriculture, Ways and Means, Government Reform and Oversight, the Judiciary, Science, and Resources, for a period to be subsequently determined by the Speaker, in each case for consideration of such provisions as fall within the jurisdiction of the committee concerned.[74]

For H.R. 1756, the Commerce Committee was the primary committee of jurisdiction. The other ten panels received an additional initial referral.[75]

When the primary committee files its report, the Speaker imposes time limits for action on the other panels. For example, the Transportation and Infrastructure Committee was designated the primary committee on a pipeline safety measure, with the Commerce Committee as the additional initial panel. When Transportation reported the legislation on May 1, 1995, Commerce was given a period not ending later than June 1, 1995, to act on the bill. Otherwise, the legislation would be automatically discharged from the committee.

In general, the switch to a primary committee of referral has worked reasonably well. This certainly was the case during the Contract with America period, when the standing committees acted in concert, with direction from the leadership. Subsequent to the contract period, there was some reemergence of jurisdictional strife, but nothing compared to the committee rivalries of the Democratic House. Competition for referrals was evident on topics such as Medicare (between Commerce and Ways and Means), telecommunications (between Commerce and Judiciary), and energy and environmental research and development (between Commerce and Science). Accommodations were made in these instances to ensure that committees to which legislation has been referred on an additional initial basis are granted a reasonable amount of time for review if the primary committee reports the measure before they do.

Deliberation

According to GOP leaders, an aim of the Republican changes of 1995 was to increase the deliberative capacity of the chamber. In August 1995, Rules Committee chairman Solomon observed, "I am pleased that our Committee has been able to keep the commitment made by our Leadership and the 'Contract with America' to a more open, deliberative and representative House."[76]

Solomon and other Rules Committee Republicans did attempt to open up floor deliberations somewhat during the 104th Congress. The broader process through which congressional Republicans devised and considered the massive 1995 reconciliation bill, however, was largely beyond Solomon's control, and many Democrats and outside commentators argued that it was anything but open or fair. The nearly two-thousand-page reconciliation package, which incorporated the GOP's seven-year plan to balance the budget by the year 2002, provoked huge consternation within the Democratic ranks. These concerns were about both policy and process. The legislation was adopted after only limited committee hearings, with little open deliberation or opportunity for floor amendment, and with limited minority party involvement. The atmosphere was replete with deadlines, late nights, partisan acrimony, intraparty fights, and electoral appeals to voters. "This reconciliation process," declared Sen. Robert Byrd (D-W.V.), "has been twisted out of all recognizable shape. It has become the antithesis of solid thorough legislating."[77]

GOP lawmakers countered that the extraordinary process they used for devising the deficit-reduction legislation actually resembled the closed, partisan, and deadline-driven approach Democratic majorities had used on previous reconciliation bills. Republicans also pledged that once work on the deficit-reduction package was complete, the House and Senate would revert to a more open and deliberative decision-making process. Still, the reconciliation measure was by far the most significant legislation considered in 1995, and it must loom large in any evaluation of deliberation or openness during the first session.

More generally, throughout the year key decisions about legislation tended to be made in closed meetings without formal Democratic participation. Democrats complained that the hearings process and committee markups were too often truncated in the rush to bring legislation to the floor. Democratic aides claimed that they were frozen out of the process by their GOP counterparts. One noted, "They don't return phone calls, they give you short notice on hearings, and everything's a secret or a surprise."[78] However, such comments are remarkably similar to the kinds of complaints often made by Republican staffers during the years of Democratic control. Overall the GOP record on openness appears to be mixed.

OTHER REFORM AREAS

During the 104th Congress, important developments also occurred in the other three areas of congressional reorganization—congressional integrity, policy-driven reforms, and congressional resources and interbranch prerogatives.

Congressional Integrity

Most of the House reforms implemented in January 1995 were intended to improve public confidence in the integrity of Congress.[79] Four reforms, all included in the Contract with America, were particularly relevant: the appli-

cation of workplace laws to Congress; the independent audit of House operations; enhanced congressional "openness;" and the pledge for a floor vote
on term limits for members of Congress. As discussed in Chapter 4, the provision applying labor laws to Congress was quickly passed by the House and
Senate and signed by the president in January. Its enactment appears to have
removed congressional exemptions (Congress above the law) as a reform priority of the general public.

Audit

The independent audit of House administrative practices was conducted by
Price Waterhouse & Company, a respected national accounting firm. The results of the audit, released in July 1995, were sharply critical of the House's
administrative practices under the Democrats. At a hearing before the House
Oversight Committee, the lead auditor testified that because of shoddy
record keeping, "We are unable to provide an opinion of any sort about the
reliability of the House financial statements" from October 1993 through
December 1994. The institution's financial practices were described as
"among the weakest I've seen."[80] Among other shortcomings and possible
violations, the audit found that House financial records were kept manually;
bills were paid late or even overpaid; between twelve and twenty members
may have violated chamber regulations regarding overspending of office
funds; and there may have been 2,200 duplicate payments for travel ex-
penses. No individual violators were named. Instead, the Price Waterhouse
report emphasized the need for greater privatization of House services to increase efficiency and reduce patronage. Although the audit results were covered by the media, they did not trigger public outrage, as did the House bank
scandal of 1991–1992.

Sunshine

As part of their House rules, Republicans also adopted sunshine provisions,
which narrowed the criteria for closing committee sessions or blocking radio
and television coverage. For example, television and radio coverage of open
committee sessions is permitted as a matter of right and not by authorization
of the committee. Under the Democratic majority, most committee meetings
were open, with broadcast media allowed. There were certain exceptions,
mostly dealing with committees such as Rules, Ways and Means, and Appropriations. These exceptions were sharply criticized by the minority Republicans, who tried to generate public opposition to closed meetings. In 1993,
GOP members of the Joint Committee on the Organization of Congress offered a number of openness proposals; these provisions were included in the
Contract with America and adopted in January 1995. One result was that
the Appropriations Committee, which often had considered legislation in
closed session, now holds drafting sessions in public. The 1995 rules changes

also require committee reports accompanying legislation to include the names of lawmakers voting for and against amendments to the bill, as well as the motion to report measures on the floor.

Term Limits

The Contract with America pledged a "first-ever vote on term limits to replace career politicians with citizen legislators." This provision, titled the Citizen Legislature Act, included two distinct term limits proposals—one limiting House members to six years and senators to twelve years of service, the other limiting lawmakers in both chambers to twelve years. GOP leaders included the term limits plank in the contract because the issue taps public concerns about the basic accountability and integrity of Congress. Opinion polls show that three-quarters of Americans consistently favor term limitations for national lawmakers.

Among politicians from both parties, however, term limits are controversial. A majority of congressional Democrats oppose limiting terms. Many prominent Republican members of Congress also oppose term limits, including House majority whip Tom Delay, House Judiciary Committee chairman Henry Hyde, House Ways and Means Committee chairman Bill Archer, Senate Appropriations Committee chairman Mark Hatfield (R-Oreg.), and Senate Judiciary Committee chairman Orrin Hatch (R-Utah).

Opponents of term limits argue that the expertise of lawmakers increases with time in office and that limiting terms will shift power to staff, lobbyists, and executive branch officials. They also argue that the ballot box is sufficient to induce significant turnover. In the 104th Congress, for example, more than half the House has served less than four years. Supporters of term limits argue that citizen legislators can better understand and respond to the concerns of ordinary Americans. "The American people are better served by dentists, teachers, and football players than by career politicians," said Rep. John Linder (R-Ga.), a former dentist.[81]

At the beginning of the 104th Congress, twenty-two states had moved to limit the terms of members of Congress. On May 22, 1995, however, the U.S. Supreme Court (*U.S. Term Limits Inc.* v. *Thorton*) ruled that such state-imposed limits on congressional terms are unconstitutional because they establish restrictions on congressional service not included in the Constitution. Congressional term limits, the Court found, can be imposed only via constitutional amendment, the approach adopted in the Contract with America.

Initially, House Republican leaders intended to consider term limits on the floor in early March, but whip counts revealed that none of the term limit initiatives under discussion could win the two-thirds support required to pass a constitutional amendment. As a result, the vote was put off for three weeks while Republican leaders sought to mobilize grassroots and member support on the issue.

On March 29, using a "Queen of the Hill" procedure, the House considered and rejected four different versions of term limitations for members of Congress. First, Democratic representatives John Dingell and Pete Peterson (Fla.) offered a proposal calling for twelve-year *retroactive* limits. If ratified, the Dingell-Peterson proposal would have required the retirement of eighty-two House members in 1996. By offering the amendment, Dingell, a term limits opponent, hoped to publicize what he viewed as the hypocrisy of senior Republican backers of the limits, who would be grandfathered under the three main GOP proposals. As expected, the Dingell-Peterson alternative was soundly defeated. The second version, sponsored by Bob Inglis (R-S.C.), provided for six-year limits on House members and twelve-year limits on senators. It was defeated 316 to 114, with a majority of Democrats and Republicans voting no. Next was a proposal by Rep. Van Hilleary, a freshman Republican from Tennessee, which would have capped congressional terms at twelve years, while allowing states to impose stiffer limits. Hilleary's amendment also went down, 265 to 164.

Coming fourth was the main proposal, sponsored by Bill McCollum (R-Fla.). It limited lifetime service in each chamber to twelve years. McCollum's initiative failed to secure two-thirds support by a wide margin (227 to 204, with one "present"). Most GOP members voted for this amendment; most Democrats voted against it. In both parties, senior lawmakers were more likely to be term limit opponents. Although forty Republicans voted against the McCollum proposal, Speaker Gingrich told reporters that Democrats were to blame for the defeat of term limits. He warned, "It is coming back. We're going to talk about it all year. We're going to talk about it next year."[82] He promised to make term limits the first vote of the 105th Congress.

Following the House defeat, Senate backers of term limits brandished a letter from majority leader Dole that pledged to bring "term limits legislation to the Senate floor for consideration as early as possible in the next six months, perhaps in June."[83] With less than half the Senate backing term limits, however, the chances for passage in that chamber during the 104th Congress were minimal. Term limits supporters, such as Sens. Hank Brown (R-Colo.), Fred Thompson (R-Tenn.), and John Ashcroft (R-Mo.), still pushed for a vote, hoping to mobilize the public and force senators to go on record on the matter. In October 1995, the Senate defeated (49 to 45) a nonbinding resolution calling on the chamber to pass a term limits amendment. Then, in April 1996, a constitutional amendment on term limits was yanked from the floor, because the needed sixty votes were not there to break a filibuster against the proposal.

As mentioned, most of the GOP reforms were intended to address public concerns about the institutional integrity of Congress. The Republican reorganization did receive widespread support on editorial pages across the country, but did it significantly enhance public esteem for Congress?

Early in 1995, it seemed that public attitudes toward Congress had improved somewhat. Consider, for instance, the Gallup Poll question asking citizens whether they "approve or disapprove of the way the U.S. Congress is handling its job." In December 1994, public approval of the institution was just 23 percent. By mid-January 1995, Congress's job performance rating had increased to 33 percent, and in early February it had risen to 38 percent.[84]

The enthusiasm and optimism of Republican lawmakers at the beginning of the 104th Congress, particularly during the widely covered opening-day sessions, provided compelling images of institutional renewal on Capitol Hill. The opening-day reforms were integral to public perceptions that change was afoot in Washington. As the Republican majority began confronting the difficult policy matters on its agenda, public esteem for the institution quickly declined, falling to just 30 percent by August 1995. In short, the important institutional reforms adopted by the GOP House, particularly as they relate to congressional integrity, did not significantly alter the way people view Congress.

Policy-Driven Reforms

On the first day of the 104th Congress, the House adopted certain policy-driven reforms (base-line budgeting, the prohibition of extraneous matters in emergency spending bills, and a three-fifths requirement for tax increases). For the most part, the impact of these reforms has been symbolic. On certain occasions, they have been waived.[85] House Rules Committee chairman Gerald Solomon has already stated that he plans to rewrite the three-fifths rule for tax increases for the 105th Congress because it has not worked as intended.

In addition to these opening-day changes, three significant policy-driven reforms included in the Contract with America were considered later in the first session of the 104th Congress: legislation to curb unfunded mandates, the balanced budget amendment to the Constitution, and the line-item veto. In June 1995, the House also passed a fourth policy-driven reform, called Corrections Day, to expedite the repeal of "ambiguous, arbitrary, or ludicrous" federal regulations.

Unfunded Mandates

State and local governments long have complained about unfunded mandates—federal statutes and regulations that require state or municipal governments to take some action, but without the necessary federal funding. Although legislation to curb unfunded mandates was considered during the 103d Congress, no floor action occurred in either chamber. House Republicans included in the Contract with America a highly restrictive unfunded mandates provision, which would have prohibited new mandates and significantly rolled back existing ones.

Because the contract proposal was viewed as excessively rigid, more moderate versions were introduced in the House and Senate in January 1995. Rather than ban unfunded mandates outright, these bills required the Congressional Budget Office (CBO) to identify any new unfunded mandates over $50 million. If the CBO analysis is not conducted or a bill includes unfunded mandates over the limit, individual lawmakers can raise a point of order to block action. A separate vote would be required to override such a point of order. Sen. Pete Domenici (R-N.M.) remarked, "This is not just a procedural bill. It is the start of a fundamental redefinition of the federalism system—or, some may say, a return to the Founding Fathers' principles of federalism."[86]

Broad bipartisan support existed for rolling back unfunded mandates, at least in the abstract. But the legislation introduced by House and Senate Republicans triggered complex issues of implementation and impact. In the House, efforts to move the bill in a consensus fashion were complicated by a leadership decision to truncate committee deliberations and quickly bring the matter to the floor under an open rule. When floor consideration began in mid-January, more than 150 amendments had been submitted. Democrats, complaining that no committee hearings had been conducted, dragged out debate, insisting on time-consuming roll-call votes on the amendments. Consequently, the Republican leadership temporarily pulled the bill from the schedule on January 24 to proceed with the balanced budget amendment. Later that day, President Clinton endorsed efforts to restrict unfunded mandates.[87]

Returning to the measure, the House agreed to limit debate on amendments. House members considered, and defeated, a large number of Democratic proposals aimed at excluding specific programs from the legislation's provisions. Many of these proposals were designed to confront Republicans with difficult votes against exempting highly popular programs. Rep. Paul Kanjorski (D-Pa.), for instance, offered an amendment to exempt federal mandates requiring that states help track sex crime offenders. The Kanjorski amendment was defeated 255 to 172. On February 1, the House passed the unfunded mandates legislation by a large, bipartisan majority.

Senate action on unfunded mandates likewise was drawn out by Democratic concerns and objections. On January 19, Senator Byrd led a successful Democratic attempt to block efforts by majority leader Dole to invoke cloture. After almost sixty hours of debate and more than forty roll-call votes, the Senate passed its unfunded mandates bill on January 27 by a margin of 86 to 10. As in the House, Senate floor deliberations focused on Democratic amendments aimed at exempting a range of environmental, health, and other regulations.[88] The chambers conferenced to resolve differences between the two bills, mostly relating to the role of the courts, and President Clinton signed the House-Senate compromise on March 22. The new procedures took effect in January 1996.

Balanced Budget Amendment

Congress moved quickly on the unfunded mandates legislation in part because the issue was linked politically with efforts to pass a balanced budget amendment to the Constitution. State and local officials were concerned that the federal government might balance its budget by transferring the costs of certain federal programs to them in the form of additional unfunded mandates. However, directly incorporating language in the balanced budget amendment to restrict federal mandates was unworkable. As a result, the House and Senate first passed freestanding unfunded mandates legislation as part of an effort to reduce opposition to the balanced budget provision.[89]

The balanced budget amendment included in the Contract with America was more stringent than other versions of the proposal. The contract plank required a balanced federal budget by 2002, but unlike previous renditions, it also required a three-fifths vote in both chambers to increase taxes.[90]

With the tax provision included, the balanced budget amendment could not win the two-thirds support in the House and Senate necessary to pass a constitutional amendment. As a result, Reps. Charles Stenholm (D-Tex.) and Dan Schaefer (R-Colo.) were pushing a more politically feasible alternative, which closely resembled the constitutional amendment almost passed by the House in 1994. Orrin Hatch and Paul Simon (D-Ill.) sponsored a similar alternative, also excluding the three-fifths tax provision, in the Senate.

On January 26, 1995, the House considered the balanced budget amendment under a "Queen of the Hill" procedure. The Contract with America version, sponsored by Rep. Joe Barton (R-Tex.) and backed by the Republican leadership, was considered first and received 253 votes. Then the Schaefer-Stenholm amendment was considered, receiving 293 votes. GOP freshmen had threatened to vote against Schaefer-Stenholm if the contract language was defeated, but they relented after an intensive lobbying effort by Republican leaders.[91] Four Democratic alternatives were easily defeated. On the vote for final passage, the Schaefer-Stenholm amendment, victorious in round one, was adopted 293 to 139, providing the Republican majority with an important victory.

The full Senate began deliberations on the balanced budget amendment on January 30 and spent most of February on the issue. Early whip counts indicated approximately sixty yes votes, twenty-five no votes, and fifteen undecided.[92] GOP leaders lobbied the swing voters, focusing on Democratic lawmakers who had supported balanced budget provisions in previous years.[93] As with the unfunded mandates bill, the leading Senate opponent was Byrd, the premier parliamentary expert.

During floor debate, opponents raised a number of objections. Some Senators wanted the Social Security trust fund placed off-budget. Others sought a detailed delineation of the spending cuts necessary to achieve budgetary balance. Still others were concerned that the amendment might involve the courts in budgetary decision making. Most important, senators realized that

House passage of the balanced budget amendment had significantly raised the stakes for their own consideration of the issue. Senator Dole remarked, "We have some Senators who have voted for [the amendment] in the past thinking it was a free vote who are now shooting with real bullets."[94]

As the Senate considered amendments to the balanced budget provision in February, the list of uncommitted senators gradually narrowed. On February 8, Republican senators defeated a "right to know" amendment, offered by minority leader Thomas Daschle (D-S.D.), which would have required that Congress pass a concrete plan to balance the budget before the proposed constitutional amendment was sent to the states for ratification. An amendment offered by Harry Reid (D-Nev.), which sought to exempt the Social Security trust fund from deficit calculations, was defeated on February 14. Democrats blocked a GOP attempt to invoke cloture on February 17 but agreed that the vote on final passage would occur on February 28. President Clinton quietly lobbied Democratic senators not to support the constitutional amendment, arguing that it would lead to draconian cuts in federal spending.[95] On February 28, aware that amendment supporters were still one vote short, majority leader Dole put off the final vote, drawing strong objections from Byrd. The West Virginian claimed that Dole's move was underhanded: "This has every appearance of a sleazy, tawdry effort to win a victory at the cost of a constitutional amendment . . . to go over till tomorrow so that additional pressures can be made on some poor member in the effort to get his vote." Dole responded, "We have every right to use the rules to determine if we have the votes or if we can pick up votes, and I intend to do that."[96]

After an unsuccessful, last-minute attempt by amendment backers to secure the support of Sen. Kent Conrad (D-N.D.), the final vote was conducted on March 2 in a packed and hushed Senate chamber.[97] As expected, the balanced budget amendment fell one vote short. The final tally was 65 to 35, with Dole voting no for parliamentary reasons (by voting no, he could move to reconsider the issue in the future). The lone GOP opponent was Appropriations Committee chairman Mark Hatfield, leading to an aborted, but highly divisive, attempt within the Senate Republican Conference to strip him of his committee chairmanship (see "Senate Changes" later in this chapter).

Line-Item Veto

The Contract with America recommended that the president be given the power to veto portions of spending bills passed by Congress (rather than having to sign or reject bills in their entirety). The contract provision was referred to as a line-item veto but was actually something called *enhanced rescission,* an idea promoted by Gerald Solomon and others during the 103d Congress.

Under enhanced rescission, the president can target any portion of an appropriations measure or the accompanying report language for reduction or elimination. A two-thirds vote in each chamber (the vote specified in the Constitution to override vetoes) is required to override the president's proposed rescission. Supporters of enhanced rescission argued that it would enable the president to cut congressional pork by targeting the wasteful projects buried in appropriations bills. Opponents countered that enhanced rescission would shift the power of the purse from the legislative to the executive branch. After accelerated committee action and two days of floor consideration, the House passed the enhanced rescission bill on February 6, 1995, by a vote of 294 to 134.

Senate consideration of the line-item veto was far more difficult. As in the House, most Democrats in the Senate opposed the enhanced rescission measure, which was sponsored by John McCain (R-Ariz.). GOP moderates and Appropriations Committee members at first objected to enhanced rescission, preferring a proposal for *expedited rescission* introduced by Sens. Pete Domenici and James Exon (D-Nebr.), chairman and ranking minority member, respectively, of the Senate Budget Committee. The Domenici-Exon proposal resembled the initiative passed by the House (and blocked in the Senate) during the 103d Congress. (From Chapter 3, recall that under expedited rescission, Congress must act on presidential rescission requests, but both chambers still must adopt them by a majority vote.)

Early in the 104th Congress, it appeared that enhanced rescission would not draw the sixty Senate votes necessary to end a filibuster by Robert Byrd, once again the chief opponent of a Contract with America reform. It also was clear that conservative Republicans strongly opposed Domenici's expedited rescission proposal, arguing that it was a mere fig leaf of reform. Indeed, a March endorsement of the proposal by Byrd was widely viewed as its "kiss of death."[98]

Confronted with sharp intraparty divisions, Republican senators initially adopted a third approach to the line-item veto called *separate enrollment*. A Reagan era idea, separate enrollment provides that after passage, appropriations bills would be divided by a legislative clerk into a large number of separate bills, which in turn would be forwarded to the president as freestanding measures. The president could sign or veto, but not reduce, the individual measures, which Byrd derisively called "billets" and "lawlets."[99] Critics charged that separate enrollment would create a logistical nightmare, as the thirteen appropriations bills would be divided into as many as ten thousand smaller measures. Still, the proposal passed the Senate on March 23, 1995, by a wide margin, with even supporters admitting it had serious problems.

The fundamentally different approaches to the line-item veto issue adopted by the House and Senate ensured that reconciling the two versions would be extremely difficult. Senate majority leader Dole broke the bicameral stalemate by accepting the House's plan for enhanced rescissions in

March 1996, after he had sewn up the GOP presidential nomination. The GOP leader, said pundits, wanted a legislative accomplishment to present to the voters. Asked to explain the sudden breakthrough after months of House-Senate bickering, Senator John McCain (R-Ariz.) replied, "Senator Dole said he wanted it done."[100] The Senate's foremost opponent of this Contract item, Senator Byrd, announced that he would not filibuster the legislation, which was adopted by the Senate on March 27 by a 69–31 margin. On April 9, President Clinton signed the enhanced rescission bill into law. Under a compromise agreed to by Dole and Clinton, the bill would not take effect until January 1, 1997, and would expire in the year 2005.

Corrections Day

An additional reform development, the advent of Corrections Day, was advocated by the Speaker in late January 1995, and it passed the House on June 20 by a vote of 236 to 191. Under the new procedure, the House can consider bills to repeal overburdensome laws and regulations through a streamlined process. To make it on to the Corrections Calendar, a regulatory reform measure must first be adopted by the committees of jurisdiction. Then, after the Speaker consults with the minority leader, a proposed regulatory or statutory correction can be brought up on the floor on the second and fourth Tuesdays of the month for expedited consideration. A three-fifths vote is required for adoption.

The Corrections Day reform provides a procedural means for the Republicans to promote their regulatory reform agenda and also gives the party an opportunity to focus public attention on examples of what Speaker Gingrich calls "legal, but silly," regulations. Opponents of the procedure have asked why the standard legislative process is not sufficient for such initiatives and also warn that special interests might attempt to use Corrections Day to repeal regulations that they claim are unreasonable but that in fact serve worthwhile purposes. So far, the Corrections Calendar seems to be working quite well. "I was skeptical at first," said Rep. Henry Waxman (D-Calif.), "but it has been a good procedure."[101]

Congressional Resources and Interbranch Prerogatives

Negative public opinion about Congress, combined with the overall budgetary environment of fiscal austerity, continued to provide incentives for House members and senators to streamline congressional operations during the 104th Congress.[102] In February 1995, for example, the House cut the official mailing allowance of lawmakers (the frank) by one-third. In March, the chamber reduced committee funding levels by 30 percent relative to the 103d Congress. And three months later, representatives privatized their mail and printing operations.

Republican leaders were actively involved in the streamlining process. Throughout the 104th Congress, Rep. Jim Nussle (R-Iowa), who had been appointed by Speaker Gingrich to oversee the transition to GOP management, continued to push for a complete overhaul of the House's administrative operations. When the House Oversight Committee did not move rapidly enough toward privatizing certain functions, Nussle warned Chairman Bill Thomas that the leadership might eliminate his panel. GOP leaders also threatened to shift responsibility for revamping House operations to the Appropriations Committee unless Thomas picked up the reform pace.

The primary vehicle for funding Congress, the legislative branch appropriations bill, was passed in September 1995 and featured a $200 million spending cut relative to fiscal year 1995. Among other changes, the measure abolished the Office of Technology Assessment, a congressional agency that provided the legislative branch with information about science policy. (Another appropriations bill also included a pay freeze for House members and senators.) Although President Clinton supported the content of the legislative branch appropriations bill, he vetoed it on October 3, mostly as a symbolic gesture. At the time, only one other appropriations measure had reached the president's desk, and he argued that Congress should not fund its own operations before passing more of the spending bills for the rest of the federal government. Six weeks later, Clinton signed the legislative branch funding bill.

Lawmakers in both chambers continue to focus on slashing and otherwise overhauling the resources available to lawmakers and to the legislative branch. For example, Congress eliminated or consolidated various legislative services, reduced funding for the General Accounting Office and other legislative entities, cut expenditures for committee staffing and congressional printing, and looked to privatize many congressional services. This trend likely will continue throughout the 1990s because voters still view Congress as bloated, wasteful, and inefficient.

SENATE CHANGES

During the 1980s and 1990s, calls for comprehensive congressional reform have been less common in the Senate than in the House. Still, partisan and other concerns did create incentives for senators to consider certain procedural and structural reforms during the 104th Congress.

First, following the 1994 elections, incoming majority leader Bob Dole named a GOP working group headed by Pete Domenici and Connie Mack (R-Fla.) to explore reform options. This GOP group released its reform agenda on January 23, 1995. The proposals, as noted by Domenici, who served as Senate vice chairman of the 1993 Joint Committee on the Organization of Congress, were based on the recommendations of that joint reform panel.[103] Although the Domenici-Mack plan was not brought to the floor, several components were acted on separately. For example, some panels cut back on their subcommittees, committee operating budgets were slashed by 15 percent, and committee staff was reduced by 20 percent.

Second, and more important, on July 19, 1995, Senate Republicans adopted important changes to their GOP Conference rules. These changes have potentially significant implications for the distribution of power among party leaders, committee leaders, and the Republican rank and file, and they parallel reforms ratified six months earlier by the House Republican Conference. The Senate reforms, aimed at making Republican committee leaders more accountable to their leadership and the full GOP Conference, quickly drew support because a cohesive conservative majority of the conference was concerned that Republican committee leaders, many of them party moderates, might not aggressively promote the policy agenda of the conservative-oriented conference majority. Thus, partisan rationales largely were behind the Senate GOP rules changes.

As a more informal, collegial, and tradition-dominated institution, the Senate hews more closely to seniority in the selection of committee leaders than does the House. Extraordinary circumstances are necessary to induce members to consider major changes in the internal distribution of power. The pivotal event was the vote of Appropriations Committee chairman Mark Hatfield against the balanced budget amendment to the Constitution. As mentioned, Hatfield was the only Senate Republican to oppose the measure, a keystone of the House and Senate GOP agendas. The proposal lost by a single vote. Conservative junior Republicans asked why Hatfield should be allowed to head the major spending committee in the Senate after derailing the balanced budget amendment. They were, of course, aware of the steps Speaker Gingrich had taken to ensure the party loyalty of House chairs.

Following the March 1995 balanced budget vote, Sens. Rick Santorum (R-Pa.), and Connie Mack sparked an effort within the Republican Conference to strip Hatfield of his chairmanship. GOP senators were deeply divided over the question, with members such as Robert Packwood of Oregon and Don Nickles of Oklahoma supporting Hatfield's retention. After majority leader Dole decided that the GOP Conference would not vote on the matter, Sens. Larry Craig of Idaho and Fred Thompson proposed that the conference explore how party loyalty among committee leaders might be enhanced. To diffuse the controversy, Dole created a conference task force, the Leadership Working Group, to consider the issue and appointed Mack as leader. The Floridian recruited the other members of the task force, which included Santorum, Craig, Thompson, Jon Kyl of Arizona, majority whip Trent Lott of Mississippi, and Hatfield backers Nickles and Packwood. Worth noting is that these senators were primarily former House members with close ties to Gingrich.

In early May, the working group released a reform plan that included, among other proposals, term limits for committee leaders, a provision giving the Republican leader limited authority to fill vacancies on top committees, the establishment (by a three-fourths vote) of a Senate GOP legislative agenda at the beginning of each Congress, and a provision that the Republican leader nominate each committee leader for confirmation by the full GOP Conference. Most of the recommendations were characterized as "freshmen/sophomore proposals," indicating that the momentum for change was largely coming from junior members.

Many viewed the reform plan as a bold attempt to make Senate committee chairs more accountable to the party rank and file and to bolster the authority of the Republican leader, thus tracking the direction of institutional reform adopted by the House GOP. Consider the proposed legislative agenda. A task force briefing paper described the purpose of the idea as threefold: "To provide a forum and focused discussion on the fundamental principles and priorities of the Conference. To establish direction, goals and a plan of action for the Conference and leadership in the coming Congress. To communicate these goals and principles to the public." Even if the legislative agenda was accepted by three-fourths of the conference, recalcitrant members would not be bound by the decision. However, the vote on the agenda would occur *before* the selection of committee chairs and other leaders by the conference. Some moderate Republicans, such as Environment and Public Works Committee chairman John Chafee of Rhode Island, were concerned that the vote on the legislative agenda might function as a litmus test for the nomination and confirmation of Republican committee leaders. Chafee commented, "To force us all to walk in lockstep is bad for the party." In contrast to a "big tent" approach to developing a party program, he said, "this is jamming us into a pup tent."[104]

As the working group's recommendations circulated among Senate GOP members and staff, the nature of the response varied along lines of seniority and ideology. As a group, the Republican freshmen agreed to the package on May 4.[105] The eleven first-year senators, along with six sophomore members, sent Dole a letter requesting his support for the Mack initiative: "The fact that our conference is debating these proposals is a symbol of our party's success. . . . Had we not enjoyed such a sweeping victory last fall, we in particular understand that these reforms might not be timely."[106] In addition to Chafee, however, a number of other senior and/or moderate Republicans expressed reservations about the plan, including Domenici, Rules Committee chairman Ted Stevens of Alaska (he now heads Governmental Affairs), Banking Committee chairman Al D'Amato of New York, and Jim Jeffords of Vermont.[107]

Numerous meetings about the Mack proposals occurred in June, with support for the plan mounting steadily. After a leadership meeting about the reforms on July 12, the full Republican Conference met to formally consider the package on July 19.[108] A modified version of the Mack plan was adopted.

The GOP Conference reforms are listed in Table 5.3. The terms of Republican committee leaders would be limited to six years as chair and six years as ranking minority member. However, over the objections of the freshmen, the

TABLE 5.3 Senate Republican Conference Changes

- Limit terms of committee chairs and ranking minority members to six years
- Limit terms of all GOP party leaders, except majority leader and president pro tempore, to six years
- Establish a Republican legislative agenda at the beginning of each Congress, with passage requiring a three-fourths vote
- Provide that Senators leaving a committee and then returning may not reclaim their old seniority
- Allow Republican members of a committee to select the chair by secret ballot, to be followed by a secret ballot vote in the Republican Conference
- Require indicted members to relinquish committee leadership positions
- Limit members to no more than one full or subcommittee chairmanship, except on Appropriations

---

original term limits proposal was altered so that it would not begin to take effect until 1997. The proposed legislative agenda passed without change, over the objections of party moderates. The proposal that the Republican leader nominate committee leaders failed in favor of a Domenici substitute providing that committee leaders be selected, by secret ballot, by GOP members of the panel, to be followed by a secret vote in the conference.[109] Also passing was a modified version of a Chafee amendment to limit the terms of party leaders to six years (the Republican leader and president pro tempore were excepted).[110] A few weeks later, the conference also adopted a rule prohibiting a full committee chair from heading any subcommittees (except on appropriations) but dropped the proposal extending the Republican leader's committee appointment powers.

After the meeting, Mack remarked, "I think we have accomplished a great deal here today."[111] Although substantial alterations were made in the original task force plan, significant changes were adopted, particularly the party legislative agenda and term limits for committee chairs and some party leaders. As changes to GOP Conference procedures, the reforms do not require action by the full Senate, and most will take effect at the beginning of the 105th Congress. These reforms could make Republican committee leaders more accountable to the conference as a whole. In addition, as Mack stated, they have the effect of spreading the action to junior senators, so that they "don't have to wait until they've been here 18 years to play a role."[112]

Compared to the House, however, the pace and degree of institutional change, as it dealt with the internal distribution of power, was far less pronounced in the Senate. The Senate grants enormous parliamentary powers to all its members. One senator, a small group of senators, or members of the minority party have an arsenal of procedural weapons, especially the filibuster and the right to offer an unlimited number of floor amendments, to stymie action on substantive and procedural issues. Plus, any reform that seeks to amend the Senate's rules requires sixty-seven votes, rather than the usual sixty, to shut down a filibuster against the proposed revision.

The ultimate consequence is that it is much harder in the Senate than in the House to adopt institutional reforms. Either there must be an overwhelming consensus for change or a two-thirds supermajority of senators must be committed to the revision. In January 1995, for instance, two Senate Democrats, Tom Harkin and Joseph Lieberman, tried unsuccessfully for two days to reform the filibuster rule. Their proposal was overwhelmingly rejected by a bipartisan coalition of senators who, for all the complaints about extended debate as an overused dilatory tactic, prefer things as they are.

More generally, Republicans were in the majority in the Senate from 1981 to 1987, alleviating the frustrations of long-term minority status. The Senate also is more informal than the highly structured House, reducing the potential gains from altering the chamber's internal organization. Because of their staggered six-year terms, two-thirds of the Senate was not up for reelection in 1994 and thus had no electoral connection (even indirect) with the reforms included in the Contract with America. Whereas the House moved quickly to pass the contract items, the Senate defeated, significantly amended, or delayed consideration of most of them. Although Senate Republicans adopted some potentially important party reforms in 1995, institutional continuity, rather than change, mostly characterized the chamber during the remarkable 104th Congress.

ORGANIZATIONAL RATIONALES

The ambitious policy agenda advanced by the House Republican majority triggered intense partisan, interchamber, and interbranch conflict during the 104th Congress. GOP lawmakers soon acknowledged that their revolution might not generate fundamental policy changes—at least not in the short term. However, the internal operations of Congress, particularly of the House, were altered significantly in January 1995. The process of change continued that year, with the same incentives that shaped the House transition continuing to influence the actions of reform-minded lawmakers.

Partisan rationales for legislative organization are critical for understanding institutional developments in the 104th Congress. During the first session, the House more closely approximated party government than has either chamber for many decades. And Newt Gingrich emerged as the most powerful congressional leader in a generation, perhaps since the turn of the twentieth century. The remarkable policy agreement within the majority party, combined with the scope and ambition of the GOP legislative program, led

House Republicans to support, even encourage, the aggrandizement of the Speaker's role. Such developments also resonated with Gingrich's personal power agenda. The magnitude of the Speaker's impact was partially due to Gingrich's enduring quest for influence.

Even more than expected, the importance and operating discretion of the House standing committees declined during the 104th Congress, as legislative responsibilities shifted to the leadership, a host of informal task forces, and the large and aggressive GOP freshman class. Some committee chairs complained. "Being a chairman in the Newt Congress means not being in the room when the deals are done," lamented one GOP member.[113] But the personal power agendas of Republican committee leaders were dominated by rank-and-file Republicans who wanted to center power in the leadership and in the Republican Conference as a whole. Although certain outside constituencies, such as agricultural groups, raised concerns about the reduced role of the standing committees, clientele factors also were overshadowed by partisan imperatives.

To a certain extent, House Republicans followed through on their pledge to allow more open amendment procedures on the floor. But the scope of the GOP agenda and the practical exigencies of legislating led the new majority to adopt time-structured rules that effectively limit debate. Throughout the mid-1990s, key decisions on major bills were made in private by Republican leaders rather than openly, with minority party participation, in the primary committees of jurisdiction. Minority Democratic participation in many conference committees also was circumscribed.

During the 104th Congress, the House also considered a number of significant changes in the other areas of reorganization. Here, partisan factors and public opinion help explain the outcome. The major proposals tended to be from the Contract with America (for example, unfunded mandates) or closely related to the issues raised in the contract (for instance, Corrections Day). Responding to partisan-electoral incentives, GOP lawmakers embraced organizational initiatives that they believed would resonate with change-oriented voters and thus improve their party's (and their own) showing at the polls.

In the 104th Congress, Senate rules and the presence of a pivotal coalition of GOP moderates mostly delayed, altered, or blocked passage of the various contract items, which had been quickly adopted in the other chamber. Senate Democrats, unlike their House counterparts, also possess enormous parliamentary powers, such as the filibuster, to frustrate action on the GOP initiatives. But selected organizational changes still occurred in the Senate.

Compared to the 104th House, the incentives for senators to alter fundamentally their chamber's internal distribution of power were less pronounced. All senators have important procedural prerogatives, and significantly centralizing authority in that chamber would be contrary to the personal power agendas of individual members, chamber rules, and many decades of informal custom. The two-thirds requirement for invoking cloture on Senate rules changes means that a broad or overwhelming consensus is necessary for revising key aspects of chamber procedure. And the Senate has long been less partisan (although interparty rancor has recently increased) and less committee centered than the more structured House.

However, as a response to Mark Hatfield's defection on the balanced budget amendment vote, a group of conservative and mostly junior senators, featuring former GOP House members close to Speaker Gingrich, developed a slate of reforms aimed at increasing the power of the Republican leader and making the committee chairs (many of them moderates) more accountable to the full GOP Conference. Though constituting a remarkable development for the highly individualistic Senate, these proposals did not go as far as the related House changes. In the Senate, partisan incentives for an empowered leadership were more effectively tempered by the personal power agendas of individual committee chairs such as John Chafee and Pete Domenici. Such is the nature of the contemporary Senate, where procedure and tradition inhibit a major centralization of power. Absent fundamental change, it is difficult to imagine Gingrich's leadership style transplanted to the Senate.

As mentioned, public opinion and partisan concerns were key factors behind House changes in the areas of congressional integrity, policy-driven reforms, and congressional resources. In these reform areas, the Senate responded to many of the same forces as did the House. Although the balanced budget amendment failed to pass the Senate by a single vote, the chamber did adopt proposals dealing with unfunded mandates, the line-item veto, staffing and funding cuts for the legislative branch, and the application of laws to Congress. For both chambers, then, the 104th Congress has been an important period in the institutional development of the legislative branch. And most of the changes should be viewed through the lens of the political party.

Notes

1. *Congressional Record,* January 4, 1995, H4.

2. Barabara Sinclair, *Legislators, Leaders, and Lawmaking* (Baltimore: Johns Hopkins University Press, 1995), p. 5.

3. John M. Barry, *The Ambition and the Power* (New York: Penguin Books, 1989), p. 243.

4. *Newsweek,* January 16, 1995, 17.

5. On the presidential tactic of "going public," consult Samuel Kernell, *Going Public: New Strategies of Presidential Leadership* (Washington, D.C.: Congressional Quarterly, 1986). For an application to House majority leadership, see Sinclair, *Legislators.*

6. Michael Weisskopf and David Maraniss, "Republican Leaders Win Battle by Defining Terms of Combat," *Washington Post,* October 29, 1995, A26.

7. David S. Broder, "At 6 Months, House GOP Juggernaut Still Cohesive," *Washington Post,* July 17, 1995, A12.

8. David S. Cloud, "Speaker Wants His Platform to Rival the Presidency," *Congressional Quarterly Weekly Report,* February 4, 1995, 333.

9. Marcia Gelbart, "Gingrich Redefines Role as Speaker," *The Hill,* February 28, 1996, 1.

10. Thomas Rosentiel, "Why Newt Is No Joke," *Newsweek,* April 10, 1995, 27.

11. Gabriel Kahn, "Hyde Battles Away on Judiciary Panel," *Roll Call,* February 20, 1995, 15.

12. Jackie Koszczuk, "Gingrich Puts More Power into Speaker's Hands," *Congressional Quarterly Weekly Report,* October 7, 1995, 3052.

13. Ibid., p. 3049.

14. *Newsweek,* April 10, 1995, 27.

15. *Congressional Record,* July 13, 1995, H6993.

16. Koszczuk, "Gingrich Puts More Power," 3052.

17. Walter Pincus, "Centralized Republican Power House," *Washington Post,* September 6, 1995, A19.

18. Ibid.

19. Jennifer Senior, "Gingrich Immerses Self in Key Committees," *The Hill,* March 1, 1995, 3.

20. Glenn R. Simpson, "Dingell Warns a Joint Referral on Health 'Recipe for Disaster.'" *Roll Call,* October 14, 1993, 1. See Haynes Johnson and David S. Broder, *The System* (Boston: Little Brown, 1996).

21. *Washington Times,* July 25, 1995, A6.

22. Marilyn Werber Serafini, "Who's in Charge Here?" *National Journal,* July 1, 1995, 1711.

23. Alissa J. Rubin, "Spadework on Medicare Pays Off for GOP," *Congressional Quarterly Weekly Report,* September 23, 1995, 2895.

24. Spencer Rich, "AMA, Internists, Private Insurers Big Winners Under GOP Medicare Bill," *Washington Post,* October 15, 1995, A12.

25. Eric Pianin and John E. Yang, "House Passes Medicare Reform Bill," *Washington Post,* October 20, 1995, A4.

26. *National Journal's Congress Daily/AM,* July 25, 1995, 6.

27. Stephen Barr, "Cuts Frustrate OSHA Plans to Improve Worker Safety," *Washington Post,* February 19, 1996, A1.

28. Dan Carney, "As Hostilities Rage on the Hill, Partisan-Vote Rate Soars," *Congressional Quarterly Weekly Report,* January 27, 1996, 199.

29. Derived from a compilation of the votes by *Congressional Quarterly.* See *Congressional Quarterly Weekly Report,* April 8, 1995, 1006.

30. Michael Weisskopf and David Maraniss, "In a Moment of Crisis, the Speaker Persuades," *Washington Post,* August 13, 1995, A8.

31. Lloyd Grove, "Hard-Boiled Eggs, No Waffles, No Pork," *Washington Post,* September 27, 1995, B10.

32. Donna Cassata, "GOP Leaders Walk a Fine Line to Keep Freshmen on Board," *Congressional Quarterly Weekly Report,* October 14, 1995, 3122.

33. Gabriel Kahn, "Wither the Aggies?" *Roll Call,* October 2, 1995, 20.

34. David Hosansky, "Panel Rejects Farm Overhaul in a Rebuke to Leadership," *Congressional Quarterly Weekly Report,* September 23, 1995, 2875.

35. David Maraniss and Michael Weisskopf, "As Time Ebbs, Futility of Talks Starts to Dawn," *Washington Post,* January 21, 1996, A17.

36. Gelbart, "Gingrich Redefines role," 1.

37. Kenneth A. Shepsle and Barry R. Weingast, "The Institutional Foundations of Committee Power," *American Political Science Review,* 81 (1987), 85–105; Kenneth A. Shepsle, Barry R. Weingast, and Keith Krehbiel, "Why Are Congressional Committees Powerful?" *American Political Science Review,* 81 (1987), 929–45. See also Steven S. Smith, "An Essay on Sequence, Position, Goals, and Committee Power," *Legislative Studies Quarterly,* 9 (1988), 151–77. More generally, consult Lawrence D. Longley and Walter J. Oleszek, *Bicameral Politics* (New Haven: Yale University Press, 1989).

38. Sinclair *Legislators,* pp. 193–97.

39. Gabriel Kahn, "It's Appropriators vs. Rest of GOP," *Roll Call,* October 5, 1995, 22. Republican leaders also viewed the House-Senate compromise on the Defense Department appropriations bill as a lost cause on the House floor.

40. Gabriel Kahn, "Turf Fights Absent in the First 100 Days, but Will Jurisdictional Comity End?" *Roll Call,* April 24, 1995, 20.

41. George Hager, "As They Cut, Appropriators Add a Stiff Dose of Policy," *Congressional Quarterly Weekly Report,* July 29, 1995, 2245–46.

42. Barbara Sinclair, *Majority Leadership in the U.S. House* (Baltimore: Johns Hopkins University Press, 1983), chap. 5.

43. Deborah Kalb, "Government by Task Force: The Gingrich Model," *The Hill,* February 22, 1995, 3.

44. They include Immigration Reform, Privatization, Fire Arms, California, Health, Transportation Fund, Budget, District of Columbia, Cameras in the House, Equal Opportunity, Disabilities, Committee Review, and Entertainment.

45. Rod Dreier, "Sonny Might Share Insights on Entertainment with Newt," *Washington Times,* March 16, 1995, A10.

46. William Claiborne, "Californians Redesign the Pork Barrel," *Washington Post,* March 5, 1995, A23.

47. Kalb, "Government by Task Force," 3.

48. *National Journal's Congress Daily/AM,* May 11, 1995, 4.

49. *National Journal,* April 22, 1995, 974.

50. Marcia Gelbart, "House Task Forces Find Power Fading," *The Hill,* March 6, 1996, 1.

51. "Permission to No. 2," *Washington Times,* February 27, 1995, A7.

52. Gabriel Kahn, "Life Under New Rules Causes Floor Headache," *Roll Call,* May 18, 1995, 3.

53. Gabriel Kahn, "GOP to Rethink Proxy Voting Ban," *Roll Call,* June 26, 1995, 1.

54. Ibid., p. 30.

55. Richard F. Fenno, *Congressmen in Committees* (Boston: Little, Brown, 1973), esp. chaps. 2, 4.

56. *USA Today,* July 27, 1995, 9A.

57. George Hager, "VA-HUD Panel's 'Most Difficult' Markup," *Congressional Quarterly Weekly Report,* February 25, 1995, 597.

58. David Rogers, "GOP Steps Up Efforts to Cut Funding for U.S. Agencies Opposed by Its Allies," *Wall Street Journal,* July 13, 1995, A12.

59. Most of the ethics charges against Gingrich were dismissed on December 6, 1995. The panel found that the Speaker had committed three rules violations but recommended no punishment. In 1996 the special counsel's work continues.

60. *National Journal's Congress Daily/AM,* July 28, 1995, 3.

61. Alissa Rubin, "Partisan Bickering Reaches Committee Level," *CQ's Congressional Monitor,* March 6, 1995, 7.

62. *National Journal's Congress Daily/AM,* March 7, 1995, 1.

63. *Congressional Record,* January 4, 1995, H12.

64. Jonathan Salant, "Under Open Rules, Discord Rules," *Congressional Quarterly Weekly Report,* January 28, 1995, 277.

65. See, for example, *Congressional Record,* May 23, 1995, H5390–92.

66. Ibid., p. H5394.

67. *Congressional Record,* February 27, 1995, H2235.

68. *Congressional Record,* May 23, 1995, H5395. In addition to different categorization schemes, partisan differences about the relative fairness of special rules in the 104th Congress also occurred because the two parties base their calculations on somewhat different samples. Republicans, for instance, included three noncontroversial bills brought to the floor with open rules in their statistics for the contract period. But Democrats deleted those three items from their sample, arguing that the GOP granted the bills open rules solely to pad their numbers. According to the Democrats, the three bills should have been considered under suspension of the rules (an expedited procedure for generally noncontroversial measures).

69. *Congressional Record,* July 21, 1995, H7386.

70. According to one count, from January through June 1995, Democrats presubmitted 556 amendments in the *Congressional Record,* of which 194 (or 34.9 percent) were considered in some form by the full House. In contrast, Republicans presubmitted 270 amendments, of which 91 (or 33.7 percent) were considered in some form on the floor. Clearly, these data are more suggestive than they are conclusive. Republicans shaped the base bills and thus may have had less need to offer floor amendments. In addition, these data do not contain any information about the relative importance

of different amendments. We thank Sam Ozeck for collecting and analyzing the amending data.

71. *CQ's Congressional Monitor,* July 24, 1995.

72. Jerry Gray, "Late Hours Draw Families to Floor," *New York Times,* August 3, 1995, B8.

73. The *primary* designation is determined by the House parliamentarians, who focus on "the weight of the bill."

74. *Congressional Record,* June 7, 1995, H5690.

75. The new referral language differs subtly from the language of joint and sequential referrals used previously. First, a primary committee of jurisdiction is listed. That the panels receiving additional referrals can consider only items falling within their jurisdictions is declared explicitly. And the additional referrals are subject to time constraints to be determined subsequently by the Speaker. The spirit of the new procedure is that the Speaker will not allow these additional referrals to drag on indefinitely—a common occurrence with joint and sequential referrals during the years of Democratic control. Although additional initial referrals resemble sequential referrals, there are significant differences as well. Most important, there is no requirement that the primary committee of jurisdiction report a bill before the additional panels can proceed, which is the case with sequential referrals.

76. Press release, House Committee on Rules, August 31, 1995.

77. *Congressional Record,* November 3, 1995, S16695.

78. Jamie Stiehm, "House Democratic Aides Resent GOP Treatment," *The Hill,* February 14, 1996, 1.

79. During the 104th Congress, the House and Senate also considered major initiatives in the areas of lobbying reform and campaign finance reform, which had implications for public perceptions of congressional integrity. Given our focus on the internal operations of Congress, these topics are not explored in this book.

80. Timothy J. Burger, "After Audit, IG to Probe Violations," *Roll Call,* July 20, 1995, 1, 14.

81. Benjamin Sheffner, "Term Limits' Day of Reckoning," *Roll Call,* March 30, 1995, 20.

82. Jennifer Babson, "House Rejects Term Limits; GOP Blames Democrats," *Congressional Quarterly Weekly Report,* April 1, 1995, 918.

83. Benjamin Sheffner, "Term Limits: What Next?" *Roll Call,* April 3, 1995, 22.

84. Data are drawn from various issues of the *Gallup Monthly.*

85. When concerns were raised in October 1995 that certain provisions in the GOP Medicare reform plan might be construed as tax increases, the special rule guiding floor deliberations on the legislation waived the three-fifths provision.

86. David Hosansky, "Mandate Bill Is More Moderate Than Proposal in 'Contract,'" *Congressional Quarterly Weekly Report,* January 7, 1995, 40.

87. David Hosansky, "Chipping Away at Opposition, Senate Passes Mandates Bill," *Congressional Quarterly Weekly Report,* January 28, 1995, 276.

88. Ibid.

89. Andrew Taylor, "Rejuvenated Budget Amendment Must Clear a Few Obstacles," *Congressional Quarterly Weekly Report,* January 7, 1995, 34.

90. More precisely, the contract required a balanced federal budget by 2002 or two years after state ratification, whichever came later.

91. Michael Wines, "House Approves Bill to Mandate Balanced Budget," *New York Times,* January 27, 1995, A1.

92. "Counting Senatorial Heads," *Congressional Quarterly Weekly Report,* February 4, 1995, 357.

93. Michael Wines, "Budget Amendment Slipping Among Senate Swing Votes," *New York Times,* February 28, 1995, A1.

94. Andrew Taylor, "Budget Amendment's Fate Hinges on a Handful of Democrats," *Congressional Quarterly Weekly Report,* February 4, 1995, 358.

95. Michael Wines, "Republicans Postpone a Balanced-Budget Vote," *New York Times,* March 1, 1995, A16.

96. *Congressional Record,* February 28, 1995, S3304.

97. Wines, "Republicans Postpone," A16.

98. Andrew Taylor, "Faced with Impasse, GOP Offers Line-Item Veto Compromise," *Congressional Quarterly Weekly Report,* March 11, 1995, 743.

99. Andrew Taylor, "Line-Item Veto Compromise Easily Passes Senate," *Congressional Quarterly Weekly Report,* March 25, 1995, 856.

100. Jerry Gray, "A Deal Is Reached on Line-Item Veto with Dole's Help," *New York Times,* March 15, 1996, A1.

101. *National Journal's Congress Daily/AM,* December 11, 1995, 5.

102. In the area of interbranch prerogatives, in June 1995 House Republican leaders attempted to pass an amendment to the State Department authorization bill that would have repealed the controversial War Powers Resolution. More than forty Republicans broke with their leadership, however, and the proposed repeal lost 217 to 201.

103. Included were proposals to reduce the number of subcommittees, clamp down on excessive committee assignments, curtail proxy voting in committee, cut staff resources, implement a two-year budget and appropriations process, and impose a two-hour limit for debate on motions to bring up legislation on the Senate floor.

104. Helen Dewar, "GOP Senators Consider Term Limits for Leadership," *Washington Post,* June 9, 1995, A12.

105. Mary Jacoby, "Now Senate Chairs Face Term Limits," *Roll Call,* May 8, 1995, 43.

106. "Aftershocks," *Roll Call,* May 25, 1995, 34.

107. Mary Jacoby, "Mack's Package for an Overhaul of Senate Rules Gaining Steam," 22.

108. "Aftershocks," *Roll Call,* July 6, 1995, 3.

109. Mary Jacoby, "Senate Republicans Approve Term Limits of Six Years for Their Committee Chairs," *Roll Call,* July 20, 1995, 22.

110. Ibid.

111. Helen Dewar, "Senate Republicans Put a Lid on Seniority by Limiting Terms of Chairmen," *Washington Post,* July 20, 1995, A25.

112. Paul Gigot, "Mack Uses Knife on Old Senate Order," *Wall Street Journal,* July 14, 1995, A12.

113. Charles Cook, "Lack of Leadership, Followership Produces House GOP Paralysis," *Roll Call,* March 11, 1996, 6.

6

Conclusions

I N APRIL 1996, congressional Republicans and President Bill Clinton agreed on legislation to fund the federal government through the remainder of the fiscal year, temporarily halting what had become an epic political struggle over the nation's budgetary and policy priorities. A seven-year plan to balance the federal budget proved to be elusive, but substantial progress was made in controlling discretionary expenditures. House Appropriations Committee chairman Robert Livingston (R-La.) observed, "For the first time in contemporary history, there is more substance in the rhetoric about cutting back the cost of government." Or, as House Budget chairman John Kasich (R-Ohio) put it, "There's no one running around here talking about creating new federal programs."[1]

During the spring of 1996, progress also occurred on certain other GOP initiatives, such as the line-item veto, which was passed by Congress and signed by the president in April. A resurgent Republican Party asserted that the GOP, in charge of a "do-something Congress," was fulfilling its 1994 campaign promises for change on Capitol Hill. Democrats argued that the main ingredients of the Republican program (for example, term limits, welfare reform, and a balanced budget plan) still were unlikely to become law and that the Republican majority was presiding over a "do-nothing Congress."

However, politicians and pundits from both parties remarked that Congress had changed as an institution relative to the years of Democratic control. Democrats and Republicans may differ on the value of the GOP reorganization, but they agree that the organizational revisions of the 1990s mattered. What does the 1990s reform experience suggest about the foundations of congressional procedure and structure? How long-lasting are the changes implemented by the Republican majority likely to be? We conclude with summary observations about these issues.

REFORM AND CONGRESSIONAL ORGANIZATION

Diverse factors shape the internal operations of Congress, and the relative importance of these factors varies depending on the aspect of the institution targeted for change.[2] Table 6.1 summarizes the relevance of the five organizational rationales featured in this book for the reform areas that constituted the 1990s reorganization agenda.

- *Leadership prerogatives* are key to the legislative prospects of the majority party, and changes in this area largely were conditioned by partisan incentives. But the personal power agendas of individual lawmakers also mattered because leadership prerogatives help determine the overall distribution of power on Capitol Hill.
- The *committee system* is a microcosm of Congress, with individual panels often referred to as "little legislatures." As a result, all five organizational rationales influenced attempts to reorganize House and Senate committees.

TABLE 6.1 Importance of Organizational Rationales

	Organizational Rationales				
Reform Area	Clientele	Partisan	Institutional	Personal Power Agendas	Public Opinion
Leadership prerogatives		X		X	
Committee System	X	X	X	X	X
Floor deliberations and scheduling		X	X	X	
Congressional integrity		X	X		X
Policy-driven reforms		X			X
Congressional resources and interbranch prerogatives		X			X

An X indicates that an organizational rationale is clearly significant in understanding the forces for and against change in a reform area.

- Controlling *floor procedure* and the congressional *schedule* is essential for the majority party to advance its legislative program. Not surprisingly, partisan incentives, as well as personal power agendas and institutional concerns (such as family-friendly scheduling), dominated here.
- Criticisms of *congressional integrity* resonate powerfully with a distrustful public. Attempts to enhance the institutional integrity of Congress were shaped by public opinion, partisan/electoral incentives to cast or avoid blame, and institutional concerns about the popular legitimacy of the legislative branch.
- The majority party has disproportionate control over chamber rules and tends to embrace *policy-driven reforms* in substantive issue areas that are important to the public and prominent on the party's agenda. Partisan rationales and public opinion shaped decision making here.
- In prior decades, lawmakers expanded chamber *resources and interbranch prerogatives* to enhance their electoral connections and strengthen Congress's decision-making capabilities. In the 1990s, however, institutional rationales have been dominated by highly negative public opinion about Congress. Hence, there are partisan/electoral advantages from downsizing the congressional bureaucracy.

Although all five organizational rationales help explain aspects of the 1990s reform process, certain factors are more important than others in understanding how and why Congress changed. We consider the overall significance of each rationale in turn.

Clientele Rationales

Lawmakers are highly responsive to the organized constituencies that affect their reelection prospects, and such clientele groups care about organizational matters because of the obvious linkages between procedure and policy. However, the impact of clientele pressures on congressional organization is most pronounced for the procedures and structures that directly affect the policy objectives of individual groups. On Capitol Hill, organizational matters that influence policymaking across all issue areas generally transcend the lobbying capacities of individual specialized constituencies. Thus, procedural or structural changes that shape the entire landscape of policy decisions (the Speaker's committee assignment powers, for example) are settled by partisan coalitions or the membership as a whole.

In contrast, the committee system is designed on an issue-specific basis, allowing clientele groups to focus their procedural fire on the committees that are particularly relevant to their interests. Committees also matter a great deal to interest groups because they are centers of policymaking. They remain key arenas for framing issues, crafting legislation, and building coalitions. As such, committees are the primary locus of interest-group activity on

Capitol Hill. Clientele rationales are most useful in understanding whether and to what extent efforts to reform the committee system succeed or fail.

During the 1990s, the main impact of clientele incentives was the blocking of a comprehensive overhaul of committee jurisdictions. Under both the Democratic and Republican congressional majorities, clientele groups mobilized against comprehensive changes in committee boundaries, largely to protect their investments of time, expertise, and campaign dollars in the jurisdictional status quo. House Republicans did abolish three standing committees (District of Columbia, Post Office and Civil Service, and Merchant Marine and Fisheries) at the start of the 104th Congress. All three panels had close ties to outside Democratic groups. These interests confronted (1) a new majority party hostile to their concerns and (2) a closed and fast-paced decision-making environment that left them little time to mobilize public opposition to the GOP restructuring.

Thus, the impact of clientele factors on committee structure was conditioned by other forces; the 1990s reform process does not support the view that congressional organization derives *primarily* from procedural or structural logrolling ("you support my goals, and I'll support yours") among important clientele interests. As described in Chapters 4 and 5, the key committee changes adopted by House Republicans following the 1994 elections served to make the committee system more accountable to the leadership and the GOP Conference as a whole. Clientele groups and the incoming chairs were able to block major committee restructuring, but the overall impact of the Republican reorganization was to shift power away from the standing committees to the leadership and majority party rank and file. Senate Republicans adopted similar, though more incremental, reforms in 1995.

Institutional Rationales

The key reform actors in the House and Senate seldom, except in a general or abstract way, focused on the collective procedural and structural needs of the entire membership. There is little evidence that the 1990s reforms served to enhance the informational efficiency of congressional organization. Instead, the main reform decisions were mostly responsive to the electoral and procedural imperatives of the majority party.[3]

To be sure, many reform proposals considered during the decade involved changes in House or Senate rules, which must be approved by a numerical majority of the relevant chamber. Broad-based bipartisan majorities supported many of the House GOP reforms in January 1995. However, throughout the 1990s reform process, the key arena for making reorganization decisions was the majority party caucus, rather than the bipartisan, bicameral Joint Committee on the Organization of Congress or the full House or Senate. Many of the most significant organizational changes actually implemented by congressional Republicans were alterations in GOP Conference rules and practices relating to the distribution of power within the majority party. The organizational votes that did occur in the full House on January 4, 1995, were matters of strict party loyalty for Republican members. GOP defectors likely would have drawn major sanctions from their leadership.

Partisan interests and votes came together when the 104th Congress convened to produce a revised alignment of House committees. During this early period, congressional Republicans spent little time discussing an issue important to Congress watchers: What *chamber-wide* needs should a revamped committee structure serve?

Some scholars, for instance, argue that the committee system is designed in part to address the requirements of lawmakers for unbiased policy information.[4] Consistent with this view, House and Senate committees may be structured so that their memberships are heterogeneous and their jurisdictions are configured to evoke a range of competing interests. Committees designed in such a manner are more likely to provide their parent chambers with broadly representative policy proposals, as well as balanced information about the implications of these recommendations. Our analysis of the 1990s reorganization process suggests that the collective informational needs of the full House or Senate were not a major objective of committee reformers.

Lawmakers periodically do consider proposals to create panels that are more representative of the chamber as a whole. The 1973–1974 Bolling committee proposed that House committee boundaries be adjusted to create a "balance of interests" in key policy areas such as health care, energy, and the environment. In 1993, the Renewing Congress project, led by political scientists Thomas Mann and Norman Ornstein, argued that "small and narrow standing committees . . . should be merged into larger and broader committees . . . enabling them to be more representative and to have more effective means to set substantive priorities."[5] And behind the scenes, members of the 1993 joint reform committee also considered jurisdictional changes aimed at creating more representative panels. However, as with the earlier Bolling effort, such proposals went nowhere, as clientele and other factors blocked comprehensive committee restructuring.

As part of their opening-day reforms in 1995, House Republicans did abolish, as noted earlier, three committees with narrow, relatively parochial jurisdictions. But the key reasons for this move were the GOP's commitment in the Contract with America to streamline Congress and the fact that the three panels were disproportionately of interest to traditionally Democratic constituencies. Similarly, the committee assignment reforms adopted by the House Republican majority were intended primarily to increase the leadership's influence within key committees rather than to promote an informationally efficient committee system for the chamber as a whole.[6]

Public Opinion

The impact of public opinion on the reorganization process was critical at the agenda-setting stage, but more circumscribed when lawmakers began considering specific reform alternatives. As with many past reform efforts, the 1990s reorganization process was launched because of intense public dissatisfaction with congressional operations, resulting in part from the exposure of scandal (the House bank and post office) on Capitol Hill.

Legislative organization is complex and far removed from the day-to-day experiences of most Americans. As a result, citizens may strongly advocate reform in the abstract but tend to support only specific reform alternatives that are relatively blunt and straightforward, and directly address their main concerns about Congress—for instance, that the institution is rife with corruption, perks, and waste, and filled with career lawmakers unresponsive to ordinary people. During the 1990s reform process, lawmakers advocated a variety of broad reform proposals in response to the generalized citizen concern that the legislative branch was not working very well. These recommendations included streamlining the committee system, reducing congressional staff, applying workplace safety and employment laws to Congress, opening up the institution to heightened public scrutiny, and embracing procedural changes that might reduce the federal budget deficit. Polls and focus groups demonstrated that the vast majority of Americans favored these proposals throughout the decade. Consequently, the GOP included them in the Contract with America, and most were adopted by the House.

In contrast, public opinion usually does not play a key role in the reform of arcane aspects of legislative procedure. During the 1990s, such organizational items included leadership prerogatives, floor deliberations and scheduling, bicameral relationships, and most aspects of the committee system. In these areas, other factors were pivotal to the success or failure of reform.

Partisan Rationales

Partisan incentives were the single dominant factor throughout the 1990s reform process, and partisan rationales for legislative organization are crucial for understanding decision making in all five reorganization areas. More than any other in recent memory, the 104th House resembled party government.

Partisan/electoral incentives led House Republicans to champion congressional reform during the 1980s and 1990s, as part of an effort to undermine public confidence in the Democratic Congress. The key changes adopted by House Republicans in the 104th Congress were meant to fulfill previous reform promises and to provide the new leadership with the tools necessary to advance the party's legislative program. From the line-item veto to Corrections Day, the policy-driven reforms adopted by the 104th Congress dealt primarily with GOP themes. The 104th Congress also has been characterized by record partisanship, the aggrandizement of leadership power, intensive involvement by House GOP leaders in the chamber's day-to-day legislative business, a decline in the role of committees and other competing power centers, and the use of sanctions by Republican leaders to minimize GOP defections on major legislation.

The increased centralization of power within the House majority resulted primarily from the greater cohesion of the Republican Conference on policy matters. Party conservatives were concerned that senior, relatively moderate, and less confrontational committee leaders might not be sufficiently aggressive in pushing the remarkably ambitious GOP agenda. House Republicans also had pledged to consider, if not pass, their policy program within daunting time limits. After four decades in the minority, GOP lawmakers believed that their party had to deliver or change-oriented voters would return the Democrats to power. As a result, the new Republican majority needed a stronger Speaker and a more accountable committee system than had characterized the Democratic House. Even in the highly individualistic Senate, junior Republicans helped pass potentially significant rules changes aimed at strengthening their leadership relative to the committee chairs and other influential members. In short, the 1990s reorganization process is fully consistent with studies by various political scientists who argue that increased preference homogeneity within the majority party provides incentives for structural changes that buttress party leadership powers.[7]

In addition to unity within the majority conference, other party-related variables shaped reform deliberations during the 1990s. First, particularly in the area of floor deliberation and scheduling, which relates to the distribution of power between the two political parties, the size and relative unity of the minority party influenced reform politics. Second, a large number of reform proposals provided congressional Republicans and many Democrats with useful campaign fodder. Such reorganization ideas (for example, committee staff reductions and applying labor laws to Congress) had electoral value above and beyond the intended impact on House or Senate rules. Thus, a range of incentives emanating from the partisan environment of congressional politics dominated the 1990s reorganization process.

Personal Power Agendas

The overriding importance of partisan incentives should not mask the substantial role played by the personal power agendas of individual lawmakers. On complex matters of congressional organization, individual members have considerable discretion in their procedural and structural choices. The rise of reform as a public issue can be fostered by individual lawmakers who seek to publicize alleged institutional shortcomings and create outside momentum for change. Political entrepreneurs outside the institution also can play a role. For example, groups such as Common Cause, Congress Watch, and the Heritage Foundation, as well as many congressional scholars, maintain an ongoing interest in congressional reform.

For the 1990s reorganization experience, Newt Gingrich (R-Ga.) was the pivotal figure. Gingrich convinced other conservative Republicans to adopt an increasingly confrontational stance toward Democratic management of the House, as he sought to harness public discontent with Congress behind the GOP electoral and legislative agendas. Following the stunning 1994 elections, Gingrich moved aggressively to consolidate his power within the House via a wide range of procedural changes. Some shift in power from the committee system to the Speaker's office would have occurred even without Gingrich because of the significant preference homogeneity within the new House majority. However, based on extensive conversations with members and staff, our personal observations of the reorganization process, and the record of the 104th Congress, we believe that the scope and magnitude of the Republican reorganization owed much to the political entrepreneurship of Gingrich.

The personal power agendas of individual lawmakers also played a role in blunting the momentum for major changes in certain reform areas. Because reform alters the internal distribution of power in Congress, it potentially threatens the prerogatives of influential members. Under both Democratic and Republican majorities, committee chairs mobilized against a comprehensive realignment of the committee system in order to protect their turf.

It is in the Senate, however, that personal power agendas particularly functioned as a major brake on organizational change. In that chamber, all members have significant procedural prerogatives, and senators guard their powers jealously. Although the Senate Republican majority was substantially more cohesive than the previous Democratic majority, the barriers to a fundamental centralization of power in the Senate remained high throughout the decade.

Limited steps were taken to strengthen the Senate leadership and make the committee system more accountable to the Republican Conference. For example, Senate Republicans agreed to adopt, beginning in 1997, a formal legislative agenda at the start of each Congress, with the various standing committees being required to implement this agenda. Overall, however, the pace and scope of institutional change have been much less pronounced in the Senate than in the House.

PROSPECTS

From committee procedures to leadership powers, the Republican majority implemented major changes in congressional operations. Few legislative analysts are likely to deny their significance in changing the political and policy-making dynamic on Capitol Hill. But are these changes likely to last beyond the 104th Congress? And what future institutional developments can we expect on Capitol Hill?

The longevity of a reform depends on whether significant changes occur in the field of incentives, or conditions, that led to its adoption in the first place. Consider these points about the current environment for congressional reorganization. Negative public opinion about Congress seems unlikely to diminish in the foreseeable future. Similarly, it is unlikely that institutional rationales will soon take center stage and push aside other factors that shape legislative organization. Major transformations in the clientele environment of reform decision making do not appear imminent. And the personal power agendas of lawmakers probably will continue to favor the procedural and structural status quo. If major alterations are to occur in the contemporary incentives that shape congressional organization, most likely such changes will be party related.

Two potential developments are particularly worth considering: (1) that the remarkable preference homogeneity among congressional Republicans may decline and (2) that Democrats may retake one or both chambers. Would either development lead to another wave of major organizational change, or perhaps to a systematic reversal of the Republican reforms? Probably not in either case. Consider each of the reorganization areas.

Leadership Prerogatives

The remarkable aggrandizement of the Speaker's role in the mid-1990s mostly derived from high policy agreement among the majority rank and file, as well as the demands placed on the party by the magnitude of its agenda. As more policy divisions emerge in the House GOP, the willingness of Republican members to defer to the centralized party leadership should diminish. Although we are neither in nor entering a period of "czar" rule, there is little sign that the intensive legislative involvement of the Republican leadership in the governance of the House is declining. Republicans remain relatively unified on major policy issues and strongly committed to their fundamental goal of shrinking the role of the national government. Thus, the Republicans are not reluctant to delegate significant authority to Speaker Gingrich and other party leaders. "It's a consensual authority," said Gingrich. "They [the party members] as a team gave me my authority."[8]

What if Democrats regain majority status? It is important to remember that even before the November 1994 transition, the trend inside the House was toward stronger party leaders. During the 1980s and early 1990s, the legislative role played by Democratic Speakers increased markedly because of growing policy agreement within the Democratic Caucus. The changes in leadership prerogatives engineered by Gingrich accelerated, but did not qualitatively alter, this underlying trend. In the future, Speakers from either party may lack the political support necessary to continue the Gingrich practice of handpicking committee chairs. But no matter which party organizes the House, we can expect that the increased stature of the office will be, to a large extent, sustained and perhaps further empowered as the most pivotal and public position on Capitol Hill.

In the Senate, the Republican Conference adopted party rules changes aimed at increasing the power of party leaders. The Senate reforms are an unusual experiment for that chamber. It is difficult to predict the magnitude of their impact or how long they might last. We do expect that any shift toward increased party leadership power will be sharply constrained by Senate tradition, Senate rules, and the personal power agendas of individual members.

For example, when Bob Dole (R-Kans.) functioned for a time as majority leader of the Senate and GOP presidential candidate, he quickly encountered resistance to his use of the Senate floor to campaign for the White House. Dole wanted the Senate to pass legislation that distinguished his views and goals from President Clinton's and that demonstrated his talent for being a "doer and not a talker." Senate Democrats did not cooperate, using the filibuster and other parliamentary devices to foil many of Dole's initiatives.[9] The unwieldy nature of the Senate agenda was the key reason that Dole resigned from the chamber in June 1996.

Committee System

Many of the committee reforms implemented by the 104th House were intended to make the committee system more accountable to the leadership and the full Republican Conference. However, the Subcommittee Bill of Rights and other reforms of the 1970s also were intended to promote such goals. Thus, the Republican committee changes are consistent with the underlying goals of prior Democratic reformers.

Of course, formal reforms of the House committee system in the mid 1990s did not fundamentally alter committee procedures or jurisdictions. These reforms primarily streamlined somewhat the House committee system and increased the prerogatives of the chairs within their panels. The main incentives for change were partisan needs, public opinion, and a desire to follow through on the Contract with America. These changes (the abolition of three House committees, staff reductions, and openness reforms) should last. Where specific procedural changes become inconvenient (the abolition of proxy voting and tighter committee assignment limitations), lawmakers most likely will develop incremental waivers and other exceptions to their own rules.

The major change in the House committee system in the 104th Congress is the shift in legislative activity and responsibility away from the panels of jurisdiction and toward the leadership, informal task forces, and the majority rank and file. This change builds on previous trends away from the insular and autonomous committees that purportedly characterized the pre-1970s Congress. But the degree to which the committee system has been bypassed in the 104th House is unprecedented in recent congressional history. As more divisions emerge in the Republican Conference, as the legislative agenda returns to "normal," or if the Democrats retake the chamber in November 1996, House committees should play a more significant and systematic role in the legislative business of the chamber.

Floor Deliberations and Scheduling

The Republican majority has taken incremental steps to open up floor deliberations in the House, but the level of change has not been as significant as House Republicans say (or as trivial as some Democrats claim). Floor deliberations continue to be highly structured, although the minority party generally has greater opportunity to participate in the consideration of most bills than was typical in the Democratic House.

All congressional majorities must confront the tradeoff between openness and deliberation on the one hand, and the need to pass legislation in a timely fashion on the other. The House will continue to grapple with the tensions between these competing goals. In the Senate, floor deliberations and scheduling have not been altered much by the Republican majority. Absent fundamental shifts in the makeup and mix of views within the two political parties on Capitol Hill, continuity, rather than change, should characterize this aspect of congressional operations.

Congressional Integrity

Public opinion polls reveal that reform has not significantly improved the way voters perceive Congress. Public distrust of the institutional integrity of the legislative branch likely will continue because of the nature of Congress (the legislative process is inherently untidy and unruly), the cynicism prevalent in much of the body politic and much of the media coverage of Congress, and broader political and social conditions in the country, such as job insecurity, public antipathy toward government, and citizens' anxiety about their economic prospects. No matter which party controls Congress, without fundamental changes in public opinion toward the institution, lawmakers will continue to search for perks to eliminate, privileges to abolish, and legislative business to open up to heightened media and public scrutiny. It is unlikely that the Republican reforms in the area of congressional integrity would be reversed under a new majority.

Policy-Driven Reforms

The policy-driven reforms considered by the 104th Congress reflect the issue priorities of the Republican Party. Much of the emphasis has been on procedural tools for addressing the budget deficit as a pressing policy problem. As long as the deficit remains a major concern, lawmakers will continue to search for procedural fixes. (If the president and the Congress are successful at reaching a long-term budgetary accord to reduce substantially the size of the deficit, congressional history suggests that the attention of procedural reformers will shift elsewhere.) In the end, the nature of the policy-driven reforms on the reorganization agenda depends on the nature of the broader policy agenda and which party controls Congress. A new Democratic majority, for instance, probably would reverse selected budgetary rules changes (such as the three-fifths rule for income tax rate hikes) adopted by the House in January 1995.

Congressional Resources and Interbranch Prerogatives

No matter which party organizes the House and Senate, low public esteem for Congress will continue to create an environment in which reforms focus on such topics as privatizing certain Capitol Hill functions and cutting back on congressional resources and prerogatives. As long as the public lacks confidence in the legislative branch and the general pressures for fiscal austerity continue, lawmakers will have difficulty enhancing the staff and other analytical resources available to Congress. Indeed, a perplexing issue now confronting Congress is how to modernize its research and information technologies (the "cyberCongress") when fiscal resources are so scarce.

The prospects for augmenting the formal prerogatives of Congress relative to the executive branch are less clear. Post-1996, one possible scenario is continued Republican majorities on Capitol Hill, with the Democrats controlling the White House. Under such conditions, Republicans may look for ways to strengthen congressional powers to compete with and challenge the Democratic president. Congressional Republicans already conduct aggressive oversight of the executive branch. If the November 1996 elections again result in divided government, this pattern would surely continue, with steps taken to strengthen further Congress's review functions.

REFORM AND DELIBERATION

Observers of the 104th Congress invariably are struck by the increase in party accountability, centralization, and cohesion; the GOP's success in advancing much of their controversial agenda through the House and Senate; the timeliness and pace of decision making, particularly in the House; and the sharp partisanship that has permeated both chambers and both parties. To be sure, the nature of the agenda and the transition to Republican rule were partially responsible for these attributes. Heightened congressional partisanship also characterized the last years of Democratic control. However, the Republican reorganization, which provided the procedural and structural underpinnings of the 104th Congress, served to reinforce and enhance these decision-making trends.

We believe that many of the Republican changes are constructive and important. For example, proposals aimed at enhancing congressional integrity, such as the application of workplace safety and employment laws to Congress, may not have substantially raised public confidence in the institution, but they have removed important sources of public anger about Congress. Similarly, the changes aimed at making the committee system more responsive to the leadership and majority rank and file have added valuable clarity and accountability to the national policy debate. Other reforms, such as stricter committee assignment limits, the reduction in the number of subcommittees, and the outside audit of House administrative practices were long overdue.

However, there has been a downside to the GOP's decision to centralize power within the House and to expedite the decision-making process. We believe that the Republican changes have diminished the quality and thoroughness of deliberation on Capitol Hill. Reforms of legislative organization that promote party accountability, timely decision making, and a fast-paced legislative schedule also can reduce the deliberative capacity of the institution. The hallmarks of quality deliberation include (1) rational and responsible policy exchanges among members, (2) ample opportunities for majority and minority party lawmakers to debate and offer policy alternatives, (3) sufficient time for lawmakers and interested outsiders to digest complex legislative information, and (4) because committees remain the main repositories of specialized policy expertise on Capitol Hill, robust committee consideration of important legislative matters. Throughout the 104th Congress, the Senate generally remained a legislative body oriented toward bipartisan deliberation—perhaps excessively so. However, keeping the four criteria in mind, briefly consider the performance of the 104th House.

First, the chamber has been characterized by bitter partisanship, interpersonal acrimony, and a general lack of civility—all of which inhibit deliberation and collaboration across party lines. "We used to have friends on both sides of the aisle," said Rep. John Myers (R-Ind.), who will be retiring from the House at the end of the 104th Congress. "Today's attitude is that you can't be friends with someone whose opinion is different. And you can't compromise."[10] In one effort to restore civility to House proceedings, a bipartisan group of lawmakers actually requested their colleagues to sign a "civility pledge," which urged members to "promote civility, comity, and adherence to House rules over party loyalty."[11]

Second, although the GOP has increased somewhat the ability of the minority party to offer amendments on the floor (relative to the majority Democrats), deliberations in the full House remain highly structured and amending opportunities typically are sharply constrained by time limitations. The 1995 reconciliation bill, which included large portions of the Republican policy agenda, was mostly constructed behind closed doors by Republican leaders. Minority party input in policy formulation at the committee stage was often limited or foreclosed entirely.

Third, the sheer quantity of legislation considered and passed by the House, particularly in 1995, necessitated a hectic, almost chaotic, legislative schedule, which curbed the ability of members and outside observers alike to make informed judgments about major policy questions. Some GOP-sponsored House rules also have been difficult to implement. For example, the House rule requiring a three-fifths vote, rather than a simple majority, to raise income tax rates has been waived several times because the new rule threatened to hinder timely action on GOP initiatives.

Fourth, and perhaps most important, the Republican leadership regularly short-circuited committee consideration on major legislation throughout the 104th Congress. In a number of instances, even after the committee of jurisdiction had reported a bill, the leadership stepped in and substantially revised legislation prior to floor consideration. Wide use of informal party task forces and the avoidance of hearings by standing committees—even on proposed constitutional amendments—were common occurrences in the House.

Of course, all four of these shortcomings also characterized the Democratic House to some extent. Partisan discord is not new on Capitol Hill. Amendment rules were even more restrictive during the Democratically controlled 103d Congress. Sometimes Democratic leaders brought major legislation to the floor without much warning and without committee hearings. And committee recommendations occasionally were revamped by the leadership or party task forces. Still, the issue here is one of extent, and the contemporary strengths of the GOP House (an empowered leadership, party loyalty, the fast-paced schedule) appear to have come at a significant cost: a reduction in the quality of informed discourse among participants in the chamber's legislative business.

The Senate exhibits the opposite set of problems. During the 104th Congress, senators continued to use obstructionist tactics, rooted in the filibuster, to block or impede important legislation backed by numerical majorities. They also continued to offer floor amendments that had little substantive relevance to the underlying legislation. And party and committee leadership within this highly individualistic institution continued to be a daunting challenge. Interestingly, some House Republicans have now updated the remarks of former representative Al Swift (D-Wash.) concerning the 103d Congress. "The Democrats are the opposition," these frustrated Republicans say, "but the Senate is the enemy."

Revitalizing the quality of deliberation within both the House and the Senate constitutes a key task for our elected representatives in Washington. Their task is made more difficult by the intense distrust so many Americans feel toward Congress. The public tends to favor reforms that would increase the role of ordinary citizens in congressional decision making and make the legislative process more directly responsive to constituents. Whereas James

Madison believed that Congress should distill, refine, and "enlarge upon the public mood"[12]—that it should be primarily an assembly for enlightened representation—most citizens are more interested in opening up Congress to maximum public scrutiny, constraining the legislative discretion of lawmakers in important ways, and reducing what so many view as congressional insularity via term limitations. As onetime GOP presidential candidate Lamar Alexander put it, "Cut their pay and send them home!"

Ironically, many people are seeking to make what is already a highly responsive institution even more responsive. Improving the deliberative capacity of Congress within such an environment is extremely difficult. But one useful step would be for lawmakers to educate their constituents more aggressively and effectively about the virtues of Congress's roles and the benefits of its "messy" processes and procedures.[13] Another worthwhile step might be for Congress to shed some of its individual and institutional workload so that lawmakers have more time for creative reflection and for concentration on effective policymaking.

The bottom line? On balance, we believe that the congressional reforms of the 1990s were important and often constructive and, for the most part, should last into the next century. Institutional change on Capitol Hill is an ongoing process, but it provides no guarantees for addressing what ails the legislative branch or for alleviating the public's discontent with the national legislature. At least for the foreseeable future, Congress will remain under fire.

Notes

1. Richard Wolf, "Budget Deal Still Leaves Big Bills Behind," *USA Today*, April 25, 1996, 9A.

2. A similar point is made by David W. Rohde, "Parties and Committees in the House: Member Motivations, Issues, and Institutional Arrangements," *Legislative Studies Quarterly*, 19, No. 3 (1994), 341–59. See also Eric Schickler and Andrew Rich, "Controlling the Floor: Parties as Procedural Coalitions in the House," paper presented at the annual meeting of the American Political Science Association, Chicago, 1995.

3. An important exception is Congress's efforts to establish a single, legislative-branch-wide information system to assist members and committees in making informed policy decisions.

4. Keith Krehbiel develops an informational rationale for congressional structure in *Information and Legislative Organization* (Ann Arbor: University of Michigan Press, 1991). Krehbiel does not assert that the structural or procedural choices of individual lawmakers are necessarily motivated by a desire to promote the collective informational needs of the chamber. Because organizational choices are basically majoritarian, he argues, decisions about structure and procedure are likely to reflect the preferences of the median voter in the chamber as a whole. In addition, Krehbiel does not directly

explore the informational implications from jurisdictional change, but see Thomas E. Mann and Norman J. Ornstein, *Renewing Congress: A Second Report* (Washington, D.C.: American Enterprise Institute and Brookings Institution, 1993).

5. Mann and Ornstein, *Renewing Congress: A Second Report,* p. 23.

6. Our argument is based on extensive interviews with members and staff. For an intriguing analysis of Republican and Democratic committee assignments in the 104th Congress, consult Sanford C. Gordon, " 'Outlier' Committees in a Republican House? Committee Restructuring in the 104th Congress," paper presented at the annual meeting of the American Political Science Association, Chicago, 1995.

7. For example, see David Rohde, *Parties and Leaders in the Postreform House* (Chicago: University of Chicago Press, 1991).

8. Quoted in John Aldrich and David Rohde, "Conditional Party Government Revisited: Majority Party Leadership and the Committee System in the 104th Congress," *Extension of Remarks,* December 1995, 7.

9. See, for example, Ross K. Baker, "Dole's Battleground May Be His Undoing," *Los Angeles Times,* April 25, 1996, A11; Adam Nagourney, "Dole Meets a Setback," *New York Times,* April 18, 1996, A1; Judi Hasson, "Dole Finds Dual Role Not Always Easy," *USA Today,* April 19, 1996, 4A; Katharine Q. Seelye, "More in GOP Say Dole's Senate Role Hinders Campaign," *New York Times,* April 29, 1996, A1.

10. Sandy Hume, "Rep. John Myers Calls It Quits, Saying 'Compromise a Dirty Word,' " *The Hill,* January 10, 1996, A11.

11. Amy Keller, "Is Answer to Rancor on the Floor a 'Civility' Pledge for Members?" *Roll Call,* February 1, 1996, 1.

12. Thomas E. Mann and Norman J. Ornstein, *Renewing Congress: A First Report* (Washington, D.C.: American Enterprise Institute and Brookings Institution, 1992), 30.

13. See John R. Hibbing and Elizabeth Theiss-Morse, *Congress As Public Enemy: Public Attitudes Toward American Political Institutions* (New York: Cambridge University Press, 1995).

Index